ACTA UNIVERSITATIS UPSALIENSIS
Psychologia et Sociologia Religionum
13

Taking a Step Back

Assessments of the Psychology of Religion

EDITED BY

JACOB A. BELZEN and OWE WIKSTRÖM

UPPSALA 1997

Printed with a Grant from the Swedish Council for Research in
Humanities and Social Sciences

ABSTRACT

Belzen, Jacob A. & Wikström, O. (eds.). 1997. Taking a Step Back. Assessments of the Psychology of Religion. Acta Universitatis Upsaliensis. *Psychologia et Sociologia Religionum* 13. 299 pp. Uppsala. ISBN 91-554-4018-5.

In recent decennia, there has been a steadily growing interest in work done and published by psychologists of religion, both in academic and religious circles and in the broader society. Positions have been established devoted exclusively to the discipline. The rate of publications has increased significantly and there are now several journals and series specifically focused on the field. Yet, as with psychology in a general, uneasiness can sometimes be observed, both outside psychology of religion and also among psychologists of religion themselves.

This complex state of affairs functioned as the starting point for a project which has resulted into this collection of paper by invited professors with long-standing experience and established repudiation in the field. Individually they have had to ponder over questions like the following:

What kind of enterprise is psychology of religion really? What are its practitioners doing? Are they actually doing what they say they are doing? Are they doing what 'customers' think they are doing? Is Psychology of religion a valid enterprise at all? What answer is to be given to the question of whether it can exist at all? (i.e. what systematic answer, not a trivial one pointing out that it does exist empirically in its publications and representatives). What is its position in the logic of scholarly enterprise/university structure: is it a subdiscipline of psychology, *Religionswissenschaft,* theology? Has psychology of religion yielded any respectable results? Are these results or insights that did not already exist in other disciplines like theology, humanities, history? What is it good for? Did it bring any insight into religion? What did it do to religion, if anything? Whom is it serving? And whom is it shaping? What is there to be said on the developments made in the recent past, in the last 30 years of growth, in terms of numbers and professionalization? Did quantitative growth bring qualitative improvement?

Each author was asked to contribute a scholarly/academic essay, explicitly written by one who is an insider, who has an overview, who is involved and devoted—but who here takes a step back. In addition to being scholarly, we explicitly wanted the essays to be personal, even passionate, reflecting, taking a stand. The present volume presents the thoughts of influential persons from a variety of countries, generations and perspectives. As expected and hoped for, the response to the initial invitation has been very diversified. Both the authors and editors have found the essays worthwhile and instructive contributions attempting to answer to the overarching central question 'What kind of enterprise should psychology of religion be?'

Key Words: Psychology of Religion, History of Sciences, Religious Studies.

© The Authors 1997

ISSN 0283-149X
ISBN 91-554-4018-5

Typesetting: Editorial Office, Uppsala University, 7113
Printed in Sweden by Gotab, Stockholm 1997
Distributor: Uppsala University Library, Uppsala, Sweden

Contents

The Authors 7

Preface 13

How to Assess the Identity of Psychology of Religion? 17
J.A. Belzen

Shame, Melancholy, and the Introspective Method in Psychology of
Religion 37
Donald Capps

Science vs. Religion 55
James E. Dittes

Looking from Sidelines 67
Heije Faber

Contemporary Religious Experiences. Reflections on Fifteen Years of
Research 81
Antoon Geels

Psychology of Religion. Towards a Synthesis for a Challenging
Discipline 97
Nils G. Holm

The Empirical Study of Mysticism. Retrospective and Prospective 111
Ralph W. Hood Jr.

A Proposal for a Psychology of Religious Expression 127
H. Newton Malony

The Confessions of a Theologian Interested in Religious Experience ... 137
Troels Nørager

On Second Thoughts. Personal Retrospect and Prospect 145
Conrad A.J. van Ouwerkerk

Neither Masterly nor Ancillary 159
Antoine Vergote

From 'Facts' to 'Fiction'. On the Fragility of the Scholarly Glasses 171
Owe Wikström

A Century of Psychology of Religion. Where Does It Leave Us
Today? 183
David M. Wulff

Author Index 199

The Authors

Jacob A. Belzen

was trained in the fields of social sciences, history and philosophy. He currently is Professor of psychology of religion at the University of Amsterdam and at Utrecht University (both in The Netherlands). His main research interest is in historical and philosophical questions pertaining to the field of psychology of religion. Some of his monographies: *Psychopathologie en religie. Ideeën, behandeling en verzorging in de gereformeerde psychiatrie, 1880–1940* [Psychopathology and religion; Theory, treatment and care in Reformed psychiatry]. Kampen: Kok, 1989; *Rümke, religie en godsdienstpsychologie.* Kampen: Kok, 1991; *Portretten en landschappen. Tekeningen uit de geschiedenis der Nederlandse psychiatrie* [Drawings from the history of Dutch psychiatry]. Baarn: Ambo, 1994; *Zorg voor de ziel. Een selectie uit de verslagen van het Theologisch-Psychiatrisch Gezelschap, 1945-1953* [Care for the soul]. Rotterdam: Erasmus Publishing, 1995.

Donald Capps

is Professor of Pastoral Theology at Princeton Theological Seminary in Princeton, New Jersey, USA. He received his doctorate from the University of Chicago and holds an honorary doctorate in theology from the University of Uppsala. He was editor of the *Journal for the Scientific Study of Religion* from 1983–1988 and president of the Society for the Scientific Study of Religion in 1990-1992. He is author of several books, including *The Depleted Self: Sin in a Narcissistic Age* (Fortress Press, 1992), *The Child's Song: The Religious Abuse and Children* (Westminster Press, 1995) and *Men, Religion and Melancholia: James, Otto, Jung, Erikson* (Yale University Press, 1997). He is an ordained clergyman in the Evangelical Lutheran Church in America.

James E. Dittes

is Professor of Psychology of Religion at Yale University, where he is Director of the Ph.D. program in religious studies. Since 1955, he has been a member of the faculties of the Psychology Department, the Department of Religious Studies, and the Divinity School. He has recently published interpretive essays on Augustine, Sigmund Freud, William James, and Carl Jung. His two most recent books (published in the fall of 1996) deal with the relation of masculinity and religion: *Men's Work/Faith* and *Afflicted with Hope*.

Heije Faber

wrote doctoral dissertations in both theology and psychology. Having served as a protestant minister for many years, he began teaching at Leiden University in the fifties. As one of the first Europeans to do so, he went to the USA to become acquainted with the Clinical Pastoral Movement, which he introduced to The Netherlands. In the sixties he became a lecturer in Leiden; in 1970 he was appointed Professor for psychology of religion and for pastoral psychology at the Theological Faculty Tilburg (The Netherlands). Faber authored numerous books and hundreds of articles. Best known became his *Psychology of Religion* (Philadelphia: Westminster Press, 1976; orig. Dutch: 1972). Some of his recent books: *Boven de boomgrens. Op weg naar een hedendaagse spiritualiteit* [Above the tree line; towards a contemporary spirituality] Baarn: Ten Have, 1987; *Het lichtend geheim. Perspectieven in de godsdienstpsychologie* [The lighting mystery. Perspectives in psychology of religion] Baarn: Ten Have, 1991; *Rekenschap van een zoektocht. Een autobiografie.* [*Account of a quest: an autobiography*] Baarn: Ten Have, 1993.

Antoon Geels

is Professor in history and psychology of religion at the University of Lund (Sweden). His research is focused on cross-cultural studies of mystical experience. His latest monographies are: *Subud and the Javanese Mystical Tradition.* Richmond: Curzon Press, 1997. *Att möta Gud i kaos. Religiösa visioner i dagens Sverige* [Encounter with God in chaos. religious visions in contemporary Sweden] (Stockholm: Norstedts förlag, 1991). His current research is centered around the topic of mystical death in the great theistic traditions: Judaism, Christianity and Islam.

Nils G. Holm

is Professor of Comparative Religion (Religionswissenschaft) at the Åbo Akademi University in Turku/Åbo (Swedish University in Finland). He is author of *Scandinavian Psychology of Religion* (Einführing in die Religionspsychologie) and has edited *Religious Ecstasy*. He is president of *die Internationale Gesellschaft für Religionspsychologie und Religionswissenschaft*. He has been working on Pentecostalism, tongue speaking, ecstasy, and has been writing on role theory and its development.

Ralph W. Hood Jr.

received his Ph.D. in social psychology from the University of Nevada. His main research interest is in religious experience, especially mysticism. He is a past president of the division of psychology of religion of the American Psychological Association and a recipient of its William James Award. He is a former co-editor of the *International Journal for the Psychology of Religion* and is current editor of the *Journal for the Scientific Study of Religion*. He has published over a hundred articles and book chapters related to the psychology of religion. Among his most recent books are his edited text, *Handbook of Religious Experience*. Religious Education Press, 1995 and *The Psychology of Religion: An Empirical Approach* 2nd. edition. Guilford, 1996, which he co-authored with Bernard Spilka, Bruce Hunsberger and Richard Gorsuch.

H. Newton Malony

(M.Div., Ph.D) is Senior Professor in the Graduate School of Psychology of Fuller Theological Seminary, Pasadena, California, USA. He is an ordained United Methodist minister and a graduate of Yale University Divinity School. His doctorate is in Clinical Psychology from George Peabody of Vanderbilt University. He has been the president of the Division of the Psychology of Religion of the American Psychological Association and recipient of its William Beer Award. Malony is the author/editor of over 32 books including *Glossolalia: Behavioral Science Perspectives on Speaking in Tongues* (Oxford, 1982), *A Dynamic Psychology of Religion: The Contributions of Paul W. Pruyser* (Oxford, 1993), and *Psychology of Religion: Personalities, Problems, Possibilities* (Grand Rapids: Baker, 1992). He has published numerous articles and book chapters including "The case for the inclusion of religion in psychotherapy" in *Religion and the Clinical Practice of Psychology* (E. P. Shafrankske (Ed.), American Psychological Association, 1996). He was the co-editor of the *International Journal for the Psychology of Religion* from 1990–96.

Troels Nørager

is Professor of Psychology of Religion and Pastoral Theology at Aarhus University in Aarhus, Denmark, where he also received his doctorate. He is author of *Theories of Socialization and the Problem of Anthropological Normativity* (1982, in Danish) and *System and Life World: Habermas' Construction of Modernity* (1985, in Danish). He has studied with Jürgen Habermas in Frankfurt, Germany, and has held an American Council of Learned Societies Fellowship for study in the United States. He is currently engaged in a research project on 'Metaphor and Religion' and in a Danish enterprise of establishing a fruitful dialogue between theology and psychology. His publications in English include contributions to *The Endangered Self* (1992, ed. by Richard K. Fenn and Donald Capps) and *The Struggle for Life: A Companion to William James's 'The Varieties of Religious Experience'* (1995, ed. by Donald Capps and Janet L. Jacobs).

Conrad A.J. van Ouwerkerk

studied in The Netherlands and in Italy (Rome). He graduated in both theology and psychology. After teaching moral theology in The Netherlands for several years, he became Professor for psychology of religion at Williams College (Massachusetts, U.S.A.). Early seventies he returned to The Netherlands, where he was appointed as a professor at Leiden University. He published essays on the boundaries of theology, philosophy and psychology of religion, e.g. *Religie in het netwerk van alledag* [Religion in everyday,s network] In: H. Zock (Ed.) (1993). *Geloven tussen waan en werkelijkheid* [Faith between delusion and reality] (Maarssen: De Ploeg). Some other recent publications: *In afwezigheid van God. Voorstudies tot een psychologie van het geloof.* [In Gods absence. Prolegomena for a psychology of faith] Den Haag: Boekencentrum, 1986; *Het werkelijkheidsgehalte van de theologie. De spanning tussen wat bedacht wordt en beleefd* [Theology's quality of realism; the tension between what is thought and what is experienced] Heerlen: UTP, 1993.

Antoon Vergote

After having defended doctoral dissertations in theology and philosophy at the University of Leuven (Belgium), Antoon Vergote went to Paris to study with Jacques Lacan, Claude Lévy-Strauss, and others. He was appointed Professor for psychology of religion at Leuven University at the end of the fifties. Next to his academic work, he was one of the founders of the Belgium School for Psychoanalysis. Among his recent publications are: *Guilt and desire. Religious attitudes and their pathological derivatives.* New Haven/London: Yale University Press, 1988 (original French edition: 1978); *Explorations de l'espace théologique. Études de théologie et de philosophie de la religion* [Explorations of theological space] Leuven: Leuven University Press/Peeters, 1990; *In Search of Philosophical Anthropology.* Leuven: Leuven University Press, 1996; *Religion, Belief and Unbelief: a Psychological Study.* Amsterdam/Leuven: Rodopi/Leuven University Press, 1997 (orig. French: 1983).

Owe Wikström

is Professor in psychology of religion at the University of Uppsala, Sweden. Ph. D. M. Div. psychotherapist and ordained minister (hospital chaplain) in the Lutheran Church. His main research interest is religion in relation to psychiatry and psychotherapy. He has written eleven books in the field, among others: *Den outgrundliga människan* (1990) [The ingraspable man—on religion and psychiatry], *Om heligheten* (1993) [On holiness—perspectives from psychology of religion], *Det bländande mörkret* (1994) [The blinding darkness. On spirituality, postmodernity and psychology], and *Aljosjas leende* (1997) [The smile of Aljosja—the implicit psychology in the novel *The Brothers Karamazov* of Fjodor Dostoevsky].

David M. Wulff

is Professor of Psychology at Wheaton College, Norton, Massachusetts, U.S.A. He has a Ph.D. in personality psychology from the University of Michigan and in 1993 received an honorary Doctor of Theology from the University of Lund, Sweden. He is the author of *Psychology of Religion: Classic and Contemporary* (New York: Wiley, 1991; 2nd ed., 1997; Swedish translation, 1993; other translations in preparation), which was awarded the 1990 Quinquennial Prize by the International Commission for Scientific Psychology of Religion. His most recent contributions to edited works include "The Psychology of Religion: An Overview," in E. P. Shafranske (Ed.), *Religion and the Clinical Practice of Psychology* (Washington, D.C.: American Psychological Association, 1996, pp. 43–70) and "Phenomenological Psychology and Religious Experience," in R. W. Hood, Jr. (Ed.), *Handbook of Religious Experience* (Birmingham, Ala.: Religious Education Press, 1995, pp. 183–199). He was the 1991 recipient of the William C. Bier Award given by Division 36: Psychology of Religion, of the American Psychological Association. He became president-elect of Division 36 in 1996 and is a Fellow both of Division 36 and of the Society for the Scientific Study of Religion. In 1995 he was appointed book review editor for the *Journal for the Scientific Study of Religion.*

Preface

Passionate Yet Serious—Searching for Identity

Psychology of religion is a flourishing enterprise, so it seems. After an earlier period of neglect by psychology in general, today it has managed again to obtain a stable position. In recent decennia, there has been a steadily growing interest in work done and published by psychologists of religion, both in academic and religious circles and in broader society, positions have been established devoted exclusively to the discipline, the rate of publications increased significantly and there are now several journals and series in the field. Next to what has in the meanwhile become a whole pile of introductory textbooks, even handbook-like volumes are being published now, offering broad orientation and surveying numerous investigations. Yet, as with psychology in a more general sense, sometimes uneasiness can be observed, both with psychology of religion and among psychologists of religion themselves. What is it all about? Is the psychology we are developing the one we really need? With all our activities and organizational achievements, what do we really know and what do we really offer?

This state of affairs has been taken as the starting point for a project that resulted into the present collection of papers. The underlying thought has been that—at this very moment in the development of the field—it would be good and appropriate to 'take a step back' and to take a look at the discipline, at its professionals and its 'customers', at its aims and at the way it is being conducted and presented. Therefore we invited scholars with long-standing experiences and reputation in the field to ponder over questions like the following:

"What kind of enterprise is psychology of religion really? What are its practitioners doing? Are they doing what they say they are doing? Are they doing what 'customers' think they are doing? Is psychology of religion a valid enterprise at all? What answer is to be given to the question whether it can exist at all? (i.e. what systematic answer, not a trivial answer pointing out that it does exist empirically in its publications and representatives). What is its position in the logic of scholarly enterprises/university structure: is it (a subdiscipline of) psychology, *Religionswissenschaft*, theology? Has psychology of religion yielded any respectable results already? Results or insights that did not already exist in disciplines like theology, humanities, history? What is it good for? Did it bring any insight into religion? What did it do to religion, if anything? Whom is it serving? And whom is it shaping? What is there to be said on the developments in the recent past, in the last, say, 30 years of growth in numbers and professionalisation? Did quantitative growth bring qualitative improvement?

Are the directions that you can perceive the discipline is going in, desirable ones? Or should it all, or to some extent, be (and have been) otherwise? Are there new, or still underdeveloped, schools of thought psychology of religion should take seriously? Are there any new questions to be answered? Which ones? Or are the questions that should have been answered still with us: waiting for their answer? Is there a necessity for a methodological breakthrough? In what direction is that to be expected?"

We hoped that these kinds of questions would trigger a self-critical reflexion with psychologists of religion. What would they really think about their discipline, about their job? Those persons who are making a living of it and are devoting a great deal of their time and energy to it—if they would have the opportunity to 'start anew', would they enroll again in psychology of religion? What does the field and its vicissitudes mean to them personally? What did it do or mean to them both as scholars and on a more personal level?

These and many other questions are the ones this project takes into consideration. The idea was to invite representatives of the field to state honestly what psychology of religion is to them or according to them. The question was not to ask for a handbook-like outline of how they conceive of the field, nor for their academic definition of the discipline. The question was much more: to tell colleagues and other interested persons their thoughts about the enterprise psychology of religion, whether these thoughts be pessimistic, hopeful, hesitating, reluctant, critical, euphoric, personal (how could they be otherwise?). We solicited from each of the addressed a scholarly/academic essay clearly written by one who is an insider, who has an overview, who is involved and devoted, but who takes a step back and tells what he thinks he and his colleagues are doing. Next to scholarly, we explicitly wanted the essays to be personal, even passionate, taking a stand. The texts sent to us, have been circulated among the contributors to the project in order to give everyone an idea to which kind of project and volume he had committed himself. In the light of this communication, several authors took the opportunity to revise their texts.

Of course, the project as it stands now entails several restrictions. Not every colleague whom we contacted, accepted our invitation to participate in this project. Some may not have liked the idea and this kind of self-critical questions at all. Therefore, this volume does not claim to be representative for the second thoughts of the psychologists of religion in general. Neither does it cover the latest developments in the field, or anything. Inviting people with a history, those who recently joined are by consequence somewhat neglected. Among them who include far more females and non-westerners than this volume would suggest!—different opinions may exist. However, we think we managed to bring together a balanced sample of people who survived both their enthusiasm and disappointment, who are devoted and experienced, and who know what they are talking about. Authors come from sides of the North Atlantic Ocean, from diverse educational backgrounds and from various institutional contexts. The present volume presents the thoughts of influential persons from a variety of countries, ages and perspectives. As we expected and hoped for, the response to our initial invitation has been very diversified. Both authors and editors have found them extremely worthwhile reading and very instructive as contributions to a answer to the question what kind of enterprise psychology of religion might possibly be. We hope and trust that these essays will advance the always necessary self-reflexion of a scholarly discipline.

Amsterdam   Uppsala
Jacob A. Belzen   *Owe Wikström*

How to Assess the Identity of Psychology of Religion ?

J.A. Belzen

> *It is not my wish to discover something new, but rather it is my joy and dearest occupation to ponder over that which is quite simple.*
> *Kierkegaard (p.50)*

Although not a single analogy seems capable of doing justice to the complex semantic whole which is religion, in some respects at least the case of religion seems to be like that of music: whereas it does not do a thing for one person, another gets totally absorbed in it and is increasingly fascinated by it. There are persons who practice hard and forever do their best without ever really succeeding, while others never give it a second thought but in the shower or at work simply whistle their little tune—sometimes way off-key to the dismay of the rest of us. People, in the nature of the case, make all kinds of music but it seems even more important to remember that it is music which makes the people. A musical ear is a specific historical product (Stäuble, 1990), the result of a specific formative social-cultural process. Whether and how people hear and make music, as well as the kind of music they hear or make, seems to depend primarily on their socialization and acculturation, on what they learned at home, though sometimes people also speak of natural talents. It seems that at times the analogy with music can be extended a very long way. Just as the Pythagoreans postulated an omnipresent kind of music (Plato, *Republic*, §§ 530, 617), the music of the celestial spheres, which, however, is not perceptible to the human ear, so some contemporary theoreticians speak of "implicit" or "invisible religion," even when there is no religion to be discerned. We will do well not to exaggerate the applicability of the analogy: though religion can perhaps be compared with music and though in some respects music can even be a functional equivalent of religion, the truth is that religion is not music. The analogy proposed here is one of only limited validity. Anyway, my aim in this essay is not to determine what religion is; my goal is much more modest. I only wish to venture to reflect on the question: What kind of enterprise is the psychology of religion? And what kind of study is needed to answer the question? In that connection I want to explore in how far the somewhat playful analogy between religion and music can be useful.

To some of us the question concerning the identity of the psychology of religion may perhaps seem rather superfluous. The psychology of religion, after all, is an expanding line of business. More and more studies are being published in this field; in recent years various professional journals and series have been started; congresses in the field are being attended by an increasing number of persons; professional organizations have been launched; surveys of the field exist and in recent years a handbook has come into being. All these items are signs of the manifest professionalization of the discipline.[1]

In The Netherlands in particular the discipline seems to have succeeded in definitively establishing itself at the university: at virtually all Dutch universities chairs for the psychology of religion have been instituted. What more can one want? Certainly, but this situation can also be for us an invitation to reflect all the more intensely on the ground rules and foundations, on achievements and possibly unfulfilled promises, on the appearances and actual realities of a professional discipline.

As it happens, the enterprise of the psychology of religion is not a self-evident one, to say nothing of the fact that not very long ago certain first-rate thinkers declared it to be an impossible business (cf., for example, Van den Berg, 1958). Still today the idea that religion and psychology have any connection at all has to be explained over and over to many people, not only outside the university but in the psychological laboratories as well. The fact is, however, that the connections between religion and psychology are extraordinarily numerous: religion can exert significant influence on the starting points, the view of man and epistemology, on the theoretical orientation and methodology, on the way the issues are framed and the way things are organized in a psychology that labels itself a science (cf. Jones, 1994; Ter Meulen, 1988; Van Strien, 1993a). As a rule, certainly in its theoretical articulations, religion holds to a certain anthropology and consequently to an implicit psychology which can be made explicit and confronted or harmonized with present-day secular psychology. Psychology in turn can attend in its theories or in empirical research to the religious aspects of human conduct and experience; some parts of psychology are even specifically directed toward this end and are welcomed by some believers as furnishing insight or an instrumentarium, while others only wish to take suspicious note of it. In certain parts of the West we seem to be witnessing a historical-sociological development which consists in a tendency for psychology to take over various tasks and functions of religion and its representatives.[2] According to some observers, psychology has even

---

[1] To mention a few facts: since 1976 the leading American Psychological Association has had "division 36" which in 1993 was rechristened "Psychology of Religion"; new periodicals are *The International Journal for the Psychology of Religion* (began publication in 1991); *Journal of the Psychology of Religion* (began publication in 1992); in The Netherlands since 1989, there has existed a series named *Studies op het terrein der godsdienstpsychologie* ("Studies in the field of the psychology of religion"); in 1990 the *International Series in the Psychology of Religion* was added. Nowadays the "European Psychologists of Religion" meet once every three years while specialized symposia occur between times; the "World Federation for the Psychology of Religion" is in process of being organized. Comprehensive surveys, among others, those of Meadow & Kahoe (1984), Spilka et al. (1985), Crapps (1986), Brown (1987 and 1988), Grom (1992), and for some time the standard work has been that of Wulff (1991).
[2] As representative of many others I will merely mention London (1986), who spoke about psychotherapists as "a secular priesthood."

assumed the air of a (new) religion (Vitz, 1994). Thus one could cite considerably more examples of various possible relations, on very different levels, between religion and psychology, without, however, necessarily having in view the *psychology of religion*. In this essay we will have to take account of the latter, and only of this specific relation between religion and psychology. But the fact that there are such diverse possibilities of relating the two should make us cautious: the question which of these relations may or may not (yet or any longer) be subsumed under the heading "psychology of religion" would presumably be assessed very differently by different judges.

One must not underestimate the conceptual problems in this field. They are, by and large, linked with the more general problematics of the definition of psychology and its object. It is well-known that members of "professional circles," as they are called, are not at all agreed on that definition. And the problem does not become any easier when one tries to define a form of psychology which addresses itself to a domain of reality which equally resists attempts to force it in the straightjacket of a concept or definition. When are we specifically dealing with the psychology of religion and when is a person considered a psychologist of religion? Does this require a degree in psychology, being accepted by the APA, or having a job in a psychological laboratory? If this is how we reason, we may end up in a situation analogous to the one Duchamp referred to when he placed a urinal in a museum. It is better for us to look at what people in fact do. Take Freud, for example, a person reputed to be one of the patriarchs of the psychology of religion. Was he then a psychologist of religion? In his *opera omnia* the part devoted to religion is very modest; moreover, according to many, psychoanalysis is not psychology in the strict sense at all. So then Freud was not a psychologist of religion? Persons like William Stern, whose name is never missing in any serious account of the history of psychology, is never mentioned anymore in the psychology-of-religion literature. Still, did he not write about the psychology of religion as well (Stern, 1928, 1931)? When Augustine writes about psychologically relevant phenomena (to put it cautiously) in his unmistakably religious autobiography, then is he writing psychology of religion?[3] Does an important book like that of Don Browning (1987) in which he shows that large sections of present-day psychology, especially of clinical psychology, are in fact versions of religious-ethical reflection, belong to the psychology of religion? Pursuing such questions gets us nowhere. The questions are not formulated well.

A rather simple way to stop the process of questioning is, of course, to introduce a strict definition which draws a sharp line between the sheep and the goats. However attractive, fitting, or even necessary this procedure may be under many circumstances, it is not the way we will proceed in this essay. The reason is that the act of definition can easily become arbitrary: "According to

---

[3] To date the beginnings of the psychology of religion later—on the occasion, say, of the opening of a laboratory in Leipzig, as is frequently done for general psychology—is historical nonsense.

one, the answer is yes, but according to another, it is no. . . ." A person runs the great danger that there is much more beauty in the field than the eye of the accidental beholder can discern. It would, furthermore, be scarcely in accord with today's thought to treat an identity, even that of the psychology of religion, as a definitive and univocally definable matter. Just as a person does not primarily exist in and by himself but is constantly being molded by interaction with fellow human beings, so something like the psychology of religion will also change its form depending on the environment in which it operates. Mindful of what Wittgenstein taught concerning games and family resemblances (Wittgenstein, 1960, §66–67), in this essay I want to treat the psychology of religion as belonging to a much larger family, indeed to an old and venerable clan with a family tree reaching back to the days when human beings began to observe themselves in a religious context. In this connection I regard the many and diverse relations between religion and psychology as the numerous descendants who sprang from the contacts between the two. From that larger clan I will choose a family living in the present, the daughters of which I will attempt to portray, daughters who will of course exhibit greater resemblance to each other than to their second cousins, and about whom I as portrait-painter—let me be honest here—do not know everything. To avoid misunderstandings I want to point out that every daughter is a type of her own—this last expression to be understood in the sense of Weber: they do not occur as such in reality (1904). In presenting these provisional sketches I want to go back to the analogy with which this essay begins and attempt to characterize some of the relations of psychology to its object as young ladies in their relation to classical music. By way of the imagery I am now forced to maintain, I invite you to join me on a visit to the Amsterdam *Concertgebouw* (Concert Hall).

Ancilla

The first lady I want to introduce here shares the fate of many an eldest daughter in a large family. She is admonished to cooperate and faithfully offers her services. One finds her in various places in the *Concertgebouw*: she cleans the floors and polishes the brass, she helps people find their way in the building, and offers refreshments to the visitors. Ancilla is her name. All her efforts are aimed at getting people to come and to come eagerly, and especially to keep coming. This daughter is of service to the parental cause and puts herself or remains entirely "within the circle" (Tillich): she helps religion reach its goal. And she does it in various ways, of which I will list three. The first is the attempt to discover, articulate, and give insight into the (classic) psychology which is, implicitly or not, inherent in the great religions—if necessary or useful, with the aid of (present-day) psychological (and/or anthropological) categories. In this manner, the way of life and the spiritual developments as they were presupposed by the religions are disclosed and made accessible to contemporary humans.[4]

A second way consists in those forms of psychology whose aim is to help support religious professionals in their work or become better prepared for their task. The situations for which psychology can be useful to a pastor, or anyone else who works with people, are of course countless, whether it concerns the early detection of a psychic disorder, knowledge of the stages of human life, discussion techniques, or organizational psychology in the interest of church development. Also when this so-called pastoral psychology understands itself more as researcher for the pastor, the persons being pastored, and/or their interaction, its aim continues to be improving the pastor's own functioning.[5]

In the third place, there is the gigantic field of psychological assistance and accompaniment in which, professionally or otherwise and after extensive or little training, religion is chosen as the point of entry in an attempt to foster human well-being. Here, too, the range of variation can be very wide: from counseling by a pastor in the case of, say, relational problems (cf. e.g., Miller & Jackson, 1985; Wicks et al., 1993), via appealing to religious values (cf. Burton, 1992), to and including the offer of or the wish to change a religious frame of reference in an otherwise secular psychotherapy (cf. e.g., Wapnick, 1985; also someone like Frankl belongs in this category). For the moment we will pass over in silence the fact that there is discussion, and that there does need to be thorough discussion, about several of the practices mentioned here by way of example. Here our concern is solely to report that this is one of the ways in which psychology and religion go hand-in-hand and are sometimes contaminated by each other. Even when the primary goal here is different, the effort is by its nature religious and seeks to create and to foster that which one views as the right religious disposition and lifestyle. As stated above, one must remember that Ancilla operates "within the circle": reflectively or not, she serves her own religion.

Critica

A second daughter from the family I wish to introduce is—especially to the mind of the older sister introduced above—a totally different type. Whether this is really true or not remains to be seen. Many family members and ac-

---

[4] In the Netherlands one finds fine examples of this approach in the work of H. de Wit (1987, 1993). Although to some extent I endorse his criticism of large sections of the psychology of religion, I believe that De Wit is needlessly mean towards it: to dismiss it as "third-person psychology" is imprecise in my opinion (as I still hope to show in the text); his plea for "first-person psychology" blocks one's access to the other person and runs the risk of solipsism. In order to avoid the problematics rightly flagged by De Wit, I expect more from an orientation to a hermeneutically-informed psychology, as voiced, for example, by Shotter in his plea for "getting in touch" and for a "second person making sense" perspective (cf. Shotter, 1992, 1993).

[5] Pastoral psychology is currently thriving. As instructive surveys we can mention the works of Rebell (1988), Blattner (1992a, 1992b), and Baumgartner (1990).

quaintances think that precisely these two resemble each other most. It cannot be denied, however, that their public conduct differs considerably: whereas the one performs her task diligently and without much fuss, the other is a noisy and recalcitrant person. She more or less fits the stereotypical image many persons in our society retain of the student of the sixties: nonconformist in behavior and dress, ideologically animated, ever ready to engage in noisy discussions but not productive, always critical, always in opposition, negative, nonconstructive. To many people this is what the psychology of religion is: a kind of critique of religion, an attempt to undermine faith and devotion, a child of the Enlightenment who neither understands herself nor her opposite correctly, an iconoclast. Ignoring all the nuances, people then view the psychology of religion as an essentially reductionistic affair: its aim is allegedly to reduce religion to nothing but psychic processes. All this naturally has to do with the legacy of the father of the psychoanalytic psychology of religion whose probing questions and methodical comparisons in numerous areas very often made waves and whose personal atheism is, mistakenly, attributed also to his intellectual offspring (Freud, 1913, 1927). But the works of other psychologists, in reality much more innocent, have often been treated with the same suspicion: why did Stanley Hall (1904) have to deviate from the standard spiritual discussion on conversion and relate it to such trivial seeming matters as gender, age, and adolescence? And though William James (1902), with the Bible in his hands as it were, wished to judge religious experience by its fruits—why did he neglect to speak about the source of that experience and why did he not employ a religious criterion?

However, though people have often been alarmed by what psychologists propounded about religion, one must nevertheless distinguish the various forms of criticism. Not all criticism springs from aversion. Just as an approach from the perspective of history was initially often experienced as a threat, so also the approach from within the human sciences proves to be something one has to get used to and even today the psychologists of religion must regularly explain that methodological agnosticism does not yet imply ontological atheism. On the contrary: I have a strong impression that the critical questions sometimes posed from within psychology regarding religious phenomena and practices commonly intend—as in the case of prophets and reformers—to call the attention of religion to what those psychologists believe is its "true" core. They wish to differentiate between true religion and its—admittedly many—distortions. The clearest and perhaps the most endearingly naive case of this was that of Oskar Pfister, a Swiss clergyman who embraced psychoanalysis as a means of purging the faith (Pfister, 1928) and in his enthusiasm went so far as to count Freud among the best Christians of all times (Freud/Pfister, *Briefe,* 64).

The enterprise of the psychology of religion seems often to be sustained by a personal concern about (certain aspects of) religion, as the enfant terrible Benjamin Beit-Hallahmi—at times unfairly—never tires of charging (Beit-Hallahmi, 1992, 1993). Sometimes this concern comes out in incidental comments or in non-scientific publications. Allport's (1960) familiar distinction between "extrinsic" and "intrinsic" religion, for example, is certainly not in the last place connected with the observation—one which initially disturbed him—that religiosity shows a high correlation with ethical prejudices (cf. Allport, 1962, 130). His use of the twin-concepts "extrinsic-intrinsic"—already known from older literature—restored people's peace of mind: the existence of forms of religion which associate themselves with prejudice and other vices need not be denied, provided one at the same time bears in mind that intrinsic religiosity is "very different" and does not do this. The extensive and—at least in The Netherlands—influential oeuvre of Han Fortmann is similarly marked by concern for (the restoration of) religious experience.

It would be worthwhile to go through the work of the psychologists of religion precisely with an eye to their presuppositions and implicit biases: it is likely that the two daughters we have so far introduced will then turn out to be much more alike than appeared to be the case at first, or even at second, sight. It is not without significance that Paul Pruyser, an author who wrote a good many prickly articles, in the middle of a piece which dealt, note well, with the "seamy side" of faith, makes the paradoxical-sounding statement: "Thank God for the critics of religion" (1991, 49).

This second daughter is very much like so many non-conformist youth and other dissidents: rebellious in their puberty, they later conform themselves all the more rigorously to the conduct of the parent they at one time criticized. Actually this daughter does not even wish to enter the *Concertgebouw*: she would most like to occupy the building, keep others from entering it, or organize a big protest demonstration at the entrance, all with a view to boycotting the music that is being performed inside. Or, if she has no choice but to be inside the building, then it should be at the ticket counter, reminding everyone who comes in that a price has to be paid for this music. But she does not do this because she is against music as such. By no means; she does it because she thinks that the music being played either cannot be called music, or is not the right music, or because she thinks it scandalous that the music presented in our beloved *Concertgebouw* is being performed in such a hideous way. She does not hate music, only its deformation; she lives for music but is a purist. Though she is considered by many to be a degenerate child, hidden behind her rebellion there is a strong love for the father.

Scientia

Another daughter seeking to be briefly introduced here does again have a seat in the *Concertgebouw* and that in a very favorable location. She is seated in the big hall and watches or listens. Much psychology-of-religion research presents itself as it were in precisely that way—as interested in music and, accordingly, as really attending the concerts, where it takes note of what the performing musicians are doing. In this kind of research people send out questionnaires, subject performers to tests, and registrate reactions in laboratories. In all these activities Scientia seeks to be as unbiased and objective as possible: she continually remembers and keeps saying that there is a gap between her and the people she is examining. The religious experience and praxis studied need not be hers. Methodologically she does not care whether she has to examine people at their prayers, sitting in front of a TV set, or making their rounds at a supermarket. She would preferably do all three and compare the several groups in terms of as many presumably relevant variables as possible. She asks herself, for example, what recreational function a pilgrimage fulfils as compared with viewing television. She wants to know in how far the phenomenon of coping with stress is present when people perform ritual ablutions, when they are queued up in a long line before a cash register, or going to communion. She investigates how frequently and under what circumstances people pray and how these frequencies relate to watching TV and other forms of leisure-time activity. If the parents used to pray one way or another, do the children do the same or do they "zap heaven" in a different way from their parents? Scientia, always careful to present herself as being above all strictly empirical in her orientation, reasons as it were as follows: for people it is basic that they do something with their time; so if people do not pray or no longer pray, they have to spend their time in some other way. How? She will if at all possible publish her results in such prestigious journals as, say, the *Journal for the Scientific Study of Religion*.

Numerous studies have been made in this way and produced significant results. This form of psychological research requires modesty. Each time someone offers a compelling talk about certain psychological aspects of religion, Scientia, with a touch of haughtiness as the true scientist, asks: How does it actually all fit together? How often have you been able to observe the stated sequences empirically? This attitude has produced much that is valuable. To mention just one example: in the broad field of religion and mental health, a field that seems relevant to society, she has invalidated numerous aprioris and sweeping assertions and noted that the relation between these two is far from unambiguous. Whatever can be imagined proves actually to occur in real life as well: religion can be an expression of psychic disturbance, but it can also be the designated manner of channeling or repressing psychic disturbances. Religion can be a danger to mental health but just as well a therapeutic agent or even a means of preventing mental illness (Spilka et al., 1985; Schumaker, 1992). In her endeavor to maintain methodological neutrality and to avoid walking into the trap of one's own preferences, Scientia as much as possible distances herself from contents and meanings and only looks for psychological structures (cf. e.g., Brown, 1987). For that reason she not only examines the religion she knows—accidentally of course—from her own past, but also presents her attitude scales and measuring instruments for cognitive styles to new and/or allochthonous religious groups. She does not shrink from cross-national research. The scientific prestige which the psychology of religion has steadily built up in recent decades is attributable in large part to the effort and tenacity of this distinguished lady. She has proven herself academically competent and open-minded: being interested in music in general, she will listen to a concert with interest and pleasure; whether the musicians play romantically or authentically, she will offer her good will and applause equally to experimental music and to Viennese classics. Tearing herself away from her busy career, this third daughter enjoys going to a concert and, closing her eyes, to surrender herself to the harmonies which surround her, musing and relaxing. . . .

The Music Critic

The fourth daughter, too, is in the hall of the *Concertgebouw* but she sits there for a different reason. To her it is not at all immaterial what music is played and how and by whom it is performed. She has come solely for this concert and is all ears as she listens. The reason is that she wants to learn something about the actual concert given on this particular night. She is perhaps, like her sister, a distinguished person as well, but she is intensely involved. She is looking for an answer to a number of questions: What kind of music is it from this particular composer? How is the music rendered by this conductor? How does the orchestra play a certain passage or other? What is the soloist doing at that particular spot? With a notepad on her lap, she sits erect on her chair. If necessary, she will not hesitate to approach any one of the musicians personally to ask why he interprets the music as he does. This lady listens to the music in virtue of her occupation, you could say: she has chosen to be a professional critic. In this connection she focuses especially on the performing musicians. The psychology of religion, after all, studies concrete persons, persons who are involved in the practice of a particular religion. Its concern is definitely not religion in general.

Psychology of this sort deliberately does not distance itself from the material aspects of religion. Just as the reviewer is not asked to write about music in general but about the how and what of a specific performance, so this psychology is not out to test a definition or an essentialistic determination of religion in general but to study the psychic aspects of a concrete, always historically- and-culturally-situated religious experience or behavior. In so doing it does not, certainly not primarily, focus on the biggest common denominator religion shares with all sorts of other functional behavior possibilities of the human species (as does, for example, Wenegrat, 1990), unless this could serve to bring out the specificity of the subjectivity being examined. This psychology is convinced that, in order to interpret a specific expression of religiosity, it must in fact take notice of precisely the religion in question. If one fails to do this, one does not understand what one is looking at; one does not even know what to look for: one does not *see* anything. For a music critic to be able to give a fitting report on a particular performance, she has to know a lot about music and musical performance practices; so psychology, to do justice to the structure and meaning of, say, a religious experience, has to place it in the framework of the religious references which preceded its genesis (cf. Vergote, 1984). According to the music critic, the discussion of an internal or external perspective as it is often carried on with regard to the study of religion is framed in the wrong terms. Of course, let it be said with emphasis, the critic is not reporting on music she has herself performed; she is talking about music performed *by others*, but this does not at all mean that the subjectivity of the author plays no role in the review. To call this the external perspective, therefore, is hardly adequate; in the psychology of religion one's goal is always to enter into the life and world of the religious other—and how could that happen if one remains outside? On the other hand, the psychology of religion does not identify itself with the religion and its subjects under review inasmuch as it plans to report, at the forum to which she herself belongs, concerning that which is happening inside. Were it to speak completely from within, it would not be producing psychology of religion but documents for the psychology of religion which themselves could be subjected to examination. Certainly the psychology of religion as hermeneutic science lives by metaphors, but one still does better to abandon the metaphors "internal" and "external" as quickly as possible to escape the snares of a dialectic created by concepts which, while conjured under reviewup by oneself, one may no longer know how to get rid of.

To meet the conditions for a correct execution of the task of a music critic is not a simple matter. To do justice to the performers the critical reviewer must not only have a good grasp of the music but must, ideally speaking, also know what it means and what is required to make music. An ideal critic knows of the years of disciplined practice and laborious progression, of enthusiasm, stress, and setbacks during the performance.

Let's try to take a closer look at that special involvement of the psychology of religion with its object, whether as critic with a special interest in the performers or otherwise.

On the Historiography of the Psychology of Religion

We have now introduced four daughters from a much bigger family which has sprung from the relation between religion and psychology. Each of the daughters has of course been described much too briefly and inadequately. We have attempted to highlight the differences, but anyone even slightly involved with them will soon remark that the features which seem so obvious in one are not totally lacking in another. From the very beginning, however, by referring to Wittgenstein I have tried to call attention to this reality. Roughly speaking, one can say that as a rule the psychology of religion remembers that it has to maintain the distinction between itself and the performing musicians: the psychology of religion is called to function as a science seeking understanding, to gather scientific insight, to give an account to "reason", and not to act as an articulator of religion and certainly not at all to construct a religion of its own. Nor must it take it upon itself to make a material judgment with respect to the truth claim which in different ways lies embodied in every religion, nor must it ignore the importance of these truth claims for the people involved. If it does, it loses sight of one of the specific aspects of the religious life form in question and threatens to lose its object even before the investigation has begun. It then becomes trivial, merely still looking for illustrations of things already discussed and familiar everywhere else. But it does not identify itself with the religious truth claim. The psychology of religion, accordingly, is not a form of spiritual direction, not religious psychotherapy, nor pastoral psychology, though use may be made of its insights in each of these other fields. Like such sister-disciplines as, for example, philosophy, history, and phenomenology, psychology possesses its own perspective and focuses attention on the manner in which integration and autonomy as criteria of well-being express themselves in a person's interaction with his environment and in the dynamic interplay among the elements and functions of the psychic life. From its own angle of vision and critical responsibility it inquires into how the activities essential to human life—working, communicating, loving, and enjoying—manifest themselves and develop in the religiosity under review (Vergote, 1988). By its nature, therefore, the psychology of religion is not *ancilla*, the handmaiden of religion.

Now this sounds like a very firm statement and it must certainly not be retracted. We indicated earlier, however, that in many an apparently critical form of the psychology of religion there is in fact a tendency to be protective of the religion recognized as true. In a manner very different from the rather obvious one of the first daughter, the "ancilla" aspect is not lacking in the second daughter and it would be interesting and also relevant to trace the way this aspect plays a role in the other daughter's behavior. In the history-of-science work, which—in ways other than what the logical positivists had in mind—is necessary for reflection on the psychology of religion and the problematics of its foundations, we will do well to bring these questions to bear on the recontextualization of the research. Just as the psychology of religion as such must exert itself to develop insight into the specificity of the religious life form under review, so the relevant history-of-science research must also keep an eye on the presuppositions—often kept implicit—and choice-determinations with respect to this specificity. The contextualism and constructivism which in recent years have been so profitably introduced in the historiography of psychology,[6] must be expanded and radicalized, certainly for the psychology of religion. Foundational research must not occupy itself only with social

---

[6] Cf. Bem (1985, 1990), Ash & Woodward (1987), Danziger (1990) and discussions regularly conducted in *Psychologie en Maatschappij* and in the circles of *Cheiron, European Society for the History of the Behavioral and Social Sciences*.

aspects and techno-economic conditions but involve personal and ideological contexts in its reflections as well. In any case the psychology of religion is much too small a province of psychology to be able to conduct its historiography totally along the lines of, say, Danziger's excellent *Constructing the Subject.* One will have to develop a *modus operandi* that matches its dimensions. To mention a small example, if one wishes to understand why in The Netherlands the psychology of religion could not strike root at the Free University in Amsterdam despite the very early and broad attention which it enjoyed at this private university, this would seem to have a lot to do with social factors—hardly at all with economic conditions—but everything with what, for the sake of convenience, we will simply but nonpejoratively call its ideological climate: with presuppositions not only relative to psychology but equally as much with regard to religion and religiosity. Critical reflection as it has developed in psychology—certainly since the sixties— still leaves us with the question concerning the *ancilla* role of the psychology of religion in all its forms, including that of the detached practitioner of the discipline. Who was being served by the psychology of religion? What interests were at issue? What values are manifest in what it offers as the results of its research? Why did people set aside time, money, and personnel for it? Who or what determined its agenda in teaching and research? In this connection what themes were ruled out and for what reason? In short: who benefited by it and why? All these questions need to be answered if we are to determine what the psychology of religion is. The psychology of religion does not consist solely in its theories; it has presuppositions beyond the merely philosophical and theological.

Let me say a word here about the personal context in which all the work done in the psychology of religion can be and, in my opinion, needs to be framed. In the identification of all those for whom the psychology of religion is or has been the *ancilla,* we can make fruitful heuristic use of the relational model described by Van Strien (1993b) for the historiography of psychology in general, provided we expand it with the notion, important in any case to the psychology of religion, that she is also the *ancilla* of the psychologists of religion *themselves.* (And I do not mean this in the trivial sense that they derive income and academic positions from it.) Just as, especially since Foucault, we are beginning to discover that (scientific) knowledge is not only a matter of knowing but also (an exponent of) power, so some parts of psychology call attention to the fact that knowledge can also be deconstructed as the reproduction of the dynamics of a life history.[7] Psychoanalysis in particular demonstrates that the nature and content of the work of any thinker whatsoever shows the traces of the dynamic configurations and conflicts which belong to the personality structure of the individual in question.

The will to start (at last!) considering this can be a significant boost to the

---

[7] For that matter this insight has been operative in the formation of feminist theory for some time (cf. Riger, 1992); for an example which functions in the psychology of religion, cf. Goldenberg (1990).

still reluctantly evolving psychology of science[8] and can enlarge the still barely existing social-psychology-informed historiography of psychology (cf. Graumann, 1994; Van Strien, 1991) with an individual-psychological orientation. To slip in an aside, let me comment that the resistance of the philosophers of knowledge, primarily those of a normative disposition, against what they mistakenly dismiss as psychologism, bears a strong resemblance to the accusation which was directed, in a past that is still with us, against the psychology of religion. The desire to give up Popper's strict separation between a "context of discovery" and a "context of justification" and to recognize that in the establishment of truth and validity, aside from logic, subjective factors basically and necessarily play a role as well, seems to them virtually equivalent to blasphemy. It would be interesting to take a closer look at this pseudo-sacralization of science and to consider the extent to which the latter also speaks to the position of religion in our society.

It is presumably a dread of a supposed relapse into the so-called "great-men-approach" which makes the historians of psychology skittish toward everything that looks like psychohistory (just as this, in a more general way, is also still the case in the historical sciences; cf. Röckelein, 1993). The permanent and necessary methodological gains which the sociology of knowledge and social historiography have contributed in general are not abandoned, however, if one acknowledges that all knowledge (and therefore also the knowledge that is given formalized scientific shape) remains a human creation. Certainly, if thanks to hermeneutic reflection we do not by way of reaction lose sight of the critical insight that human beings are the products rather than the producers of culture, there is no danger of psychological reduction, neither in the human scientific study of religion, nor in the history of psychology.

When I stated a moment ago that we should explore in how far the psychology of religion is and has been the *ancilla* of the psychologists of religion themselves, I had in mind something other and more than a possible salute to a psycho-historical approach in historiography. This, as I indicated, would definitely have to be combined with a critical analysis of the presuppositions which psychologists of religion entertain with regard to their object of study. By this process it will become evident that much of what has entered history as the theory formation of the psychology of religion is marked by a personal struggle to gain intellectual clarity and a personal position with respect to what can and may be believed. We may suppose that the psychologists of religion, as forerunners of their generation and/or as grassroots members of a religious-community, sensed in advance and sometimes also grasped the confrontation of their own religion with, and the necessary acculturation in, the changing times. Anxiously, in their own usually undogmatic but seldom antidogmatic way, they searched for a contemporary articulation of the faith, one that was in the first place satisfying to themselves but to their religious community as

---

[8] Cf. The recent theme issue of *Psychologie en Maatschappij,* 1992, *16* (4), 347–425.

well. This community, after all, inhabits them even more than they inhabit it. These psychologists who, note well, often first received a theological training, devote themselves to the study of religion because, from their own involvement in it, they are in search of insight in and a personal relation to that phenomenon.

On the one hand, of course, this is no big thing: why should a person study a subject if he were not deeply interested in it? But for many people who still understand science in accordance with the ideals of modernity and think that subjectivity may not play a role in it, this is reprehensible. Like the third daughter we described earlier, they believe that, methodologically, it should not make any difference whether the psychologist studies soccer players, cheese merchants, or believers. The psychologist *as psychologist,* we are triumphantly told, has no judgment of his own about—let us say—the taste of the different kinds of cheese being sold. He or she only records whether and how many people buy and eventually consume them. Again: it is indeed true and the gains of such happy sayings may not be lost. At the same time it is also naive, for the psychologist as psychologist does not exist empirically: he is an invention of modernistic signature. The psychologist always remains a human being of flesh and blood, the point at which culture and the life history of an individual intersect. Accordingly, in his study of religion he remains codetermined by his subjectivity. Even when he methodologically opts for giving primacy to the voice of the objective or, in any case, detached man of science, the background choir of many other incarnate voices continues to shape the tone color as a whole. The researcher who ignores or denies his own subjectivity resembles a listener in a music hall who does not care what is being played and how it is played on the stage up front: he listens with an appropriate degree of attention or politeness but when he returns to his home his head is already focused on other matters and he is no longer able to submit a report of any interest. Such a form of psychology of religion produces, along with all the good things, a multiplicity of facts and factoids without much insight or coherence, superseded as quickly as they are forgotten. Such a psychology was harshly judged in the well-known Gergen article of 1973, and in a historiography aiming at the determination of identity we certainly need not study it extensively. On the other hand, the approaches which are still remembered are those which have really had something substantive to say, however one-sided at times. Ideally, the psychologist of religion learns not to forget his own subjectivity but to employ it in such a way that it serves to make clearer what he studies rather than to conceal it.[9] If a reviewer indulges in a display of personal feelings or value judgments, she does not know her business. But if, in order to do justice to the performance, she brings her knowledge and enthusiasm to

---

[9] With increasing frequency, in other places as well, it is stated that psychological research needs to let go of its detachment, in order to find something meaningful; that it must not separate subjects from their everyday reality but employ experience-friendly techniques (cf. Voestermans, 1992).

bear on it, no one will hold the inevitably subjective coloration against her, though this does not mean at all that readers will endorse her every opinion. The psychology of religion—now that according to some people modernity seems to be on its last legs—must learn even more rigorously than in the past to abandon the last remnants of positivism and to view subjectivity not as an inescapable evil but as part of the royal road of knowledge that does not need to be immediately furnished with moral labels. In this connection it is worth calling attention to the epistemological discussions carried on in present-day psychoanalysis on the theme of "countertransference". Put in very simplified terms, what it comes down to is that it is increasingly being recognized that to gain access to the subjectivity of the person being investigated there is no other way than the subjectivity of the investigator himself (cf., e.g., Hirsch & Aron, 1991).[10] Also in the historiography of the psychology of religion, therefore, one must not neglect the subjective relation of the psychologist in question to religion.

In distinction from what has happened in the case of Scientia—the daughter who presented herself as "the truly scientific investigator"—the subjectively-colored reviews of the fourth daughter have often been preserved. Although they were sometimes rather personal and therefore probably one-sided, often she gave very striking descriptions of certain parts of the concert, sometimes in such a way that at later performances the orchestra even attempted to reckon with them. Remarks about religion as neurosis (Freud, 1907), for example, have not yet been forgotten, in contrast to stocktaking surveys such as *The Social Psychology of Religion* (Argyle & Beit-Hallahmi, 1975). They may have been made from a one-sided perspective but they did proceed from a subjective involvement which, far from wanting to be religious, was a lifelong critical and restless engagement with religious figures, ideas, and behaviors.[11] The *Zeitschrift für Religionspsychologie* which was at one time published by the *Internationale Religionspsychologische Gesellschaft,* had as motto on the title page of the first installment: *Deum et animam scire cupio* ("I desire to know both God and the soul"). It would be a historical error, of course, to trot out Aristotelian, Augustinian, and whatnot psychology as the direct forerunners of today's psychology. Still with this motto the editor, Karl Beth, seems to have had a good sense of the fact that psychologists of religion, by way of the detour of the human religiosity they were examining, were definitely also—obviously and simultaneously—on a search mission for insight into the specific disclosure of reality offered by religion. They share the earlier desideratum of Augustine and of so many spiritual and/or theologi-

---

[10] Let dilettantes beware: learning to cultivate and handle "free-floating attentiveness" is laborious, is seldom totally successful, and requires much training and self-knowledge. In many respects it is easier, by means of cognition alone, to pass a doctoral exam, say in psychology.
[11] In the meantime this has been endlessly described, specifically in the case of Freud, the "unmasker" (Ricoeur) par excellence. I will only mention one recent publication: Rice (1990), particularly because he so neatly counters the central thesis of the much better-known work of Gay (1987).

cal thinkers before them: like those earlier ones, the psychology of religion as *quaerens intellectum* ("seeking understanding") is an expression of *fides* (faith). Just as earlier thinkers often believed that based on their reflection on the fides *quae* they should definitely have to say something about the fides *qua,* so many psychologists of religion similarly attempt to discover something about the *fides quae* by way of an analysis of the *fides qua*. Present in the psychology of religion, even when like her distinguished sister Scientia, she tries to conduct herself as academically as possible, there is the genetic potential of Ancilla, while she belongs to the same blood-type as Critica. Sometimes—just as this sometimes happens in the case of such totally different thinkers as Buber, Levinas, or even Derrida (1987)—she threatens to lose sight of the boundary between academic exposition *about* and an actualizing resumption *from within.* For herself and others she is looking for a genuine, purified faith that can stand the criticism of science and culture, in the process occasionally running the risk of speaking only about ethereal figures and forgetting that many of the actually encountered forms of religion and religiosity are fairly monstrous in nature.[12]

Just to make one more allusion to family likenesses: at this point even theology and psychology prove to be shirt-tail relations. They are both, be it in very different ways, forms of *fides quaerens intellectum.* It would be useful to investigate to what extent psychologists of religion have also been the spiritual leaders of their respective communities. How were their publications received? Did they in fact make a contribution to present-day thought and conduct relative to religion or are they much more a reflection of a shift to the subject, as that seems to have been the case in so many areas of twentieth-century culture? To cite a few examples from The Netherlands[13]: was not the work of Fortmann so widely read because, vicariously, on behalf of the Catholic part of the Dutch population, he was in search of a religious posture which could stand the critical test of psychology? Is not Faber's own liberal search for spirituality perceptible in his pendulum-like movement toward the psychology of religion? On the other hand, are not the strategic highways Vergote built to the place where theology, philosophy, and psychology meet typical for his own—still religiously reasonably homogeneous—flat Flemish homeland? Had he lived in The Netherlands, would he not have built more bridges and in Switzerland more tunnels? In short, could the work of any thinker and by implication the psychologist of religion ever be understood in isolation from socio-historical and autobiographical-spiritual elements? Would that even be desirable? Aside from those elements, would that understanding not be largely mythical?

---

[12] In this connection, cf. the critical (and sometimes incorrect) discussion of Smith & Handelman by L. Balter (1993).

[13] For some information on psychology of religion in The Netherlands, cf. Belzen (1994).

Bibliography

Allport, G.W. (1960). Religion and prejudice. In: G.W. Allport. *Personality and social encounter* (pp. 257–267). Boston: Beacon Press.
Allport, G.W. (1962). Prejudice: is it societal or personal? *Journal of Social Issues, 18*, 120–174.
Argyle, M. & B. Beit-Hallahmi (1975). *The social psychology of religion.* London: Routledge & Kegan Paul.
Ash, M.G. & W.R. Woodward (Eds.) (1987). *Psychology in twentieth-century thought and society.* Cambridge: Cambridge University Press.
Balter, L. (1993). [Review J.H. Smith & S.A. Handelman. *Psychoanalysis and religion.*]. *The Psychoanalytic Quarterly, 62*(3), 481–486.
Baumgartner, I. (Ed.) (1990). *Handbuch der Pastoralpsychologie.* Regensburg: Pustet.
Beit-Hallahmi, B. (1992). Between religious psychology and the psychology of religion. In: M. Finn & J. Gardner (Eds.). *Object relations theory and religion: clinical applications.* Westport, Connecticut/London: Praeger.
Beit-Hallahmi, B. (1993). Three ideological traditions and the psychology of religion. *The International Journal for the Psychology of Religion, 3* (2), 95–96.
Belzen, J.A. (1994). Between feast and famine. A sketch of the development of the psychology of religion in the Netherlands. *International Journal for the Psychology of Religion*, 1994, 4, 181–198.
Bem, S. (1985). *Het bewustzijn te lijf: een geschiedenis van de psychologie in samenhang met culturele en maatschappelijke ontwikkelingen van 1600 tot het begin van de 20e eeuw.* Meppel: Boom.
Bem, S. (1990). Contextuele geschiedschrijving. In: P.J. van Strien & J.F.H. van Rappard (Eds.). *Grondvragen van de psychologie: een handboek theorie en grondslagen.* Assen: Van Gorcum.
Berg, J.H. van den (1958). *Psychologie en geloof: een kroniek en een standpunt.* Nijkerk: Callenbach.
Blattner, J., B. Gareis & A. Plewa (Eds.) (1992a). *Handbuch der Psychologie für die Seelsorge* (Band 1: Psychologische Grundlagen). Düsseldorf: Patmos.
Blattner, J., B. Gareis & A. Plewa (Eds.) (1992b). *Handbuch der Psychologie für die Seelsorge* (Band 2: Angewandte Psychologie). Düsseldorf: Patmos.
Brown, L.B. (1987). *The psychology of religious belief.* London/Orlando: Academic Press.
Brown, L.B. (1988). *The psychology of religion: an introduction.* London: Society for Promoting Christian Knowledge.
Browning, D.S. (1987). *Religious thought and the modern psychologies.* Philadelphia: Fortress.
Burton, L.A. (Ed.) (1992). *Religion and the family: when God helps.* New York: Haworth Pastoral Press.
Crapps, R.W. (1986). *An introduction to the psychology of religion.* Macon, Georgia: Mercer University Press.
Danziger, K. (1990). *Constructing the subject: historical origins of psychological research.* Cambridge: Cambridge University Press.
Derrida, J. (1987). Chora. In: *Poikilia: études offertes à Jean-Pierre Vernant.* Paris: Editions de l'Ecole des Hautes Etudes en Sciences Sociales.
Freud, S. (1907). Zwangshandlungen und Religionsübungen. In: *Gesammelte Werke: chronologisch geordnet. Band VII: Werke aus den Jahren 1906–1909* (pp. 129–139) (Eds. A. Freud et al.). London: Imago, 1941.
Freud, S. (1913). *Totem und Tabu: einige Übereinstimmungen im Seelenleben der Wilden und der Neurotiker (Gesammelte Werke: chronologisch geordnet. Band IX.)* (Eds. A. Freud et al.). London: Imago, 1940.

Freud, S. (1927). Die Zukunft einer Illusion. In: *Gesammelte Werke: chronologisch geordnet. Band XIV: Werke aus den Jahren 1925–1931* (pp. 325–380) (Eds. A. Freud et al.). London: Imago, 1948.

Freud, S. & O. Pfister (1963). *Briefe 1909–1939* (Eds. E.L. Freud & H. Meng). Frankfurt am Main: Fischer.

Gay, P. (1987). *A godless Jew: Freud, atheism and the making of psychoanalysis.* New Haven/London: Yale University Press.

Gergen, K.J. (1973). Social psychology as history. *Journal of Personality and Social Psychology, 26* (2), 309–320.

Goldenberg, N.R. (1990). *Returning words to flesh: feminism, psychoanalysis, and the resurrection of the body.* Boston: Beacon.

Graumann, C.F. (1994). Die Forschergruppe: zum Verhältnis von Sozialpsychologie und Wissenschaftsforschung. In: W.M. Sprondel (Ed.). *Die Objektivität der Ordnungen* (pp. 381–403). Frankfurt: Suhrkamp.

Grom, B. (1992). *Religionspsychologie.* München: Kösel.

Hall, G.S. (1904). *Adolescence: its psychology and its relations to physiology, anthropology, sociology, sex, crime, religion, and education* (2 vols.). New York: Appleton.

Hirsch, I. & L. Aron (1991). Participant-observation, perceptivism, and countertransference. In: H.B. Siegel, L. Barbanel, I. Hirsch, J. Lasky, H. Silverman & S. Warshaw (Eds.). *Psychoanalytic reflections on current issues* (pp. 78–95). New York: New York University Press.

James, W. (1902). *The varieties of religious experience. A study in human nature.* Hammondsworth: Penguin, 1982.

Jones, S.L. (1994). A constructive relationship for religion with the science and profession of psychology: perhaps the boldest model yet. *American Psychologist, 49* (3), 184–199.

Kierkegaard, S. (1980). The concept of anxiety: a simple psychologically orienting deliberation on the dogmatic issue of hereditary sin. In: *Kierkegaard's writing, vol. VIII* (edited and translated with Introduction and notes by Reidar Thomte in colloboration with Albert B. Anderson) Princeton: Princeton University Press.

London, P. (1986[2]). *The modes and morals of psychotherapy.* Washington, DC: Hemisphere.

Meadow, M.J. & R.D. Kahoe (1984). *Psychology of religion: religion in individual lives.* New York: Harper & Row.

Meulen, R.H.J. ter (1988). *Ziel en zaligheid: de receptie van de psychologie en van de psychoanalyse onder de katholieken in Nederland, 1900–1965.* Nijmegen: Katholiek Studiecentrum.

Miller, W.R. & K.A. Jackson (1985). *Practical psychology for pastors.* Englewood Cliffs, NJ: Prentice Hall.

Pfister, O. (1928). Die Illusion einer Zukunft. In: E. Nase & J. Scharfenberg (Eds.). *Psychoanalyse und Religion.* Darmstadt: Wissenschaftliche Buchgesellschaft, 1977.

Pruyser, P.W. (1991). *Religion in psychodynamic perspective.* New York/Oxford: Oxford University Press.

Rebell, W. (1988). *Psychologisches Grundwissen für Theologen: ein Handbuch.* München: Kaiser.

Rice, E. (1990). *Freud and Moses: the long journey home.* Albany, NY: State University of New York Press.

Riger, S. (1992). Epistemological debates, feminist voices: science, social values, and the study of women. *American Psychologist, 47* (6), 730–740.

Röckelein, H. (Ed.) (1993). *Biographie als Geschichte.* Tübingen: Diskord.

Schumaker, J.F. (Ed.) (1992). *Religion and mental health.* New York/Oxford: Oxford University Press.

Shotter, J. (1992). 'Getting in touch': the meta-methodology of a postmodern science of mental life. In: S. Kvale (Ed.). *Psychology and postmodernism* (pp. 58–73). London: Sage.
Shotter, J. (1993). *Conversational realities: constructing life through language.* London: Sage.
Spilka, B. et al. (1985). *The psychology of religion: an empirical approach.* Englewood Cliffs, NJ: Prentice-Hall.
Stäuble, I. (1990). Historische Psychologie und kritische Sozialwissenschaft. In: M. Sonntag (Ed.). *Von der Machbarkeit des Psychischen.* Pfaffenweiler: Centaurus.
Stern, W. (1928). Zur Religionspsychologie des Jugendlichen. *Zeitschrift für Pädagogische Psychologie, experimentelle Pädagogik und jugendkundliche Forschung, 29,* 584–585.
Stern, W. (1931). Religiosität als "absolute Introzeption". *Zeitschrift für Religionspsychologie (Beiträge zur religiösen Seelenforschung und Seelenführung), 4,* 57–60.
Strien, P.J. van (1991). Zu einer Psychologie der Wissenschaftsentwicklung. In: H.E. Lück & R. Miller (Eds.). *Theorien und Methoden psychologiegeschichtlicher Forschung* (pp. 54–65). Göttingen: Hogrefe.
Strien, P.J. van (1993a). *Nederlandse psychologen en hun publiek: een contextuele geschiedenis.* Assen: Van Gorcum.
Strien, P.J. van (1993b). The historical practice of theory construction. *Annals of Theoretical Psychology, 8,* 149–227.
Vergote, A. (1984). *Religie, geloof en ongeloof: psychologische studie.* Antwerpen/Amsterdam: De Nederlandse Boekhandel.
Vergote, A. (1988). *Guilt and desire: religious attitudes and their pathological derivatives.* Yale: Yale University Press.
Vitz, P.C. (1994). *Psychology as religion. The cult of self-worship.* Grand Rapids: Eerdmans.
Voestermans, P.P.L.A. (1992). Cultuurpsychologie: van cultuur in de psychologie naar psychologie in 'cultuur'. *Nederlands Tijdschrift voor de Psychologie, 47,* 151–162.
Wapnick, K. (1985). Forgiveness: a spiritual psychotherapy. In: E.M. Stern (Ed.). *Psychotherapy and the religiously committed patient.* New York: Haworth.
Weber, M. (1904). Die 'Objektivität' sozialwissenschaftlicher und sozialpolitischer Erkenntnis. In: *Gesammelte Aufsätze zur Wissenschaftslehre.* Tübingen: Mohr, 1988[7].
Wenegrat, B. (1990). *The divine archetype: the sociobiology and psychology of religion.* Lexington, Mass.: Lexington Books.
Wicks, R.J., R.D. Parsons & D. Capps (Eds.) (1993). *Clinical handbook of pastoral counseling, volume 1.* Mahwah, NJ: Paulist (expanded edition).
Wit, H.F. de (1987). *Contemplatieve psychologie.* Kampen: Kok. (English translation: *Contemplative psychology.* Pittsburgh, Pa.: Duquesne University, 1991)
Wit, H.F. de (1993). *De verborgen bloei: over de psychologische achtergronden van spiritualiteit.* Kampen: Kok.
Wittgenstein, L. (1960). *Schriften.* Frankfurt am Main: Suhrkamp Verlag.
Wulff, D.M. (1991). *Psychology of religion: classic and contemporary views.* New York: John Wiley & Sons.

Shame, Melancholy, and the Introspective Method in Psychology of Religion

Donald Capps

The editors' invitation to "take a step back" in order to "take a look at the discipline" of psychology of religion brought to mind—by way of contrast—viewers' reactions to the paintings of J.M.W. Turner, the 19th Century English artist whose works typically featured an overwhelmingly bright sun. So effective was Turner's replication of the sun's brightness that one early observer said that the sun in a Turner painting "absolutely dazzles the eyes" while another noted: "The only way to be reconciled to the picture is to look at it from as great a distance as the width of the gallery will allow". A contemporary art critic notes: "These early critics recognized some obscure danger involved in looking at this picture. It is like looking the sun in the eye. There is danger of being blinded. Best is to look at a safe distance, from the other side of the room" (Miller, 1992:134). He also notes, however, that the dazzling brilliance of color and light that Turner was able to achieve was subject to "solar retribution". An early critic, John Ruskin, describes what typically happened to a Turner painting with the brief passage of time:

> No picture of Turner's is seen in perfection a month after it is painted. The Walhalla cracked before it had been eight days in the Academy rooms; the vermilions frequently lose lustre long before the Exhibition is over; and when all the colors begin to get hard a year or two after the picture is painted, a painful deadness and opacity comes over them, the whites especially becoming lifeless, and many of the warmer passages settling into a hard valueless brown, even if the paint remains perfectly firm, which is far from being always the case (Miller, 1992:165).

Thus, Turner's project to "create out of paint a second sun that would not be an imitation of light, but a light-source itself" (p. 135) was successful, but his achievement was unstable, subject to almost immediate decomposition.

If we are being asked to take a single step backward, the implied message is that contemporary psychology of religion is not nearly as "dazzling" or "obscurely dangerous" as Turner's artistic achievements. Nor is there any suggestion that what is being done invites "solar retribution" in the form of an almost immediate decomposition of the dazzling achievement. As the editors point out, "In recent decennia psychology of religion has managed to obtain a stable position: there has been a growing interest in work done and published by psychologists of religion, both in religious circles and in broader society; a number of academic positions have been established devoted exclusively to the discipline, the number of publications has increased significantly and there are now several journals and series in the field." Stability has been achieved, and there is little danger that the discipline will decompose itself.

On the other hand, the editors have not asked contributors to write essays that necessarily celebrate these achievements. There is a note of disquiet in their invitation, for they have also asked us to consider whether psychology of religion is a valid enterprise at all, and what we think of recent developments? Did quantitative growth bring qualitative improvement? And this personal question: "If you would have the opportunity to 'start anew', would you enroll again in psychology of religion?"

With these questions, the editors are asking us to "take a step backward" so as to gain some perspective on the discipline, but, especially in that last question, they are also asking us to "take a look inside," to be introspective. This is an invitation that I greatly appreciate, as I believe it is precisely the introspective character of psychology of religion that we are most in danger of losing. It survives largely because, no matter how rigorous we may be in disallowing it, it cannot be gotten rid of entirely. As E.G. Boring wrote in 1953, "Introspection is still with us, doing its business under various aliases, of which *verbal report* is one" (quoted in Bakan, 1967:95).

Introspective Observation: First, Foremost and Always

What psychology of religion is in danger of losing, or perhaps never really possessed except in a few eccentrically dazzling displays, is an adequate appreciation for the role that introspection plays in making psychology of religion a unique and distinctive discipline. Without an appreciation for introspection, psychology of religion is hardly different from any of the other disciplines in religious studies: sociology of religion, anthropology of religion, history of religion, and so forth. If I now answer in the affirmative the personal question, "If you would have the opportunity to 'start anew', would you enroll again in psychology of religion?" this is because it was the only discipline in religious studies at the time I was searching for a field of study that affirmed introspection as the way to discover the meaning of whatever phenomenon was the subject of study. History of religion, which had attracted me for its breadth of subject matter, did not have the commitment to introspection that I experienced in courses taught by James E. Dittes at Yale Divinity School and by David Bakan at the University of Chicago. (Their commitment to introspection is discernible in most everything they have written, but writings that make it explicit are Dittes [1977] and Bakan [1967].) What these two mentors impressed upon me was that psychology of religion is less identifiable for its subject matter (as this would be anything deemed religious or relevant to it) or its primary literature (neither taught courses that took the student systematically through the major schools or traditions), but for its way of going about the study of religion, and this was that introspection was a fundamental, not incidental or expendable feature of the process.

In *The Principles of Psychology*, William James suggests that psychology has three methods of investigation, the experimental, the comparative, and introspective observation, and it is the latter that "we have to rely on first and foremost and always" (James, 1950, I:185). He notes that "The word introspection need hardly be defined—it means, of course, the looking into our own minds and reporting what we there discover". What we "there discover" are "thoughts" about phenomena outside the mind, or believed to exist outside the mind; but the word "thoughts," he suggests, may be misleading because our minds are as likely to contain inchoate feelings and sensations as clear perceptions and ideas. In fact, it is not until the psychologist reports and writes about these "states of mind" (which are his own) that he is able to "name them, classify and compare them and trace their relations to other things. Whilst alive they are their own property; it is only *post-mortem* that they become his prey" (p. 189). James does not dismiss the common charge that introspection is difficult and also fallible:

> But since the rest of this volume will be little more than a collection of illustrations of the difficulty of discovering by direct introspection exactly what our feelings and their relations are, we need not anticipate our own future details, but just state our general conclusion that *introspection is difficult and fallible; and that the difficulty is simply that of all observation of whatever kind*. Something is before us; we do our best to tell what it is, but in spite of our good will we may go astray, and give a description more applicable to some other sort of thing. The only safeguard is in the final *consensus* of our further knowledge about the thing in question, later views correcting earlier ones, until at last the harmony of a consistent system is reached. Such a system, gradually worked out, is the best guarantee the psychologist can give for the soundness of any particular psychological observation which he may report. Such a system we ourselves must strive, as far as may be, to attain (pp. 191–192).

It is fair to say that much of what goes by the name of psychology of religion today is non-introspective. Introspection places the investigator's state of mind—and hence, one's own subjectivity—at the very center of the process of observation, and this is precisely what most psychology of religion today is systematically against. For most of our colleagues in the discipline, introspection is a contaminant, an illegitimate introduction of a subjective element into what is supposed to be an objective procedure. The result is that psychology of religion becomes indistinguishable from sociology of religion, and the irony is that the results of this "objective" process may not tell us anything that is interesting or worth knowing about the object of observation. In contrast, the introspective method never fails to reveal something that is interesting or worth knowing about the world around us because this method registers our own reactions to this world. If *our* reactions to any object of investigation are neither interesting to us nor worth our own reflecting upon, then we can only conclude that the object itself has no attractive power, nothing that piques our interest, our desire to investigate, to know it better, more fully, more intimately. In his chapter in *The Principles* on "The Perception of Reality," James writes:

> The mere fact of appearing as an object at all is not enough to constitute reality. That may be metaphysical reality, reality for God; but what we need is practical reality, reality for ourselves; and to have that, an object must not only appear, but it must appear both *interesting* and *important*. The worlds whose objects are neither interesting nor important we treat simply negatively, we brand them as unreal... *In this sense, whatever excites and stimulates our interests is real*; whenever an object so appeals to us that we turn to it, accept it, fill our mind with it, or practically take account of it, so far it is real for us, and we believe it. Whenever, on the contrary, we ignore it, fail to consider it or act upon it, despise it, reject it, forget it, so far it is unreal for us and disbelieved. Hume's account of the matter was then essentially correct, when he said that belief in anything was simply the having the idea of it in a lively and active manner (James, 1950, II: 295).

Much of what is called "psychology of religion" today simply does not stimulate my interest, is therefore unreal to me, which is also to say that I simply do not believe in it. As the editor of the *Journal for the Scientific Study of Religion* for five years (1983–1988 issues), I found myself in the awkward position of having to defend my discipline against the charge by my theologian colleagues that psychology of religion is just a lot of "numbers crunching." In one sense, it wasn't difficult to defend my discipline against these particular critics, because, after all, James, in my view, had gotten it right when he said in *The Varieties* that we will always have theologians because someone will always be needed to serve as the museum curators for dead religion (pp. 446–447).

But James does not spare the scientists either, and his charge against them strikes much closer to home as it applies to so much that goes by the name of psychology of religion. His complaint against the scientists is that they cast a deathly pall over the observable world by reducing it to "mathematical and mechanical modes of conception" and thus eliminating its "human suggestiveness":

> For our ancestors... most things were taken into the mind from the point of view of their human suggestiveness, and the attention confined itself exclusively to the aesthetic and dramatic aspects of events. How indeed could it be otherwise? The extraordinary value, for explanation and prevision, of those mathematical and mechanical modes of conception which science uses, was a result that could not possibly have been expected in advance. Weight, movement, velocity, direction, position, what thin, pallid, uninteresting ideas! How could the richer animistic aspects of Nature, the peculiarities and oddities that make phenomena picturesquely striking or expressive, fail to have been first singled out and followed by philosophy as the more promising avenue to the knowledge of Nature's life? Well, it is still in these richer animistic and dramatic aspects that religion delights to dwell. It is the terror and beauty of phenomena, the "promise" of the dawn and

of the rainbow, the "voice" of the thunder, the "gentleness" of the summer rain, the "sublimity" of the stars, and not the physical laws which these things follow, by which the religious mind still continues to be most impressed (pp. 497–498).

"What thin, pallid, uninteresting ideas!" Doesn't this complaint, this lament, apply to much that goes by the name of psychology of religion today? And what is the fate of "religion" in the process? Doesn't it become thin, pallid and uninteresting as well?

James's own lifelong struggle with melancholy provides the introspective fulcrum from which these criticisms of both theology and science are made. As he points out in his chapter in *The Varieties of Religious Experience* on "The Sick Soul", for melancholiacs, the observable world has become dead and lifeless, a scene of unrelieved, unremarkable grey. The melancholiac knows the spell is lifting when he perceives a yellow jonquil on an early day in March, when the world comes alive again, virtually daring the observer to try *not* to notice (pp. 63, 476–477). If the theologians are the closet-naturalists of the deity, reducing the unseen world to "a set of titles obtained by a mechanical manipulation of synonyms ... verbality stepping into the place of vision" (p. 446), the scientists are guilty of another reductionism, that of describing the seen world by means of "mathematical and mechanical modes of conception". There is a special irony in this as far as the scientist *of religion* is concerned, because his methods of observation kill the very phenomenon that he has chosen for study, for religion lives to the degree and extent that it draws on its "animistic" roots. Are our "scientific studies" of religion, then, even worse than the theologians' obituaries of religion—are they not more like casualty reports, enumerating the dead and injured?

James suggests that the "abstract definitions and systems" of the theologians and the "mathematical and mechanical modes of conception" which science uses are both poor substitutes for the likes of a Saint Augustine whose "speculations" about the world he bids us "listen to". Saint Augustine writes:

> Who gave to chaff such power to freeze that it preserves snow buried under it, and such power to warm that it ripens green fruit? Who can explain the strange properties of fire itself, which blackens all that it burns, though itself bright, and which, though of the most beautiful colors, discolors almost all that it touches and feeds upon, and turns blazing fuel into grimy cinders?. . . Then what wonderful properties do we find in charcoal, which is so brittle that a light tap breaks it, and a slight pressure pulverizes it, and yet is so strong that no moisture rots it, nor any time causes it to decay? (in James, 1950, p. 496).

James adds: "Such aspects of things as these, their naturalness and unnaturalness, the sympathies and antipathies of their superficial qualities, their eccentricities, their brightness and strength and destructiveness, were inevitably the ways in which they originally fastened our attention" (p. 496).

The same, of course, could be said of the individuals who people our world, especially those who "stand out" for us among the masses because they have been our parents, our grandparents, our sisters and brothers, our spouses and children, our friends and enemies. It was the sympathies and antipathies of their superficial qualities, their eccentricities, their brightness and strength and destructiveness that were inevitably the ways in which they originally fastened our attention.

In a recent volume on Hjalmar Sundén, Owe Wikström relates how he has recently been poring over almost-illegible diaries from his early years at the University of Uppsala in the 1960s in quest of the impact of his mentor. What he has found is "an unruly mess of notes about appointments, exams, tennis, money and other trivialities" (Wikström, 1995:17). But this exercise recalled the day he had come to the University to matriculate. He had just walked past the History Department:

> Fascinated, I had watched the jackdaws circling around the spires of the Cathedral: in my home town of Lulea, in the north, no such creatures existed. The reason that I recall them so vividly is that I stood there a long time, pondering which subject I should take first for the career which I had mapped out for myself as a teacher in Swedish and Religious Education: Literary History (as it was called in those days), or Theology. Just opposite the statue of Geijer, I tossed a stone, to allow chance to decide, and Theology won. Later I learnt from Hjalmar Sundén that Chance is really Fate drained of meaning: a secularized religiosity; but that was an interpretation I had not yet achieved (pp. 17–18).

Having decided on Theology—or, rather, having allowed a stone-toss to decide for him—disappointment followed:

> Most of our lecturers and teachers, however, left me unmoved. Obviously, they must have affected me; but between those for whom systematic theology was synonymous with well-intentioned Lutheran apologetics, and those who had surrendered to positivist paranoia, replacing theology's claim to truth by questions concerning the philosophical meaningfulness of religious utterances or language game theory, *only Hjalmar Sundén stands out* (pp. 18–19, my emphasis).

The reader of this account of a young man's struggle to find his own place in the world cannot mistake its introspective quality. Among his observations of the world around him, two realities stand out: the jackdaws circling around the Cathedral spires, and Hjalmar Sundén, the professor who was unlike all the others. Further introspection might have suggested a convergence of these two "outstanding" perceptions, as Wikström's description of Sundén's style of lecturing puts the reader in mind of the jackdaws circling the Cathedral spires:

> When he came in, he would often sit hunched over the lectern, with his hands clasped together. Turned in on himself, he would begin to speak in his low and slow bass voice like a private monologue, leading us into the psychology of the mystics, the physiology of the brain, Freud's Jewish background, the psychological function of religious rites, or the visions of Ramakrishna. Often he would half-doze, and then, in the quiet fascinated room, as if from an inner slumber, he would alternately tell stories, critiques, or analyses. Occasionally this monologue

would be interrupted by a pedagogical eruption: an (illegible) sentence might be written on the board; or he might stand up and theatrically act out an improvised play in order to illustrate a thesis about the psychology of role-taking (pp. 23–24).

If Wikström were asked the question he and his co-editor have asked us to answer, "If you would have the opportunity to 'start anew', would you enroll again in psychology of religion?", could he possibly say anything but "yes"? The fact that Sundén, alone among his professors, provided a valued interpretation of his stone-tossing experience ("Chance is really Fate drained of meaning") may account in part for his "yes," but the more important factor was that, for reasons only Wikström himself can know, and then, perhaps, only imperfectly, Sundén "stood out" for him, and, in "standing out," also "stood for" things deep inside of him that others did not "stand for," even, perhaps, "stood against" by signalling that they would not "stand for" such things being thought, felt or intuited by others.

Introspection, Self-Consciousness, and Shame

The story of my own awakening to what we are now calling the psychology of religion is somewhat similar, especially in the fact that chance seems to have played so much a part in it, and in the fact that it, too, involved the discernment of a professor who "stood out" among the others. In my first year as a Bachelor of Divinity student at Yale Divinity School, I took the required course in Church History from the renowned church historian and Luther scholar, Roland Bainton. One day Bainton came to class in what seemed an especially combative mood. We were on the subject of Martin Luther, and for the better part of the hour Bainton condemned a recent book on Luther, Erik H. Erikson's *Young Man Luther* (1958), a book of which I was blissfully unaware. As I recall—I have no lecture notes to assist me—Bainton challenged Erikson's right to write a book on Luther because he lacked the professional qualifications that Bainton, by implication, amply possessed (see Bainton, 1959, 1971). I left the lecture hall in something of a combative mood myself and went over to the seminary library where I found a copy of the book that Bainton had just vilified. As I read it, I felt that I was not only beginning to understand for the first time a figure—Martin Luther—who had "stood out" for me, but in a very ambivalent sort of way, throughout my youth (after all, I had been raised a Lutheran from birth); but also, and more importantly, I was discovering some things about myself, things which Erikson's phrase "identity crisis" named exceedingly well. Without having the name for what I was doing, I later came to realize that it was a process of introspection.

But if this book enabled me to name my problem—*my* religious pathology—it did not lead to any immediate solution. Having devoted my first year in seminary to the thought that I might become a systematic theologian, I devoted the second and third years to entertaining the prospects of becoming an ethicist and a historian of religion. By the end of my B.D. years, I had decided to leave the theological world entirely. I subsequently returned (to explain why would take too long to tell), and I found myself at Yale Divinity School once again, now enrolled in the Master of Sacred Theology program, grateful for a second chance, but no clearer than before about the direction in which I wanted to go. Among the courses for which I signed up was one taught by James E. Dittes. While I do not recall the actual title of the course, it was clear from his opening introduction that it was very atypical of courses taught at Yale Divinity School, for it was based on the proposal that each week we would explore the relationship between the personal life and the theological ideas of the theologians whose ideas we were learning about in other courses. It now seems strange to me that all the years I had been at Yale Divinity School, I had not taken a course from Dittes, and had not known that there was one faculty person who *was* favorably disposed to the kind of investigation that I had discovered—virtually by accident and contrary to what Bainton intended—in Erikson's *Young Man Luther*.

Throughout the year that I was back at Yale Divinity School, James Dittes "stood out" for me because he "stood for" something that the others would not "stand for" (i.e., would barely tolerate). What Bainton explicitly ruled out of bounds in a respectable seminary, the others implicitly ruled out by their condemnatory attitude toward "psychology" as being "reductionistic," as if the theologies that they themselves proclaimed were somehow immune from "reductionism" by virtue of the fact that they were called "theology," or written by professional theologians. (*Their* reductionisms were reflected in their weakly developed concepts of self or psyche.) However, what made Dittes "stand out" for me was not that he was a proponent of psychology, but that he encouraged us to look inside of ourselves for the insights we were struggling for in our efforts to understand the connections between the personal lives and theological ideas of the individuals we were studying. I don't recall whether he actually used the word "introspection," but this is what he was encouraging us to do (and be). He did not intervene very much in our discussions, but when he did, it was usually to point out that our theological categories and our reliance on the psychological theories developed by others (for different circumstances) were perhaps inhibiting our understanding, impeding the process of insight and enlightenment. The implicit message was that if these categories and theories lead to genuine insights, let us by all means use them; but, if not, let us not be afraid to let them go and rely solely upon ourselves—our own experiences and experiencings—as the basis for our observations. Is it any wonder, then, that our seminar challenged us to focus on ourselves as we sought to understand the figures we had chosen to study and discuss?

An especially important insight came for me when I was reading John Henry Newman's *Apologia Pro Vita Sua*. Newman was the figure I had chosen for my contribution to the seminar, a rather ironic choice in light of my dawning interest in becoming a psychologist of religion; for, as Carol Zaleski has recently pointed out, "[William] James is particularly puzzled by John Henry Newman, perhaps because he senses that Newman is a kindred spirit facing him from the other side of the looking-glass" (Zaleski, 1993–1994:139; cf. James, 1982:458–461).

One important consequence of my having chosen Newman, who was subsequently the subject of my doctoral dissertation at the University of Chicago, was that my chosen figure had written an autobiography, and that his own commitment to introspection was therefore, in part, self-directed. In his *Apologia Pro Vita Sua*, Newman becomes his own object of introspective observation. I came to appreciate the personal risks involved in this act of self-observation while reading his chapter on the "History of My Religious Opinions from 1839 to 1841". This chapter begins in a very self-conscious manner, and is especially concerned with the difficulty and potential fallibility of the exercise of self-observation:

> For who can know himself, and the multitude of subtle influences which act upon him? and who can recollect at the distance of twenty-five years, all that he once knew about his thoughts and his deeds, and that, *during a portion of his life, even at the time his observation, whether of himself or of the external world, was less than before or after, by very reason of the perplexity and dismay which weighed upon him,—when, though it would be most thankful to seem to imply that he had not all-sufficient light amid his darkness, yet a darkness it emphatically was?*. . It is both to head and heart an extreme trial, thus to analyze what has so long gone by, and to bring out the results of that examination. I have done various bold things in my life: this is the boldest: and were I not sure I should after all succeed in my object, it would be madness to set about it (Newman, 1956:199–200, my emphasis).

What is striking about this passage is Newman's suggestion that he is about to recount a period in his life when his own introspective capacities were not as strong as before or after this period because, at the time, he was living in a kind of personal darkness. In other words, he will be writing about a time in his life when his introspective capacities were themselves at a low ebb, when he was seeing neither himself nor the world around him with any real degree of clarity.

What follows this introduction is an account of how he went from his "supreme confidence in my controversial *status*" in the Church of England to concluding that the theological position he had so carefully and laboriously formulated was untenable and had to be abandoned. I will not take time to summarize his account of this period of darkness, but I *do* want to draw attention to the experience in which he began to see matters clearly again. He had been involved during the Long Vacation of 1839 in a careful study of the Monophysite heresy of the 5th Century and

> it was during this course of reading that for the first time a doubt came upon me of the tenableness of Anglicanism. I recollect on the 30th of July mentioning to a friend, whom I had accidentally met, how remarkable the history was; but by the

end of August I was seriously alarmed... My stronghold was Antiquity; now here, in the middle of the fifth century, I found, as it seemed to me, Christendom of the sixteenth and nineteenth centuries reflected. *I saw my face in that mirror, and I was a Monophysite* (Newman, 1956:217, my emphasis).

This statement, "I saw myself in that mirror," is a declaration of his having become clear about himself and about his situation in the world. He now saw his earlier period of "supreme confidence" for what it was—an erroneous, fallacious perception of Christianity, a perception in which he had been profoundly self-involved. This was the beginning of the end of his relationship to the Church of England, as he now understood that he and it were in fundamental, irreconcilable opposition.

But what of the reader of this deeply introspective text? I have to say that, like James, I was unable then—as now—to press my sympathies for Newman's ecclesiastical plight very far, having very little idea then—as now—why a 5th Century heresy was such an emotionally charged matter for Newman himself. But the thought that he had believed he knew himself and knew what he was doing—"supremely confident in his controversial status"—and now discerned how untenable and hollow it had all been—this thought hit home in a very powerful, personal way. I realized that what he was describing here was a profoundly shaming experience, one that was especially painful because it attacked what he had most prized in himself, his ability to take an unpopular stand because he knew that he was right. What was so shaming was the realization that he had been wrong and that his controversial position, while courageous, was finally quite hollow, unsupported by the evidence. The very thing that he prized about himself had become the cause and source of profound shame. And this is what I realized was shaming for me as well. I, who secretly relished in taking controversial positions, felt my own shame in reading about his discovery that he had been both controversial *and wrong*.

On the other hand, Erik H. Erikson's observation that shame involves the feeling of being "self-conscious" now assumed a new, and oddly positive meaning for me. Previously, it had meant a desire for "invisibility" in the face of others, owing to a basic shyness. Now it suggested that it is precisely in my experiences of shame—when I am "*self*-conscious"—that I become aware, genuinely aware, of who I am. This insight made the pain of shame seem more bearable, as it suggested that shame has two faces: It reveals our obtuseness about ourselves but at the same time it proves self-revelatory (Erikson, 1963: 252–253). We come away from an experience of shame knowing ourselves better than we did before.

In the course of the next few years, I focused a great deal on the role that shame plays in autobiographical writings, and made a special point of the fact that Augustine's *Confessions* is more about shame than guilt, especially if one focuses less on the text's subject matter and more on its introspective process (Capps, 1990a, 1990b, 1994, 1995a). Over the past twenty-five years that I have been a professor, I have viewed the course I offer in psychology of religion (which focuses on several major classics in the field) as being "about" the discipline itself, whereas the course I offer in religious autobiography invites students to become engaged with and in the introspective process itself. By reading the life stories of others, as I had read Newman's *Apologia*, they come to valued insights concerning themselves.

Introspection, World-Awareness, and Melancholy

In recent years, I have been shifting my emphasis somewhat from shame to melancholy, a shift that reflects my increasing awareness of the possibilities and difficulties that attend our observation of the world around us. I had already begun writing about melancholy before I underwent surgery for a detached retina (Capps, 1995b), but my experience of temporary loss of eyesight in my left eye and the fact that my eyesight in that eye remains impaired has given unexpected impetus to my interest in melancholy (Capps, 1995c, 1995d). (A book that was personally therapeutic was Trevor-Roper, 1988.) As already noted, James gives considerable attention to melancholy in *The Varieties*, suggesting that the melancholiac views the world around him as lifeless and dead, or threatening and sinister. While we might dismiss the melancholiac's view of the external world as mere pathology, James instead considers it one essential way by which we come to an understanding, simultaneously, of the world that we inhabit and the "world" that lies hidden inside each human breast, the world that inhabits us. It is the struggle for life and the evil that issues from it (both social and personal) to which melancholy is so profoundly attuned. In commenting in "The Sick Soul" chapter on the inadequacies of "the religion of healthy-mindedness", James writes:

> The method of averting one's attention from evil, and living simply in the light of good is splendid as long as it will work. It will work with many persons; it will work far more generally than most of us are ready to suppose; and within the sphere of its successful operation there is nothing to be said against it as a religious solution. But it breaks down impotently as soon as melancholy comes; and even though one can be quite free from melancholy oneself, there is no doubt that healthy-mindedness is inadequate as a philosophical doctrine, because evil facts which it refuses positively to account for are a genuine portion of reality; and they may after all be the best key to life's significance, and *possibly the only openers of our eyes to the deepest levels of truth* (p. 163, my emphasis).

He continues with a horrific description of the world that the melancholiac sees with unusual clarity:

> The normal process of life contains moments as bad as any of those which insane melancholy is filled with, moments in which radical evil gets its innings and takes its solid turn. The lunatic's visions of horror are all drawn from the material of daily fact. Our civilization is founded on the shambles, and every individual existence goes out in a lonely spasm of helpless agony. If you protest, my friend, wait

till you arrive there yourself! To believe in the carnivorous reptiles of geologic times is hard for our imagination—they seem too much like mere museum specimens. *Yet there is no tooth in any of those museum-skulls that did not daily through long years of the foretime hold fast to the body struggling in despair of some fated living victim.* Forms of horror just as dreadful to their victims, if on a smaller spatial scale, fill the world about us to-day. . . Crocodiles and rattlesnakes and pythons are at this moment vessels of life as real as we are; their loathsome existence fills every minute of every day that drags its length along; and whenever they or other wild beasts clutch their living prey, the deadly horror which an agitated melancholiac feels is the literally right reaction on the situation (pp. 163–164, my emphasis).

In light of these realities, "It may indeed be that no religious reconciliation with the absolute totality of things is possible. Some evils, indeed, are ministerial to higher forms of good; but it may be that there are forms of evil so extreme as to enter into no good system whatsoever, and that, in respect of such evil, dumb submission or neglect to notice is the only practical resource" (pp. 164–165). If introspective observation has as its ultimate objective the achievement of a "consistent system," the melancholiacs view of the world is that ultimately no such system exists, and, in any case, we find ourselves, for practical reasons, choosing to "neglect to notice" some features of the world (and of ourselves) that are too horrible for us to observe. What melancholy impresses upon us, therefore, is the fact that "the practically real world for each one of us, the effective world of the individual, is the compound world, the physical facts and emotional values in indistinguishable combination" (p. 151). The world outside and the world inside correspond to one another, and it is the melancholiac who has the introspective capacity to see that this is, unfortunately, the case, as both—by virtue of their struggle for life—are implicated in radical evil.

On the other hand, to dismiss the melancholiac's insight into the real world around us would make religion unnecessary (i.e., without practical effect), for, as we saw earlier, the "practical real world" for the religionist—or for the religious self that resides in us—is also a compound world, the physical facts and emotional values in indistinguishable combination, so that the religious self's perception of the "promise" of the dawn and the rainbow, the "voice" of the thunder, the "gentleness" of the rain, and the "sublimity" of the stars is no less true than the melancholiac self's perception of the world as one where "every individual existence goes out in a lonely spasm of helpless agony". Both perceptions are true, and both need each other even if they are ultimately irreconcilable.

As for psychology of religion, James insists that it cannot avoid—turn its eyes away from—these experiences of melancholy:

Painful indeed they will be to listen to, and there is almost an indecency in handling them in public. Yet they lie right in the middle of our path; and *if we are to touch the psychology of religion at all seriously*, we must be willing to forget conventionalities, and dive below the smooth and lying conventional surface (p. 145, my emphasis).

Thus, as shame is to self-knowledge, melancholy is to knowledge of the practically real world around us, for, as Newman understood, self-knowledge cannot be realized without true knowledge of the very aspect of the world that caught his attention (as expressed in his "controversial status"); and, as James recognized, our knowledge of the world around us is determined by what we find ourselves able to take interest in (thus, by what we discover to be true of ourselves). Newman and James are, indeed, kindred spirits, facing each other from opposing sides of the looking-glass.

The common link between shame and melancholy is that, in terms of "emotional value," both exhibit—and conceal—the observer's own profound sense of rage. In spite of the fact that they are quite different emotional experiences, rage is the one feature they share in common. In *Childhood and Society*, Erikson observes that shame "is essentially rage against the self" (1963:252); and, in *Young Man Luther*, he quotes the whole passage from *The Varieties* in which James describes the world as "an agitated melancholiac" feels it, and adds:

> James is clinically and genetically correct, when he connects the horror of the *devouring* will to live with the content and the disposition of melancholia. For in melancholia, it is the human being's horror of his own avaricious and sadistic orality which he tires of, withdraws from, wishes often to end even by putting an end to himself. This is not the orality of the first, the toothless and dependent, stage; it is the orality of the tooth-stage and all that develops within it, especially the prestages of what later becomes "biting" human conscience (p. 121).

This is what Erikson calls "the mood of severe melancholy, intensified tristitia, one would almost say tristitia with teeth in it" (p. 120); and lest we miss the fact that the melancholiac's rage against the world—internalized as self-hatred—has its origin in the toothy child's rage against his mother, Erikson prefaces his discussion of tristitia with a quotation from Luther concerning the Christchild "hanging on a virgin's tits" (p. 119). It requires a deliberate act of emotional myopia to miss the word "tit" in tristitia.

Art, Animistic Religion, and the Child's Eye for the World

The editors have asked contributors to this volume to set forth, if possible, a new direction for the discipline if they judge the current directions to be undesirable or inadequate. My suggestions here will be relatively brief, but they build rather naturally on my emphasis throughout this article on the importance of introspective observation. They suggest an affinity between animistic religion, art, and the psychology of childhood.

Two decades ago, Paul W. Pruyser gave his presidential address for the Society for the Scientific Study of Religion on "Lessons from Art Theory for the Psychology of Religion" (1976: 1–14). In this address, Pruyser suggested that

"Certain concepts in the theory of art might be applicable to the psychology of religion, particularly when one realizes that in ontogenesis the individual tends to be introduced at once to art and religion" (p. 1). The first section of his address sets about to describe "the reciprocal reinforcement between art and religion in childhood and subsequent cultural experience" (p. 1).

I find myself responding appreciatively to Pruyser's suggestion that we give more attention to "the reciprocal reinforcement between art and religion in childhood," though I do not have a clear idea of where this may take us, and, indeed, I think we should be quite wary of setting forth a program for how we might proceed, even one as tentative as Pruyser's was. In *Memoirs of the Blind* (1993), Jacques Derrida suggests that one reason artists have produced so many paintings of blind persons is that these serve as self-portraits. Artists almost without variation paint blind persons with hands venturing forth, preceding the rest of their bodies, as if testing the area in front of them before actually stepping forth. So, too, suggests Derrida, artists lead with their hands, as they approach the blank canvas before them. What will they "see" on that canvas? What will they cause to appear there? (pp. 2-5). Or, as Denis Hollier writes, "The space of painting is space where someone who has torn his eyes like Oedipus feels his way, blinded. Thus it is not the eye but to the missing-eye that painting corresponds" (quoted in Jay, 1993:230). What follows, then, is nothing more than an initial venture, literally, a stab in the dark.

In *Young Man Luther*, toward the conclusion of his chapter on "The Meaning of 'Meaning It'", Erikson suggests that Luther gave new meaning to the very idea of work. As he prepared and delivered his lectures on the Psalms,

> he became affectively and intellectually alive. This is not works; it is work, in the best sense. In fact, Luther made the verbal work of his whole profession more genuine in the face of a tradition of scholastic virtuosity. His style indicates his conviction that a thing said less elegantly and meant more truly is better work, and better craftsmanship in communication (p. 220).

Thus, if Luther spoke against works, "he spoke against holy busywork which has nothing whatsoever to do with the nature or the quality of devoted craftsmanship" (p. 219). Only introspective observation, in which one is oneself the observed, can answer the question whether one's work as a psychologist of religion is "holy busywork" or "liberated craftsmanship." Yet, Erikson also suggests that the fact that Luther had liberated himself from the bonds of the past was discernible to others, for "when this monk spoke up he presented in his words and in his bearing the image of man in whom men of all walks of life were able to recognize in decisive clarity something that seemed right, something they wanted, they needed to be" (pp. 223-224). The "inner state" of liberation required the world's—or some aspect of that world's—confirmation. As Erikson puts it in his discussion of how "Renaissance sensuality (in contrast to the medieval alternation of asceticism and excess) tried to make the body an intuitive and disciplined tool of reality", and "insisted on a full interplay between men's senses and intuitions and the world of appearances, facts, and laws", this

> makes the verification of our functioning essence dependent on the meeting between our God-given mental machinery and the world into which God has put us. We need no proof of His identity nor of ours as long as, at any given time, an essential part of our equipment and a segment of His world continue to confirm each other (1958:192).

As for whether psychology of religion gives evidence of the liberated craftsmanship that this principle of introspective observation envisions, two books—James's *The Varieties* and Erikson's *Young Man Luther*—are surely discernible as such. Not incidentally, both authors had become accomplished painters before turning their attention to other fields, and their backgrounds as artists are unmistakably evident in the way they have constructed their texts. Joan M. Erikson has recently written, "About Erik's work and his way of looking at things it seems most important to stress—always—that he was an artist" (personal communication, February 20, 1995). Or, as he puts it in the foreword to *Childhood and Society*:

> I came to psychology from art, which may explain, if not justify, the fact that at times the reader will find me painting contexts and backgrounds where he would rather have me point to facts and concepts. I have had to make a virtue out of a constitutional necessity by basing what I have to say on representative description rather than on theoretical argument (1963:17).

But the book that most informs my current gropings is Jean-Paul Weber's *The Psychology of Art* (1969), a book that my underlinings suggest I, as a graduate student, read only portions of. Carefully marked, however, was his chapter entitled "The Ontology of the Work". Here, Weber suggests that "aesthetic emotion" derives from childhood and, therefore, "aesthetic creation roots itself afresh in childhood (certain events of which are so deeply engraved in memory that they remain always to haunt the life and works of the artist as personal themes)" (p. 138). He suggests that the reason certain scenes acquire an "aesthetic quality" for us—a mist-covered hill, a tree or bridge mirrored in a river, a light at nighttime, bright enough to create sharp contrasts between light and dark—is because "they cause 'adult' realities to appear within one of the primitive optical perspectives of infantile vision" (pp. 145–146). He explains:

> The child's vision is incapable, among other things, of exact accommodation, somewhat like that of myopes. This natural "myopia" has the effect of shading out sharp degrees, of making objects fluid, of surrounding them with a vague corona, of depriving them of their structure, and one sees instead only a confused irradiation. At night, in particular, a mere bright point becomes a sort of flower or sun bursting open and dancing in the shadow. It seems to me that this is the origin of the aesthetic quality of certain objects whose contours are somewhat uncertain, whose colors are delicate and unspecifiable, whose complex structures our eyes are too lazy to pick out in detail. For example, in flowers or in the dense crown of

a tree or the play of light through the foliage; and, in a tropical night, the exaggerated shimmer of the stars. The aureole of brightness or color that light sometimes leaves around certain objects appears to depend on the same explanation (p. 146).

Does this not also explain the various "animisms" that James identifies as being so fundamental to the religious point of view? Are such religious animisms not also the "transformations" that occur when "adult realities" appear "within one of the primitive optical perspectives of infantile vision"?

And then there is the matter of the individual person who "stands out" in a group—e.g., in the group photograph of a theological faculty—whose other members are, for this viewer, quite indistinguishable from one another. Weber notes that, initially, "the child cannot grasp the *substantial identity* of the object—which it therefore dissociates into a host of *pictures* that are identical, but variously located" (p. 148). In time, however, the child begins to see in three dimensions, and Weber equates the third dimension that the painter achieves through artifice with "the new dimension which the child's vision little by little, as a result of maturation and practice, discovers before and behind fluid, unintelligible, mobile frontal planes" (p. 149). What especially interests Weber here is the

> moment of transition in which the new-born space is simply suggested, or barely felt in the context of the superficial, direct experiences of the child. In this, I believe, is found the explanation of the aesthetic quality attached to the *surfaces* through which the painter brings to the fore and offers existence to total visual space (p. 149).

If, then, identifying a person who "stands out" from the crowd is an aesthetic experience, is it not also religious, for it forges an emotional bond that is indissoluble, even though death intervenes? As Richard Brilliant points out:

> Making portraits is a response to the natural human tendency to think about oneself, of oneself in relation to others, and of others in apparent relation to themselves and to others. *To put a face on the world catches the essence of ordinary behavior in the social context*; to do the same in a work of art catches the essence of the human relationship and consolidates it in the portrait through the creation of a visible identity sign by which someone can be known, possibly forever (1991: 14; my emphasis).

From here, it is only a small, though certainly fateful step toward what Pruyser says James himself saw, namely, that "in religion the universe acquires a face for us" (1976: 11).

But reminiscent of whose? Brilliant suggests that the infant's ability to make out its mother's face is the beginning of all portraiture:

> The dynamic nature of portraits and the "occasionality" that anchors their imagery in life seems ultimately to depend on the primary experience of the infant in arms. That child, gazing up at its mother, imprints her vitally important image so

firmly on its mind that soon enough she can be recognized almost instantaneously and without conscious thought; spontaneous face recognition remains an important instrument of survival, separating friend from foe, that persists into adult life (p. 9).

If making out the mother's face is the beginning of all portraiture, is it not also the originary religious experience? In a footnote in the chapter, "The Reality of the Unseen", in *The Varieties*, James quotes B. de St. Pierre: "Nature is always so interesting, under whatever aspect she shows herself, that when it rains, I seem to see a beautiful woman weeping. She appears the more beautiful, the more afflicted she is" (p. 58; see also Capps, 1995d). Which is to say that, when the universe acquires a face for us, reminiscent of our mother, it is a face that evokes ever-so-mixed emotions—of empathy and rage for the one perceived, and shame and melancholy in the one who is perceiver.

I am proposing, in other words, that if we are to recover the method of introspective observation for psychology of religion, we would do well to take seriously Pruyser's insight that art theory holds lessons for the psychology of religion. At the same time, we will need to take seriously the legitimate critiques of introspectionism, and address them as best we can. A valuable, if incomplete, effort in this regard is Bakan's "A Reconsideration of the Problem of Introspection" (1967), in which he addresses the standard criticisms of introspectionism (i.e., that its data are not public; that the very act of introspection modifies the experiences we wish to observe; that various errors, such as distortion, rationalization and displacement, are common; and that the social and cultural prejudices [or prejudgments] of the observer were inadequately recognized by its earlier practitioners). These problems do not, however, lead Bakan to conclude that the introspective method should be avoided, because he believes that, like other scientific methods, it can be self-correcting, a point that is supported by my illustration of John Henry Newman's realization that what he had taken to be true of the world and of himself was, on further reflection, a grievous error. Perhaps this means that those who are able to recognize and publicly acknowledge their errors in self- and world-perception (who can, in other words, live with their shame) are best suited for the use of the introspective method. These will be the ones who are convinced—on religious grounds?—that there *is* such a thing as "solar retribution." For did we not learn this hard lesson in childhood: That the world in whom we found recognition and instrument for survival could also retaliate our rage, mocking our efforts to fathom her meanings and to appropriate her powers?

Bibliography

Bainton, R. (1959). Luther: A psychiatric portrait. *Yale Review, 48,* 405–410.
Bainton, R. (1971). Psychiatry and history: An examination of Erikson's *Young Man Luther. Religion in Life, 40,* 450–478.
Bakan, D. (1967). A reconsideration of the problem of introspection. *On method: Toward*

a reconstruction of psychological investigation (pp. 94–112). San Fransisco, CA: Jossey-Bass.

Brilliant, R. (1991). *Portraiture*. Cambridge, MA: Harvard University Press.

Capps, D. (1990a). Augustine's *Confessions*: The scourge of shame and the silencing of Adeodatus. In D. Capps & J.E. Dittes (Eds.), *The hunger of the heart: Reflections on the Confessions of Augustine* (pp. 69–92). West Lafayette, IN: Society for the Scientific Study of Religion Monograph No. 8.

Capps, D. (1990b). Augustine as narcissist: On grandiosity and shame. In D. Capps & J.E. Dittes (Eds.), *The hunger of the heart: Reflections on the Confessions of Augustine* (pp. 169–184). West Lafayette, IN: Society for the Scientific Study of Religion Monograph No. 8.

Capps, D. (1994). An Allportian analysis of Augustine. *The International Journal for the Psychology of Religion, 4,* 205–228.

Capps, D. (1995a). *The child's song: The religious abuse of children*. Louisville, KY: Westminster/John Knox Press.

Capps, D. (1995b). Enrapt spirits and the melancholy soul: The locus of division in the Christian self and American society. In R.K. Fenn & D. Capps (Eds.), *On Losing the Soul: Essays in the Social Psychology of Religion* (pp. 137–169). Albany, NY: State University of New York Press.

Capps, D. (1995c). "That shape am I": The bearing of melancholy on James's struggle with religion. In D. Capps and J.L. Jacobs (Eds.), *The struggle for life: A companion to William James's The Varieties of Religious Experience* (pp. 72–106). West Lafayette, IN: Society for the Scientific Study of Religion Monograph No. 9.

Capps, D. (1995d). Prayer, melancholy, and the vivified face of the world. In D. Capps & J.L. Jacobs (Eds.), *The struggle for life: A companion to William James's The Varieties of Religious Experience* (pp. 250–264). West Lafayette, IN: Society for the Scientific Study of Religion Monograph No. 9.

Capps, D. (1995e). The mysterium tremendum: Its childhood origins. *Psychology of Religion Newsletter, 20,* 6–15.

Derrida, J. (1993). *Memoirs of the blind: The self-portrait and other ruins*. (P-A. Brault & M. Naas, Trans.). Chicago, IL: The University of Chicago Press.

Dittes, J.E. (1977). The investigator as an instrument of investigation: Some exploratory observations on the compleat researcher. In D. Capps, W.H. Capps & M.G. Bradford (Eds.), *Encounter with Erikson: Historical interpretation and religious biography* (pp. 345–373). Missuola, MT: Scholars Press.

Erikson, E.H. (1958). *Young Man Luther*. New York: W.W. Norton.

Erikson, E.H. (1963). *Childhood and society*, 2nd rev. ed. New York: W.W. Norton.

James, W. (1950). *The principles of psychology*, 2 vols. New York: Dover Publications.

James, W. (1982). *The varieties of religious experience: A study in human nature*. New York: Dover Publications.

Jay, M. (1993). *Downcast eyes: The denigration of vision in twentieth-century French thoughtt*. Berkeley, CA: University of California Press.

Miller, J.H. (1992). *Illustration*. Cambridge, MA: Harvard University Press.

Newman, J.H. (1956). *Apologia pro vita sua*. New York: Doubleday.

Pruyser, P.W. (1976). Lessons from art theory for the psychology of religion. *Journal for the Scientific Study of Religion, 15,* 1–14.

Trevor-Roper, P. (1988). *The world through blunted sight: An inquiry into the influence of defective vision on art and character*, rev. ed. New York: Viking Press.

Weber, J-P. (1969). *The psychology of art*. (J.A. Elias, Trans.). New York: Dell Publishing Company.

Wikström, O. (1995). The integrity of the religious experience: The role of Hjalmar Sundén as teacher and mentor. In N.G. Holm & J.A. Belzen (Eds.), *Sundén's role theory—An impetus to contemporary psychology of religion*. Finland: Åbo Academy.

Zaleski, C. (1993–1994). Speaking of William James to the cultured among his despisers. *The Journal of the Psychology of Religion, 2–3,* 127–170.

Science *vs.* Religion

James E. Dittes

How do we achieve a *science* of *religion* when science and religion are, fundamentally, adversaries. That is the dilemma still besetting the psychology of religion, no less today than a century ago when psychology and religion were more obvious rivals. It is the dilemma that chronically harasses and thwarts the field and underlies most of its anguished statements of identity crisis, such as those occupying this volume.

How exercise the authority of science and yet honor the authority of religion? Psychologists of religion appear fated to compromise the integrity of one or the other. Either we must forfeit some of the power of the science of psychology or else neglect some of the richness of the religion we propose to investigate. Statements in the psychology of religion are destined to leave either psychologists or religionists (or both) feeling that their perspective has been minimized, attenuated, rendered shallow.

Psychology and religion compete for the human soul. They compete for its loyalty. They compete for access. They compete for the privilege and authority of identifying the dis-eases of the soul and of prescribing its care and cure. They offer the soul competing vocabularies with which to understand itself. They compete to teach the soul how to perceive its creation and its destiny and how to understand and relate to the universe in which it finds itself.

The science of psychology (almost always) implies unambiguously a metaphysics and epistemology, an anthropology of human nature and destiny, and norms for human demeanor—traditionally concerns of the realm of religion. Religion (almost always) identifies the components and the resources of human nature, the motives and mechanisms of human functioning, the nature and source of its dysfunction and disablement, and the means of remedy. Religion, in other words, usually imparts a psychology.

Since psychology and religion are often both expressions of the same broad cultural forces, they often coincide. (A large industry adjunct to psychology of religion has tried to chart these parallels, in a spate of "psychology-*and*-religion" publications, perhaps more in mid-century than today, and perhaps more in Jungian circles than others.) But since psychology and religion are also the expressions of deliberately distinct sub-cultures, they more often compete. Even when their doctrines or world-views or psychologies do seem to coincide, they still compete for the authority to make these assertions.

Which Language?

It is a struggle for prescribing which language shall be used, a struggle quite analogous to that in the clash of cultures in such places as Quebec or Belgium, Miami or Barcelona, where disputes about philosophy and identity are often waged in terms of disputes over choice of language. Which language shall be used to characterize the behavior or affect or experience which is deemed "religious"—that of the psychologist or that of the religionist? For language is the vehicle of ideology, and the competition of ideologies is waged as a competition between languages. You can't use both. You can be bi-lingual only serially not simultaneously. To use the language of the psychologist and thereby invoke the worldview and anthropology which that language represents is to disregard the language of the religionist, and vice versa.

Take your choice. The limitation may be roughly analogous to that depicted by Werner Heisenberg, who in 1927 (the same year Charles Lindbergh had to choose between carrying a radio and enough fuel to cross the Atlantic, and the same year Sigmund Freud insisted that humans had to choose between putting their trust in science or religion) reminded physicists of the humbling but obligatory trade-off imposed by the "principle of indeterminancy": You can't know both the position and the velocity of an electron; take your choice. (Or get along without either.)

When psychologist confronts religionist, who controls the agenda? Whose conceptual scheme will govern the data to be selected, the questions to be asked of it, the interpretations to be rendered, the conclusions to be drawn?

This, I propose, is the fundamental and insoluble dilemma of psychology of religion. Either choice is unsatisfactory to most of us. We certainly can't get along without the power and illumination of the language of psychology—whether that language is abstract conceptualization, clinical perception, empirical operational categories, or statistical findings. (*Within* psychology, of course as well as within religion—there is also competition among languages, or perhaps, dialects. Clinicians and researchers seldom understand each other.) To dispense with such language is not to be a psychologist. That is precisely the accusation—"You are not a psychologist!"—sometimes flung at researchers who are more phenomenological or taxonomic or ethnographic in method, those who tend to adopt the language used by religious practitioners, either to describe or interpret the religion, i.e., those who would say that they are truly honoring the "subject" as a subject.

But to exercise the psychological language is to disregard the testimony of the religionist, which may be wise and reflective and insightful, psychologically as well as theologically. The religionist usually has a thorough and elaborate understanding of what is happening to and within the self during religious experience and religious activity—a thorough and elaborate psychology, but in the religionist's language. To discard the religionist's language and self-understanding may seem like aborting the whole point, like pinning a butterfly into a collection, and pretending what you've caught is the same thing as the butterfly on the wing; like cutting off your nose to spite your face. Some psychologists are comfortable with this choice, sometimes as a rueful renunciation required by their discipline, sometimes as a triumphant conquest. The accusation such psychologists are readily vulnerable to is the opposite of being called "not psychologists"; they are accused of letting their psychology preempt and suffocate the religion, of practicing "psychologism" or "reductionism" or committing the "genetic fallacy". "How can you study religion when you throw away the religion", is the complaint.

This dilemma—the language of psychology or the language of religion?–subsumes, or generates, some of the traditional disputes and dilemmas that are commonly identified in the field.

Reliability or Relevance?

Especially, the dilemma of "which language?" is closely related to the dilemma between aspiring, on the one hand, to the objectivity and reliability and precision of scientific method and aspiring, on the other hand, to depth of meaning and interpretation. All students in psychology of religion face the dilemma and choice between knowing something small and relatively superficial but knowing it reliably, or else knowing something grander and more profound but knowing it more precariously and disputably. It is simply one of the limits of life that we cannot have it both ways. Most of us compromise a little on both sides, achieving *some* depth and *some* reliability.

We all *want* to have it both ways, to discern highly significant patterns at the heart of the religious enterprise *and* to do so precisely, reliably, and indisputably. But it doesn't happen that way. I can't prove, as Heisenberg could, that it *can't* happen. But the testimony and evidence is overwhelming: It doesn't. Whatever the significant interpretation aspired to, whether the precision of method is empirical virtuosity or elegance of theoretical categories, the trade-off remains between rigor of method and meaningfulness of results. Show me someone who seems to have illuminated something of genuine significance about human religiosity, and I will show you someone vulnerable to (and quite possibly already victim of, perhaps deservedly so) methodological attack. Show me someone in rigorous control of data and reasoning, and we want to respond, "So what?"

The dilemma, the trade-off, is hardly different, in kind, in psychology of religion from what it is in any of the human sciences, or any science, for that matter—so that neither side can legitimately claim exclusive title to the mantle of "scientific." But it seems different in degree; it looms especially excruciatingly for the aspiration to illuminate and interpret something as complex and momentous as religiosity. Studying *religion* seems to raise the stakes on both sides of the dilemma: It seems to make it more crucial to be profound, and it also seems to make it more crucial to be right.

A Personal and Vocational Choice

There is no "right" way to choose the trade-off. Either choice is a professionally respectable and valid aspiration. Whether one aspires more for reliability or aspires more for depth is a personal vocational choice, like the choice to pursue psychology of religion at all, or like the choice of topic within psychology of religion. (Probably the P-J scale of the Myers-Briggs Type Indicator would be as good a predictor as any; and both P and J traits are legitimate and healthy personality characteristics.) What "kind" of psychologist of religion one chooses to be is not fair game for attack any more than the choice to be a psychologist of religion at all—for all the heat and anguish that is often generated by disputes between the champions of one criterion or the other who scold each other for not being more "rigorous" or more "relevant." Everyone has the right and responsibility to make their own choice, and no one has the right to fault another's choice.

Nor are personal regrets appropriate as one looks back at the choices made and is tempted to rue their limits. One can too easily look back at a mass of data and close analysis and lament "I should have aimed higher", or consider a corpus of ingenious interpretations and ponder "What if it's all a house of cards." The trade-off choice is imposed by the way things are, and the choice one makes is the best choice one can make; "should have" and other second-guessing is out of place. The limits of any chosen strategy are imposed by the way things are, not by any personal failings.

It might seem plausible and reasonable to agree to disagree, to adopt a "politically correct" norm of multi-culturalism—or, to use William James's plain speech, to recognize the "varieties"—in which it is agreed that either language is valid and appropriate for its own speakers: Religion and psychology ask different questions about the same phenomena and therefore can be expected to reach different and essentially incommensurate conclusions. That is usually the recommendation when this issue is discussed in abstract. But in practice too much is at stake.

In the remainder of this paper, I shall illustrate these dilemmas and choices in the thinking of some of the major writers on psychology of religion. The conclusion will be that just stated: To paraphrase the title of William James's classic, there are *varieties* of psychology of religion; there can be no such thing as *the* psychology of religion.

Freud and His Clinical Dialect

If the *clinical* "dialect" of psychological language is spoken, then one must fit to religion such words of appraisal as "healthy", "mature", "dysfunctional", (or their opposites), as well as the entire available array of diagnostic categories. The gain is in the focus such terms bring; the loss is in their narrowness and exclusiveness. To take a classical instance: Simply because he spoke such a clinical language, quite apart from any alleged hostility to religion, or other agenda or motives, it was inevitable that Sigmund Freud, once he turned his attention to religion, would find the practices of religion matching such words as "obsessiveness" and "neurosis" (1907) or "dependence" and "hostility" and "Oedipal" (1913, 1927, 1930). This was the only vocabulary available to him. He did not know and did not try to learn the language of the religionists. He can hardly be faulted for speaking his own language, and speaking it fluently, in this case, any more than he can be faulted for writing in German.

If he is to be faulted, it is for not acknowledging that his clinical psychological (or psychiatric) language is not the only language, for not acknowledging that there are varieties of languages, including those of the religionists themselves. It is, of course, common and easily understandable psychologically that a speaker exalts and relies on his own language as though it provides exclusive (or superior) comprehension. Freud "knew" better, in principle: When Freud (1927) directly addressed the issue of reductionism, he disclaimed, in principle, the exclusive authority of his psychological or scientific language; science, too, may be an "illusion", he acknowledged. But in practice, Freud and probably all speakers of the language of clinical psychology give the impression of clearly implying an "only" in their statements. All that Freud actually said was that religious practice resembles obsessive neurosis. But because that is all he said, he is heard to be saying that religious practice is *only* an obsessional neurosis. In principle, one may disclaim the "only". But in practice, it's unavoidable; one speaks only one language at a time.

William James's Religious Language

To cite another classic case, William James (1902) attempted to steer a middle course by rejecting the extremely insistent dialects of both medical psychology and religious establishment. In the opening lectures of his Gifford Lectures (published as *The Varieties of Religious Experience* 1902), he challenged and rejected the authority of medical diagnosis, on one hand, and of established theological and ecclesiastical pronouncement, on the other, precisely for their exclusivistic reductionism. Both missed, he said, the vitality of the religious experience they purported to account for.

In practice, James relied primarily on the vocabulary of individuals recounting whatever they deemed to be religious experience. He recorded their own words, taking them at face value, without need to be translated into psychological language. He regarded the self-reports as sufficiently valid, meaningful, and insightful, in their own terms. His own contribution was, essentially, to generalize from the individual reports and to arrange them in categories.

It is very important here to notice that, although a decade before these Gifford Lectures, James had completed the monumental and comprehensive *The Principles of Psychology* (1890), he renounced that vocabulary when he approached religion. It would have been most expected for James to speak of religion by using the vocabulary(ies) which he had so laboriously worked out in the two volumes of the *Principles*. But he left that behind to approach religion on its own terms. He recorded and developed an entirely new vocabulary for *The Varieties of Religious Experience.*

While recognizing, even applauding William James for this discipline and courageous commitment to honor the perspectives of his religious subjects, it is also very important to recognize that he did not transcend the dilemma. He chose one horn of the dilemma. He chose to honor the authority of the religious experience and the experiencer's report. But the cost was the loss of the benefits of science. Unlike his psychology text, *The Principles,* there are in *The Varieties* no interpretive principles as to how and why events and experiences occur as they do, principles that can be exported from the book and used in fresh cases, principles that can be tested, confirmed, disproved, improved on. People can read the *Varieties*, but they can't *use* it. (This is ironic in the light of James's high evaluation of pragmatism, the priority he accords to what he calls the "fruits".) A scientist expects to emerge from a study with a set of interpretations and hypotheses which become an agenda for further study. James's study did not. James's work did not seed a following, a school, an accumulation of wisdom and insight built on his work, the way science does. James honored the religion, and its varieties and the varieties of approaches, but this lost him any science to be honored.

James regarded himself as an empiricist. His empiricism, however, was not that of a scientist, but the empiricism of an artist, a career James actually pursued and enjoyed before he turned to the science of medicine, which he did not enjoy, and then to philosophy. For a painter the subject sets the agenda—unlike the "subject" of empirical research, who must be fit, as well as possible, into the categories provided by the researcher, the categories of rating scales and questionnaires. The painter portrays subjects, as they present themselves. The painter's contribution is to enhance and vivify this presentation. Whatever ways the artist's portrait differs from a literal photograph are not, in good art, the results of the artist's agenda, preconceived ideas he/she brings to the encounter. Rather, they are the artist's perceptive recording, the artist's re-presentation, of what the subject brings to the encounter, how the subject presents himself or herself. This is the "empirical" task James set himself as he encountered religion.

It is also important to notice that James was a philosopher and religious inquirer before (and after) he was a psychologist (long before, if we consider the seminars conducted around the family dining table by William James's father, Henry, a maverick but earnest free lance theologian). The questions that most concern William James in the *Varieties* are the questions of religious inquiry (e.g., What can I trust to be most fundamentally true? How do/can I relate to it? What can I do to be/feel saved? What/where is good?)—the same questions that most concern those he studies. He learns *from* them, not about them. Their ideas and experience have the authority, not his judgements and theories about them. Perhaps still more to the point, he wants his hearers and readers to honor the religionists whose experiences he recounts and to learn from them. The *Varieties* is much more a thorough-going apologetic, even a tract, for religion than it is a scientific report.

The Dialect of Empirical Psychology

James renounced both of the major dialects of the language of psychology, the clinical dialect and the quantitative dialect. (The two dialects are so different, reflecting such different ideologies, that speakers of these two dialects find as much difficulty and antagonism in conversing with each other as with speakers of the languages of religion.) In his lectures, because he knew it was an ingratiating tactic with his Scots audience, it was the clinical dialect that he most explicitly and energetically attacked as demeaning (and de-meaning) of religion. But in fact, James felt much more apprehensive about the threat that empirical, quantitative languages of science posed for the religion it claimed to study.

When one speaks the language of *empirical* psychology, one speaks of rating scales, rankings, factors, scores, dimensions, etc. So it is inevitable and appropriate that when one uses such language to speak of religion, religion is construed in terms of scales, scores, factors, and the like. It is neither surprise nor flaw that the religionist does not recognize himself in these terms, any more than that the empirical psychologist finds little if anything recognizable in the religionist's language. They simply are speaking different languages.

As with the speaker of the clinical dialect, what *is* regrettable, though still probably inevitable, is the unapologetic exclusivism with which the speaker of either language declines to recognize that the other is speaking validly.

This—the use of empirical and quantitative methods in psychology of religion—is where the crucial dilemma, perplexity, and conflict is found, in the field's audacious attempt to make a science of the study of religion. This is the source of much that is troublesome and disputed about the validity and identity of the psychology of religion—as witnessed, for example, in much of the discussion in this volume. It is connection with empirical methods that the choice between rigorous reliability and depth of meaning becomes most excruciating. Both science and religion put their identities at risk when they confront empirical quantitative methods. Such language traditionally is the essence of science. And such language appears to challenge the very essence of religion, which above all claims the validity and reality of entities and dimensions of human experience that are trans-rational, singular, non-reproducible, not subject to empirical control or apprehension; the very point of religion, ordinarily, is to challenge the adequacy of an empirical, "scientific" ideology.

The *clinical* dialect, with its bent to pathologize, appears to challenge the *value* of religion, whether religion is good for human beings. But it is the *empirical* dialect that appears to challenge the *validity* of religion, whether religion is true or false.

Starbuck: Empirical Pioneer

Some maneuvers a century ago, during the period which could be regarded as the birth-time of American psychology of religion, are importantly illustrative. They were energized by William James's distrust of quantitative methods for the study of religion. It is sometimes conventional to contrast G. Stanley Hall and James: Hall the empirical researcher vs. James the phenomenologist and ethnographer, who heeded the native language of the religionist. However, I think it may be more useful to take as the empirical standard-bearer and native speaker of quantitative methods the figure of Edwin Diller Starbuck, who published the first book called *The Psychology of Religion* (1899) and who had closer and more telling personal relations with James than Hall did. Between Hall and James the only evidence we have is of cordial proper relations. James, for example, genially accepted Hall's invitation to journey from Cambridge to Worcester in September 1909 to attend the Hall-sponsored lectures by Freud and Jung. The relations between James and Starbuck, however, were more confrontational and focused on just the methodological dilemma here under discussion.

Starbuck (then Edwin Starbuck, before his marriage) was a Quaker high school science teacher in southern Indiana, discovering in his private reading and to his delight the intellectual excitement of the then-emerging historical-critical methods of Bible study: Biblical texts could be related to social contexts and functions and interpreted in the light of such analysis. Starbuck made the connection: If the Bible can be analyzed and interpreted in terms of its human and historical functions, why not study religious experience in the same way. (In his time and place "religious experience" primarily meant adolescent conversion experiences.) What human psychological functions and processes are implicated in conversion? Furthermore, why not study the matter empirically. Starbuck wrote to James at Harvard, volunteering to become his student, and was accepted. He soon began handing out to students at Harvard Divinity School and elsewhere his modest though (for the times) ingenious questionnaires, and he began tabulating the results, and interpreting the numbers. But James had no stomach for this number-crunching that ignored the throb of religious vitality that James could find only in a first-hand case study. (His annoyance comes through even James's habitual geniality in the introduction he eventually wrote for Starbuck's book). And Starbuck lost patience with James's impatience. So they enacted out the dilemma here under discussion and went their separate ways. Starbuck went to Clark University to finish his degree with Hall, and James was provoked by the encounter to finally perform the Gifford Lectures, which he had been habitually postponing, to show *his* view of how religion is properly studied.

Allport's Effort at Science and Religion

The middle of the century brought us a dramatic and influential attempt to speak simultaneously the language of religion and of a psychology, to let scientific inquiry and religious norms *both* set the agenda. It was an attempt to derive psychological categories from religious norms. It proved a dramatically *failed* attempt. The failure is not yet fully recognized—apparently many cling to the hope. But the failure needs to be recognized, as a way of recognizing the stubborn reality of the dilemma that science and religion are rivals, and in any negotiation between the two, one can prevail, or neither, not both. Because the attempt was in the form of a simple questionnaire instrument, the boldness of the attempt, and its transparent futility is more evident than in more abstract or conceptual efforts (as, for example, the attempt of Carl G. Jung and his followers to speak bi-lingually the languages of religion and psychology simultaneously.)

I refer to Gordon Allport's well-known conceptualization of the distinction between "extrinsic" and "intrinsic" religion, and to his attempt to operationalize the concepts with opinion scales (Allport 1950, 1966; Dittes 1971). Allport wanted to regard himself as a successor to William James (he was proud that his office was in William James Hall at Harvard), and he was at pains to honor the perspective of religion and religionists. Indeed, though he was an eminent professor of psychology through most of his career, his first and last faculty appointments at Harvard were to teach ethics, and he never shunned expressing, in any of his writing, the kind of value judgements one expects from a religionist rather than a scientist.

This proclivity for religious value judgement is at the heart of his formulation of the concepts of "intrinsic" and "extrinsic" religion. Allport was transparently and admittedly wanting to adopt a religionist's perspective on the distinction between "good" and "bad" religion, between true and false religion, between faithful and idolatrous religion. Allport's perspective was self-consciously in the heritage of religious prophets and reformers who scolded shallow use of the forms of religion and its social benefits without earnestness of personal commitment. He wanted to identify these "extrinsics" so he could scold them, as he wanted to identify the "intrinsics" as attractive models.

More precisely, he wanted to identify the extrinsics so he could have them to blame for racial prejudice. He was driven to invent these typologies by data which showed religious persons more prejudiced than non-religious (Allport 1954, 1966; Dittes 1969). Like the religious partisan he was, he wanted to defend religion from this stigma: There must be genuinely religious persons—who are unprejudiced—who are distinguishable from hangers-on who go through the motions of religion and who are involved in religion just for what they can get out of it; these latter "extrinsics" must account for the prejudice that appears in the data. That was Allport's reasoning.

Allport wanted to derive his categories from the religious perspective of ethicists, prophets, and reformers. He also wanted to render these categories as psychological constructs and as scientific. To this end he devised items for questionnaire or attitude scale measurement, not having the antipathy to quantitative methods of his model, William James. But, like James, he succeeded in his first objective, to render the religionist's perspective, but failed in his second goal, to make it a scientific rendering. The failure shows on several counts.

1. These categories are orphans, psychologically. Because they were derived from religious not psychological thinking, they are not related, either conceptually or empirically to any underlying psychological or personality theory or to any important psychological variables. Research and theorizing has been sterile. There are no important psychological findings as to how intrinsics and extrinsics develop or how they function. These concepts have not helped develop any psychological insights.
2. Because the concepts were generated to meet the purposes of a religious reformer, they have not been defined or measured as precisely as science requires. Prophets and ethical advocates can deal with categories that are much too broadly and loosely defined for scientific use. It is appropriate for their purposes to iterate their value message in varying conceptual forms, to call attention to varying behaviors that illustrate their evaluative message. But this conglomerate approach does not meet the needs of scientific precision, and Allport's categories and questionnaire items have not stood up well to factor analyses and assessments of reliability.
3. Similarly, it serves a religious reformer's purposes to focus diverse and homogeneous considerations into a single dimension, a "good-bad" polarity, and this is what Allport's categories do. But science advances by analyzing components.
4. The categories are highly restricted to a conventional Western Christian culture. Again, it is appropriate, perhaps necessary for a religious reformer to deal with a concrete historical and cultural context, but psychological science generally aspires to more generalizable interpretations.

Conclusion

I have used William James and Gordon Allport to illustrate the plight of the psychologist who aspires genuinely to enter into the perspective of the religionist. The cost is that the aspirations of psychology as a science are neglected. To be balanced, I should cite cases of psychologists who hold steadfast to their scientific objectivity and rigor, at the expense of dealing with religion superficially and stripped of its soul. But these instances are too well known, and already are well dealt with by other chapters in this volume. In terms of works already cited in this paper, I need only point out that no one reads Starbuck, except for historical interest.

My point is that the impediments to a thorough-going *science* of *religion* are inevitable and great, cause for vigilance, but not for fault-finding or hand-wringing, cause for balancing one approach with another, not for feuding between approaches. When we venture to write or to read psychology of religion, we should *expect* to find either our scientific conscience or our religious sensitivity dissatisfied. But we should not squander attention on that inevitable fate, but move readily beyond that dissatisfaction to attend to whatever insights can be garnered, as inevitably partial as they are.

Bibliography

Allport, G. W. (1950). *The Individual and His Religion.* New York: Macmillan.
Allport, G. W. (1954). *The Nature of Prejudice.* Cambridge, Massachusetts: Addison-Wesley.
Allport, G. W. (1966). The Religious Context of Prejudice, *The Journal for the Scientific Study of Religion.* 5: 447–457.
Dittes, J. E. (1969). Psychology of Religion, In *Handbook of Social Psychology* Second edition. Edited by G. Lindsey and E. Aronson. Reading, Massachusetts: Addison-Wesley. Vol. 5: pp. 602–659.
Dittes, J. E. (1971). Typing the Typologies: Some Parallels in the Career of Church-sect and Extrinsic-Intrinsic, *The Journal for the Scientific Study of Religion.* 10: 375–383.
Freud, S. (1907). Obsessive Actions and Religious Practices. In *The Standard Edition of the Complete Psychological Works of Sigmund Freud,* Vol. 9, pp. 115–127. Edited by James Strachey. London: Hogarth, 1959.
Freud, S. (1913). *Totem and Taboo.* In *The Standard Edition of the Complete Psychological Works of Sigmund Freud*, Vol. 13, pp. 1–162. Edited by James Strachey. London: Hogarth, 1953.
Freud, S. (1927). *The Future of an Illusion.* In *The Standard Edition of the Complete Psychological Works of Sigmund Freud,* Vol. 21, pp. 3–56. Edited by James Strachey. London: Hogarth, 1961.
Freud, S. (1930). *Civilization and Its Discientents.* In *The Standard Edition of the Complete Psychological Works of Sigmund Freud*, Vol. 21, pp. 59–157. Edited by James Strachey. London: Hogarth, 1961.
James, W. (1890). *The Principles of Psychology* 2 vols. New York: Henry Holt.
James, W. (1902). *The Varieties of Religious Experience. A Study of Human Nature.* New York: Longmans Green. New York: Random House Modern Library.
Starbuck, E. D. (1899). *The Psychology of Religion: An Empirical Study of the Growth of Religious Consciousness.* New York: Scribners.

Looking from Sidelines

Heije Faber

The invitation from the editors of this collection—to do a step sideways and have a look from the sidelines at the field on which the psychology of religion is registering its triumphs (or are we more in the phase of training and preparation?)—makes me realize, that in the present time of the disappearance of "the great stories", we are aware that science is affected by the person of the researcher: the time in which he is living, the place where he is living and the mental gifts which he has inherited. All this has an influence on what he (or she) as a scientist is achieving. The "great story" of science, psychology of religion included, does exist and it has a bearing on what we are doing, but it consists of a directive, leading idea. This is visible in many small stories.

The invitation leads me to explore my own small story, and in doing that—as I hope—a vague outline of the great story will also emerge. "Who am I and what influence have my life-history, my career, my place in the society and the environment, in which I grew up, had on this story?"

Let me start by saying, that I came to the psychology of religion rather late in my life, but that I nevertheless through my life history approached the psychology of religion with a clear vision of its possibilities and its problems and have tried to show this in my publications. I may say, that I—in my small story—have always had an eye on the great story.

Let me begin by telling something about the lifestory and my career. I was born in 1907 in the Netherlands as a son of a liberal minister in the Dutch-Reformed Church—a church which was torn apart by the fierce struggle between liberals and orthodox—and grew up in the context of this old church, which goes back to the Reformation and was originally the state-church. The Netherlands, however, have been outside the sphere of influence of this church. The country I was born was a middle-class country with an enlightened middle class, in which XIXth century Modernism had become rather solidly rooted. The idealism of the Modernists led to the endeavour to renew church-life, a great enterprise to bring the Christian heritage more in line with what modern men and women were supposed to think and believe. In the background however these liberals had already a certain suspicion that the position of Christianity in modern society was more perilous than people in general thought.

This situation was my spiritual context when in 1932—after my studies in Leiden (Holland) and Marburg and Heidelberg (Germany)—I became a minister myself: not however in the state church but in a "free" congregation outside the official Church with the intention to be there nearer to "modern, secularised" people. There—in the vicinity of Amsterdam—in these years of economic crisis and unemployment, I was suddenly confronted with the typical "modern" phenomenon of Dutch national-socialism, a sister-movement of the German one, which after 1933, the year in which Hitler came to power, overran this politically and economically weakened country. I even headed a movement against it. In my ministry in my congregation I wrestled with the problem that in Leiden with its accent on history and philosophy, I was not adequately prepared for the practice of the ministry, a gap which I tried to fill by reading psychological books. I got an opportunity to start a more systematic study of psychology, when during the German occupation of the Netherlands I was compelled to go into hiding—on account of my former political activities. I crowned this study by writing a second dissertation and obtaining a doctorate in psychology in Amsterdam in 1956. The title of my dissertation was *Over ziek sijn* (On being ill). This work was the result of a three year long cooperation with a psychosomatic researchgroup in the University-hospital of Amsterdam. It contained, in the first part, some theoretical considerations about various ways of approaching the phenomenon of illness and gave, in the second part, the result of a research project among 28 patients of the group concerning their religious development and their religious life. This dissertation constituted my first step in the field of the psychology of religion. Till that time I had moved mostly in the field of theology proper and had also made some cautious steps in pastoral psychology, particularly regarding the issue of communication in the pastoral interview. This dissertation led the theological faculty of Leiden to invite me to join their faculty to work—with an eye to improving the preparation of their students—toward a psychology for ministers. In 1960 I went to the United States to study the situation there and discovered the at that moment ground-gaining movement for Clinical Pastoral Education. I considered this movement so important for the formation of ministers in a rapidly secularising world, that I decided to introduce it in my country and, if possible, outside Holland and to contribute to its organisation. Over the years I have put a lot of energy in this endeavour.

At the same time the psychology of religion started to come alive for me. I discovered how important it is for the minister to have more insight into the origin of religious life. This also took on a great significance for me personally. As far as the first point is concerned: my interest in the problems of the critical situation of church and Christianity in modern society inspired me to do research into the possible connection between the "becoming fatherless of modern society", the title of a publication of Alexander Mitscherlich (1963), and the development of the radical theology of the sixties, in which the image of a patriarchal God was attacked. In addition my contacts with psychoanalysts in the just mentioned psychosomatic research-group aroused my interest in a psychoanalytical critique of religion and in the possibility of penetrating with the help of psychoanalytic insights deeper into the mystery of religion, especially its origin in the relation of a child to his or her parents. Out of my activities in the field of pastoral psychology and psychology of religion in this way some publications originated, some of which have also been published abroad. For me personally this field of research became meaningful. In my autobiography, published in 1993, I have given a description of my life as a double journey, one as a journey of a modern man, involved in the development of our society in the direction of Post-Modernism, wanting to find a more authentic life, and as a religious man, seeking more insight into the mystery of religion, better said into my relation to God. At this point we may ask the question, in how far in this small story something becomes visible of the great story of psychology of religion—particularly its central problems and its important perspectives, but also its "smaller" problems, like its methodology and its relation to neighbouring sciences. I realize that in asking this question I am confronted with my observations from the sidelines. This confrontation leads me to some fundamental observations. Even though I am aware of the modesty of my small story, at the same time it has for me—and I hope for a number of readers also—existential significance. By this I mean that it opens up a view of what one can describe as the "ultimate questions" of man and society.

Observations

My first observation is that in my small story a tension is hidden. I wonder, how others involved in the great story deal with this tension. In the conversation I had with my professor in psychology during the time of my hiding during the war about the possibility of starting a study in psychology, he began by discouraging me. "You as a theologian", he said, "are accustomed to reading ten books and then writing an eleventh. We as psychologists are interested in making observations; we elaborate these observations into hypotheses and we test these hypotheses with new observations. In this way we try to come to theories." It is clear what he had in mind. The workers in both these sciences have a different attitude (habitus). Thus, a theologian who wants to become a psychologist—and perhaps wants to cultivate the field of psychology of religion professionally—must make a fundamental shift. The shift from belief (reflection on "believed" truths) to observation (observation of facts, e.g. in the field of religion). These observations lead to quite another kind of reflection than the reflection of the theologian. He tries—after careful consideration of hypotheses—to formulate a theory, a "glimpse" of a truth. This truth, however is not a "believed" truth, but one founded in observations. The theologian may be inclined to force his (theological) truth upon the psychologist, i.e. he will expect that the psychologist will accept his truth as a fact. On the other side the psychologist will expect from the theologian, that he will be prepared to listen to him and to let himself be criticised by him, or at least be corrected in the believing of his truth.

This causes a tension, in the first place in the mind of the theologian-psychologist himself, but also between the students of both the sciences. This tension in our time is moreover heightened because religious truth is suffering from a decrease in plausibility and, in the lives of the believers, is impaired by doubt on the one side and by a kind of fundamentalist "petrification" on the other under the influence of a fear of losing these truths. At the same time the truth of psychology in the ongoing process of ever more observations in other cultures—and even in our own—leads to an unavoidable feeling of the relativity of all religious truth, even our own.

How does the psychology of religion find its way in this complicated situation? Looking from the sidelines my only answer must be, that I have an unhappy feeling. I do not observe much of this tension, that I experience around me. It seems that many theologians make the impression of being blind to what psychology of religion is doing. They go on, as before, writing their voluminous but often not very relevant books. And psychologists, on the other side, are busy with their research but seem to be deaf to the deep emotions, which arise in their material. There is hardly question of a tension and certainly not of an encounter. It seems as if only a few people have heard, or perceived the tremors of secularisation, or of Post-Modernism in our society, or are aware of the echos of eternity in the existence of modern men and women.

I believe consequently that my teacher was right in stating that both disciplines require a different perspective. For me, however, the question arises whether psychology of religion as such does not require a separate perspective. And together with this a separate language. Paul Pruyser saw this problem when he suggested in his book *The Minister as Diagnostician* (1976) that the minister in contacts with psychotherapists should not adapt to the concepts and the language of the therapists but should contribute his own concepts and language to the "diagnoses" of the client. Do words like conversion, freedom, love, repentance and other concepts and words not say something essential about human beings?

How do we get sight of such "facts" (if we want to use this word here)? And by what method do we bring them into a meaningful relation with each other (if we see this as the task of science)? This is asking for the most appropriate method of psychology of religion. If we pose this question to Wulff in his *Psychology of Religion: Classic and Contemporary Views* (1991) we must conclude that we in this field have only two methods, both of them rather traditional ones: the objective, as he calls it, and the subjective one, i.e. the psychoanalytic method. I am not quite fair here: Wulff mentions among the subjective methods also the interpretative one of Spranger. I will return to Spranger. But the point I want to make here, is that these two methods are characterised by the fact that they have their origin in the XIXth century. This means that the methods to study religion are in essence derived from the secular sciences, for whom religion is a cultural phenomenon next to other phenomena, that can be studied as such. The last thing I would like to suggest is, that one cannot reach important results in this way. But is religion, in last resort, a cultural phenomenon only? Does a rite like, for instance, baptism fit into a classification like this one? And the structure of the religious relation (what believers experience in their relation with their God), is it possible to penetrate to the heart of it with objective-psychological methods? We find ourselves here in the depth of our human existence, where science meets its limits and where only existential philosophy can try to sketch some fundamental structures. I think that in order to do justice to the phenomenon of religion, we must try in addition to and perhaps beyond the traditional methods—in a kind of dialogue with the existential philosophy—to find new methods more suitable to the religious experience and, perhaps also, a new more adequate language. We may ask if it is possible whether we can learn from the psychological observations and even the vocabulary of the great mystics.

It is possible to clarify what I have in mind in another way. The structure of the religious experience is—with a presently much used term—to be found on an ontological level. Modern ontology moves in the present situation as a research of Being wholly in the shadow of the phenomenological method as it was introduced by Edmund Husserl. Not only the "classical" existentialists like Heidegger, Jaspers and Sartre, but also somebody like Levinas is working in this field. A common characteristic of these philosophers is that they are taking leave of rationalism, more exactly of the modern way of thinking of Enlightenment; in their search for truth they are not finding their source in an irrationalism as a reaction on rationalism (of Enlightenment), but they fathom the structures of the pre-reflexive Self, not of the rational I. They hope to find there more authenticity. Well, this domain is also the domain of religion. In its more authentic forms religion is more present on the level of the Self than of the I. This level is with Heidegger in *Sein und Zeit* (1927) he level of the fundamental—later called "ontological" by others—feelings. Heidegger himself finds the authenticity of human existence in the fundamental feeling of anxiety. I from my side put overagainst this the fundamental feeling of "basic trust" (Erikson,1950), in the field of the religious experience. It is no coincidence, that Erikson in his life shows gradually a development—as Hetty Zock shows in her dissertation (Zock 1990)—towards an existential, one may also say, ontological psychology.

I add here two comments, to which I will come back later: first, that the fundamental role of the mother (and of both parents) as an object of religious psychological research emerges here; and second, that in this context one must point to the importance of images and in consequence of this to the role of language in the religious relation. We should not forget, that e.g. Heidegger in the second half of his life had been fascinated by the role of the poet in his search for more authenticity.

Post-Modernism

In looking from the sidelines at the psychology of religion I see thus as a shortcoming that the psychology of religion identifies itself too much with empirical and psychoanalytic psychology, although I realise that their contribution is invaluable. We must however find a connection with a new development, which—I am convinced—finds its origin in a new requirement or need. In order to explain this, some words are necessary. I see this requirement in connection with the appearance of so called Post-Modernism on the cultural scene. One can see this Post-Modernism as a reaction to and at the same time as a deepening of Modernism, that is to say of the cultural pattern of Enlightenment.

If it is true that in Post-Modernism we see a turn away from Enlightenment, we experience in these years a thorough shift in Western culture. We must acknowledge that not only psychology of religion but the whole of theology and, therefore the Western churches as well have only a dim awareness of this situation. Enlightenment meant, in the words of Immanuel Kant "the leaving of man of his *selbstverschuldete Unmündigkeit*" (the not being of age of which we ourselves are guilty). What against the background of these words does it mean, that in Post-Modernism we recognize a turning away from and—as I said before—a deepening of Enlightenment?

I see it this way: the human being has come of age and has this being of age, as it were, confirmed in both the two centuries which followed the Enlightenment. Science and technology, democracy and global cooperation did give this man come of age the reign over the world. But in looking back on these two centuries modern men and women have seen also war, oppression, genocide, poverty and criminality; these are darkening their horizon. Kant had asked: what can I know, what shall I do and what can I hope, what is man? In these words the future lays open for this man come of age. But present-day humans ask: what am I afraid of, in which can I believe, who is my neighbour, what is a human being? He is confronted with himself, with the meaning of being man in a world, which he dominates, but does not really understand. It is post-war Existentialism of people like Heidegger, Sartre and Levinas, that asks these questions.

I am aware that the comparison which I am going to make, is too general. I am convinced however, that it is right. In Post-Modernism man enters the phase of adolescence of his development, i.e. of the development of Western Society. I give an explanation. Erikson did say decisive things about the phases of human life. Man in his childhood leaves his parental home with a feeling of "initiative", of wanting to exercise the direction of his life, of wanting to come of age. Following this is the phase of "industry", of applying himself on abilities and tasks, in other words: in the XIXth and XXth centuries the phase of science and industrial revolution. In our Western society we are now in the next phase, that of puberty and adolescence. Erikson describes this phase in the human life-cycle, in which people are searching for a deeper identity, in which "all sameness and continuities relied on earlier are questioned again". It therefore is a time in which doubt and even despair may play a great role. The Dutch psychiatrist Rümke in a book on *Phases in the life of man* (1938) describes similar critical periods of transition as phases in which an integration found in a former phase via a period of disintegration of the life-pattern through a new integration can reach a newly won organisation. We in our society experience clearly a period of disorganisation: the "fatherless society" of Mitscherlich becomes more and more a society without binding structures; it has gradually achieved the character of a "permissive" society. In the world of Post-Modernism, therefore, one can see in the "deconstruction of the great stories" (one of its slogans) a search for a new integration, an identity with deeper foundations. I believe that we can see this same process in the philosophy of Existentialism. After the Neo-Kantian philosophy of the end of the XIXth and the beginning of the XXth century—with its analysis of the role and the importance of modern science—Existentialism came to the foreground— via the so called life-philosophy—as an expression of the search of man after himself and even of his doubt concerning the possibility of a proper identity.

Consequences for Religion

If this brief sketch of the present situation is right, there must be far-reaching consequences in the field of church and religion. The development of religion as well as theology must then be studied in the light of this hypothesis. We are confronted here—once again: if I am right—as psychologists of religion with the task of a very important, but rather difficult field of study. There is, up till now, nothing to lead us.

I will try to say something about it. In the field of religion we see the disappearance of fixed ecclesiastical structures, in many countries even a disappearance of organised religion itself. The decline of the participation in religious meetings and rituals in most of the Western churches is alarming. The younger generation for the greater part is alienated from church and religion. Where religion shows signs of life, it is on one side in various forms of personal spirituality and on the other side in a number of fundamentalist groups. In the field of theology itself, radical theology with its slogan "the death of God" (Nietzsche) has had more influence under the surface than has been visible in the traditional theological scene. In practically all theological publications of some importance a *Diesseitigkeit* is noticeable, which shows itself in the great interest in the problems of pluralism, of the interreligious dialogue, of pastoral theology, of liberation-theology and which points to the trend to find the "locus theologiae" more in human reality than in a definitive revelation. Does present-day theology make clear, what Chesterton may have meant with his paradoxical saying "There is no God and Jesus Christ is his prophet"? The *doctrina de*

Deo is moving into the background and is making place for Christology and pneumatology. If there is a God, he must be found in the realm of our human possibilities. In my conviction it is here at this point that the great challenge of the first decennia of the next century arises for psychology of religion. What is it, that we as psychologists of religion are able to contribute to an elucidation of this situation? My suggestion is that in the foregoing some hints can be found.

Hint no. 1

One of the hints is that we as believers or unbelievers are post-modern men and women. I presume we are able to admit that religion is psychologically rooted in the reality of human life and that therefore the relation God-man is not characterised by a *Senk recht von oben* [perpendicularly from above] (Karl Barth). That, however, religion is also rooted in the reality of society and culture is a step which we often have not yet made. People see society and church mostly as separate entities and not—in spite of their undoubtedly often strained relation—involved in each other under the "surface" with all kinds of threads and interconnections. My studies have shown me, that the development of our society in the direction of a fatherless society has also religious and theological consequences. Research into this connection is necessary.

As far as I can see, therefore a study of the influence of Post-Modernism in the field of religion and church should be a priority on our agenda.

Hint no.2

The second hint may be found in my view of the development of our society towards a phase of adolescence. If Erikson is right in saying, that in this phase "all sameness and continuities relied on earlier are questioned again", this will mean in practice that we experience in this phase a return to the origin, in which the beginning of this development in the direction of an own identity is struggled through again and this time on a deeper and more personal level. This means, that the relation to the parents again, but now in another way— from a deeper opposition and with a clearer perspective on the future—becomes an issue for investigation and dimension in ourselves. What does the young man or woman reject in his or her parents and what is he or she prepared to "learn and take with" him (or her) from them on his or her road to maturity? We on the one hand reject our parents and on the other hand we introject (with the term of Freud) them at the same time.

If I am right, we may say—with a certain reservation because of the rough comparison—that in Post-Modernism our society tries to define its relation to the "fathers"—and in the first instance: negatively—, but at the same time in its search for a deeper "identity" hopes to make new discoveries in the old tradition. It looks for the deeper sources, that stand at the origin of its development.

In this context psychology of religion encounters the question: which meaning do the parents have in the religious development of young people and which role do they play there? I wonder, whether we have sufficiently accounted for the fact, that in all religions the language is full of references to father and mother and that the father and mother-images predominate in the pantheon of God-images. Freud in *Totem und Tabu* (1913) and in *Die Zukunft einer Illusion* (1927) was more aware of the psychological meaning of this fact than we Western psychologists of religion. It seems as if only a few of us are interested enough to do research into the motherly and fatherly aspects in the image of God, but a deeper analysis of the structural connections has rarely been done. That the different relation to mother and father is at the origin of all religious life and that we find the result of this double origin in the world of religious phenomena—and so perhaps in Post-Modernism also—is a field that awaits exploration.

Hint no.3

There is a third hint in connection with this. It concerns the structure of what we call (with a term which I think more and more objectionable) "religious experience", that is the structure of the human relation to (the mystery of) God. The writer of the first epistle of John says, that nobody ever saw God (I John: IV,12), something with which we all will agree. But how are we able to say much about God and to know apparently about him? If it is true, that in the relation to God we are involved in a relation of "ultimate concern" and in this relation we find the relation to our parents, we cannot avoid the conclusion, that one of the lines of connection between the two is, that in the parent-child-relation the "ultimate concern" is an aspect as well.

I believe indeed, that introspection into our own experiences as well as observation of the lives of others shows us that the relation to the "origin" is an "ultimate concern" for human beings. The parents are for children the anchor of their existence in the time their "ontological anxiety" is awakening; they remain their anchor for many years. Later on—when our independence is growing—they are a lasting background, in relation to which each of us must define his or her relationship till late in life. Erikson is right in saying, that old age brings with it "a new and different love of one´s parents". The "ultimate" of this concern is more vague, but it is still to be felt.

Everyone, including those who have not known their parents, makes for him- or herself an image of father or mother. And through these images we express out of which fundamental feelings we give form and contents to this relation. Everyone has—with Jungs terminology—an archetype of father or mother. In the course of life we remain confronted with the ontological mystery, that at our origin our parents have answered for us. They awakened an "ultimate, basic trust". This trust they are not in a position to give always. But the "ontological mystery" at that turning point arises out of the trust they have created: the image of the Father and the Mother, which was already embedded in their archetype. They represented in our trust the God, whom nobody can see, but who is yet able to have a relation to us.

In the foregoing we have more than once used the word image. In my conviction, image is indeed essential to understand the God-man-relation. Nobody has seen God, but we do speak in the language of religion and of theology extensively about him. We are able to do this on account of the images we have of him. I have said before that in the domain of the Self some fundamental feelings play a role: for Heidegger, for instance, anxiety. He explains in *Sein und Zeit* (1927) that feelings have to do with possibilities of being a human being. In anxiety man experiences which possibilities he is realizing. He does not mention images, but some reflection makes us conscious that the image, which man has of himself—so: that he is a dead tree or a wave in the ocean—, gives expression to an understanding, that is included in a fundamental feeling. Heidegger says that each understanding of ourselves is an emotional understanding.

We are able to apply this easily to the understanding of God. Our understanding of God is an emotional understanding and is expressed in an image. So the father-image of God expresses the basic trust we have concerning God. In this image we show which feeling we cherish concerning the invisible mystery of God. There may be also other feelings important in the relation to God and they perhaps will lead to a more motherly image.

Our thesis therefore is that fundamental religious feelings arise in the original relation to our parents and from there have a decisive influence on our later development. Schildmann in a study of the dreams of Karl Barth has shown that Barth's relation to his father led to his father-image of God, that it got its confirmation and depth in the *Du* (Thou) that he during his lecture of Paul's epistle to the Romans heard speak to himself in the figure of Christ (Schildmann, 1991). Our conclusion therefore is that the parents as well as the images play an essential role in the religious relation. They even belong together.

Comments

In concluding this contribution I make some comments. In the first place, re-reading this paper I come to the conclusion that my small story has been born in a confrontation with my own personal development, but also in one with the development of Western society in this XXth century. This is no coincidence. Looking from the sidelines at the psychology of religion in action and reflecting on it I realize that psychology—including psychology of religion—which in this century has got its impetus out of the great need for psychological insight, is more and more in danger of getting stuck in an isolation of a science, which refines itself steadily, but at the same time becomes sterile. I consider the confrontation with the reality of the man and woman of to-day essential for the vitality of particularly the psychology of religion.

In the second place: this asks for more reflection on the problem of the method in psychology of religion than we are accustomed to. The danger for all psychology is that the example, that stood before its eyes in the XIXth century at its origin, i.e. that of natural science, has become a "hidden agenda"; neutrality of the researcher, the quantification of the data, the rational control of the object of research are aspects of this agenda. I will be the first to acknowledge, that the attitude of objectivity and distance, which is required for this type of science, is a necessary condition for every psychological research. But the data of the natural sciences are different from the data of human sciences. My fear is that a psychology which orients itself on behaviorism, for example, will forget this. My impression is that psychoanalysis in this respect wrestles with a problem, that it has difficulties in resolving.

I do not pretend to have a clear answer, but I hope—with some foundational observations—to have made a small contribution to a possible discussion. One of the human sciences—cultural antropology, as we have called it—shows a way. It has adopted the method of participant observation: on the one hand to participate in the social life of the tribe, which it studies, and on the other to observe as objectively and from a distance as far as possible. We recognize that this brings the scientist in a clear tension: he must identify with his object and at the same time put himself overagainst it. But it is just in this tension, that he can hope to do justice to the nature of his object: fellow human beings, who experience in their rituals their deepest anxieties and joys. In this way only will he be able to understand their religion, the heart of their rituals. In the relation of these men to their gods, as it realizes itself in their rituals, we clearly meet an understanding of these gods, that expresses itself in intense feelings. Their religion is—with the words of Heidegger—*gestimmtes Verstehen*. (We may try to translate: the felt understanding).

In his participation the researcher enters as far as possible into this *gestimmtes Verstehen,* in order to describe this later from a distance and with the utmost objectivity in concepts, which are understandable for Western scientists, and to look for internal and external connections with the intention of making it scientifically accessible.

I believe that in this kind of participation we utilize the best method for psychology of religion. It represents a middle way between the subjective and the objective method, which Wulff (1991) distinguishes. Objective methods will be necessary to collect and to sort out the material for research, but this material must be worked at in a participant observation. The problem is how the psychologist of religion un-covers in this material the *gestimmtes Verstehen* , that is the heart of it? Two steps are necessary: first *Einfühlung* (empathy), an empathic entering into the world of feelings, which he finds among the believers, and second realizing in this empathy and at the same time not hampered by it, which understanding becomes noticeable in those feelings. This understanding he must try to make intelligible, i.e. intelligible in the language, which is accepted in a discourse of psychologists of religion.

What I try to formulate here, resembles the *verstehende Psychologie*, as

Spranger developed this years ago in his *Psychologie des Jugendalters* (1924) in the line of Wilhelm Dilthey. Spranger however was interested in the content, the "ideology" of adolescence. His picture of the concrete human being in adolescence remained vague. Psychology of religion stays with its interest with the feelings and therewith with the religious man or woman as a living person. The religious content is the object of other theological disciplines. Psychology of religion is interested in the ways religion originates and develops in the human psyche.

The Problem of Language

It seems clear to me, that a perspective like this on the psychology of religion and its method puts us before the question, whether our language is adapted to an understanding that is essential for religion. It is of course unavoidable, that in our use of language the same tension will be visible, which also played a role in participant observation. One takes part in a *gestimmtes Verstehen* of a particular character and must at the same time express this understanding in general (understandable for outsiders) words. What we see however, is that psychologists of religion use words and concepts of general psychology or psychotherapy and try to impose them on the religious understanding. The particular character of this understanding is then not reached. I plead therefore to try as an example to observe the development of our own religious life in a period of seeking and doubt and to "understand" it with a "language", that does justice to the task of every scientific research, which is therefore not apologetic or propagandistic, but is understandable for "believers" and at the same time discussable for "unbelievers". I believe that the contemplative tradition may be able to help us.

It is perhaps also a help if we realise that existentialist philosophers like Heidegger and Levinas wrestle with a similar problem. We see that they either call in the help of poets (Heidegger) or look out for images and give them an objective, and so for scientific discourse usable meaning (Levinas). William James in his *Varieties of Religious Experience* (1902) and Rudolf Otto in his *Das Heilige* (1917) are examples of what I have in mind.

Conclusion

I hope that in the above my ideal of what psychology of religion as a science can do has become clear. It has a double purpose; on the one hand to render service in the concrete situations of the moment and on the other to try to achieve a universal validity. In other words it must have the will and the courage to be a small story, a story of people in the limited situation in which they are working and which requires them to fulfill a small, necessary task: To help people on the way to more clarity concerning belief. And besides this to claim a great story: to offer a perspective in the small story on the life of human beings, of every man and woman sub *specie aeternitatis* .

Bibliography

Erikson, E.H. (1950). *Childhood and Society.* New York: Norton.
Faber, H. (1956). *Over ziek zijn.* Assen: Van Gorcum.
Faber,H.(1993). *Rekenschap van een zoektocht. Autobiografie.* Baarn: Ten Have.
Freud, S. (1913). *Totem und Tabu. (Gesammelte Werke, Bd. IX,* eds. A. Freud et al.). London: Imago, 1940.
Freud, S. (1927) *Die Zukunft einer Illusion. (Gesammelte Werke, Bd. XIV,* eds. A. Freud et al., pp. 325–380). London: Imago, 1948.
Heidegger, M. (1927). *Sein und Zeit.* Halle a.d. Saale: Niemeyer.
James, W. (1902). *The Varieties of Religious Experience. A Study in Human Nature.* Hammondsworth: Penguin, 1982.
Mitscherlich, A. (1963). *Auf dem Weg zur vaterlosen Gesellschaft.* München: Piper.
Otto, R. (1917). *Das Heilige.* Breslau: Trewendt & Granier.
Pruyser, P.W. (1976). *The Minister as Diagnostician.* Philadelphia: Westminster.
Rümke, H.C. (1938). *Levenstijdperken van den man.* Amsterdam: Arbeiderspers.
Schildmann, W. (1991). *Was sind das für Zeichen?* München: Kaiser.
Spranger, E. (1924). *Psychologie des Jugendalters.* Leipzig: Quelle & Meyer.
Wulff, D.M. (1991). *Psychology of Religion. Classical and Contemporary Views.* New York: Wiley.
Zock, H. (1990). *A Psychology of Ultimate Concern.* Amsterdam: Rodopi.

Contemporary Religious Experiences
Reflections on Fifteen Years of Research

Antoon Geels

Taking a step back and observing your own work is perhaps just as necessary as doing the job itself. This counts not only for research but also for teaching. In this chapter the focus will naturally be on some fifteen years of research on so called intense religious experiences from a cross-cultural perspective. From an overall point of view this research can be characterized by a search for new psychological models. Is this the proper strategy to follow also in the future? In my reflections on these questions I will first present a review of the most important parts of my research and then discuss a possible strategy for the future.

During my travels in Asia and the Middle East I often came across statements illustrating the discrepancy between the scholarly study of religion and living religion. When I studied repetitive prayer in Istanbul, Turkey, a few dervishes took me on a walk through Old Istanbul, showing me a number of Sufi premises which since the time of Kemal Atatürk, in the twenties, function as museums. We came to talk about Western, scholarly studies of Sufism. "That's not us", one of the dervishes exclaimed. This remark reminded me once again that academic interpretations seldomly manage to be confronted with the type of religion they are supposed to study. The religion of books often has very little to do with practised religion.

From one perspective this is, of course, not at all surprising. Scholars specialized in religious studies usually study texts. This category of textual oriented specialists, working with philological methods, do not have the habit of asking questions like 'What kind of people read this text?' or 'How is this text used in the context of religious practice?' The distance between these learned scholars and the religion they study is about just as far as the distance between the basement of the university library where they found the text and the geographical area where the type of religion is a living reality. An example could be an indologist who translated and edited an obscure Hindu text—a kind of work I certainly do admire!—and Hindus in one of the numerous villages, covering eighty percent of the Indian population, Hindus who are more interested in their crop or their own digestion. Possibly the indologist decides to travel to the country of his studies and finds difficulties to adapt to a culture which, so far, only has been the object of textual and literary analysis. The culture shock can be severe, leading to a new decision: back to the secure study room, surrounded by all those familiar books.

Although I present this problem in a satirical form, there is, of course, a serious dimension connected with this situation. It could be labelled as the *text and context* problem. It is one of my basic convictions that textual data should be studied in relation to the context where they are used, which includes the interpretation of the persons using it.

Another possibility is that scholars working with texts, for example a specialist in the philosophy of Ibn 'Arabi, deal with the ideal world, whereas dervishes practising repetitive prayer (*dhikr*) represent the real world. My work with dervishes in Turkey taught me that very few of them study classical Sufi texts. Tradition is transmitted from person to person, primarily from the Shaykh to the dervish or from the *murshid* to the *murid*. In addition, there exist pamphlets and other types of simply printed material, which presents the basic *tarekat*-jargon, i.e. the language used in the circles of the dervishes. Let's regard this as the problem related to *the ideal and the real* world.

Reconstruction and Interpretation

Book-shops in Sweden as well as in other countries offer quite a few books about people having all kinds of religious experiences. In the USA a book about guardian angels turned out to be a real best-seller, selling about half a million copies. From one point of view this is a sign of our time, witnessing perhaps the great spiritual need in a world, which by so many people is experienced as chaotic. Why is there war, conflict and corruption? Why does the human being have to hover between the angel and the beast? The genre of literature referred to can have a comforting function: there is, after all, another dimension in our existence, a dimension which some people would call divine. Now, the reading of this kind of books can certainly have a reinforcing value for the readers faith, but from a scholarly perspective this genre is of little or no value. The primary reason for this is that the biographic perspective is too limited or even missing. Religious experience, including the vision of angels and other types of encounter with a dimension interpreted as divine, has to be studied in the context of the individual's biography.[1]

It is my proposal to label this part of the research process as the *reconstruc-*

---

[1] At the conference for European Psychologists of Religion in Lund, Sweden, in June 1994 I asked prof. L.B. Brown what he intended to do with the thousands of letters telling about all kinds of religious experiences, gathered for many years in England. The answer was that he really did not know. One of the basic problems, I think, is that these documents were collected without asking the informants about the biographical context of the experience. This means that a systematic analysis of the documents can only be arbitrary—you never know whether the issue studied really is missing or just a part of the untold story!

tion phase, a phase which is absolutely fundamental for a proper *interpretation* of the experience studied. Let me mention from the outset that there are now sharp dividing lines. The process of reconstruction is also a kind of interpretation. Let's return to this question later.

One of the guiding principles in a reconstruction process is the ambition to *search* for all data relevant to the research problem. The second principle would be to *use* all the discovered data. When I started to search for data to be used in my dissertation study on the Swedish mystic and shoemaker Hjalmar Ekström (1885–1962) I tried to follow in his footsteps, so to speak, searching for archival data in all places where he lived and worked, all institutes he was related to. In addition I searched for personal documents, primarily letters, by contacting friends and acquaintances who were still living, or their relatives. In many cases a few phone calls or a letter were sufficient; in other cases I stubbornly but politely reminded relatives that there should be letters, so please ask your siblings, or search again at attics and in basements. Most of the time this stubbornness was most rewarding. In extreme cases my informant owned important letters written by Ekström, letters from a period which I had not covered with other data, then showed them to me without giving permission to read or copy them! In the case referred to it took me about half a year to convince the person that the documents would not be misused in such a way that the name of his father would be insulted. After all, I was not making a study of his father, but of Ekström, who during a turbulent period in his life contacted the father, who functioned as a support at that time.

When writing the thesis I tried to integrate all data available and to reconstruct the childhood, adolescence, and adult life of a person who has been characterised as a 'wash proof Lutheran mystic'. One of my critics told me that I had written a biography, putting it in such a way as to imply negative criticism. I thanked him for this, because it had been my intention to write a biography, preferably in such a way that his two daughters, his siblings, as well as his friends would recognize him, which they certainly did! If Hjalmar Ekström could be regarded as a Lutheran mystic in our time I thought it wise to concentrate on his development. As far as classical mystics are concerned we usually lack biographical data. My decision was, then, to find and use all data available. The only part that is regrettable, I think, is that I did not at that time make a sharp distinction between reconstruction and interpretation. This meant that the theoretical perspective, chosen from social psychology and the sociology of knowledge, is intertwined with the biographical reconstruction. Since about five years ago I try to avoid this mixture.

Biographical reconstruction could be compared to the work of publishing critical editions of religious texts, a kind of work done by the same kind of philologists I satirically presented above. Critical editions have a lasting value. What would an historian of religion without training in anthropology do if he or she did not have access to texts? In a similar way we could ask: What would a psychologist of religion do without a proper biographical context? (see note

1.) As far as the interpretations are concerned, well, they can be changed, possibly because the interpreter at a later date has chosen another position. In addition, it goes without saying that everything in the reconstruction cannot be interpreted with the chosen perspective. But this fact should not have any influence on the reconstruction. After all, colleagues have better chances to present *their* interpretations if the reconstruction is covering as much as possible of the individual's development. One of the dangers of the hermeneutic approach, I think, is what I would call a procrustes-technique, i.e. to adapt the interpretation to the chosen theory, leaving out an unknown number of data. I am afraid that this approach is not uncommon. Instead of presenting all the evidence, the case functions as an illustration to the theory.

To interpret religious experience and behaviour is a way of looking. We could call it perspectivism. The perspective chosen is meant to shed new light on the phenomenon studied. In other words, it has a heuristic value. We should always remember, however, that it is one of innumerable possible perspectives. Part of the interpretitive work is, then, to be aware of the perspective chosen, its merits and its limitations, to discuss what we 'see' and the aspects we do not 'see'. After all, there are other perspectives, shedding light (or darkness) on other parts of the descriptive representation of the data. The hermeneutical scholar oscillates, I think, between the two poles of nearness and distance. We are near, sometimes 'under the skin' of the informant; at other times we have to keep distance in relation to the object studied and to ourselves. With the last remark I am referring to the kind of self-distance leading to questions like 'Why do I choose this topic? Why this method? Why this theoretical orientation?'

As mentioned above, a reconstruction is already a form of interpretation, a way of structuring the data in a meaningful manner. In the case of Ekström I chose a biographical structuring because the main research task was to study his religious development. In another biographical study I chose a different approach. The topic was to study the relation between religious experience and artistic creation. The object of the study was the internationally successful Swedish artist Violet Tengberg (b. 1920). Critics had observed the mystical dimension in her symbolic expression, but they could not point at any specific subjective influence. I contacted her and she agreed to cooperate. During a period of about six years she supplied me with all kind of data: her correspondence, notes, diaries, as well as her personal archives containing recensions of exhibitions, articles about her, and so on.

In a first, purely descriptive part, I alternated between describing the artist's 'outer' and 'inner' world, i.e. a world possible to study for anybody who bothers to dig up published data, and her inner world of reflections, associations, and intense religious experiences. During the twelve years of her life that were carefully studied (1965–76) she struggled with intense problem of meaning, both with artistic creation and life in general. "Life", she wrote in a letter to a well-known literary historian, "is meaningless if it doesn't aim at something higher and bigger than that which man can bring about. If this didn't exist, than everything would be as a soap-bubble, which easily can be punctured, and life would be one great roar of laughter."

The most important of her religious visionary and auditive experiences happened to her in Paris. In one of her visions she saw two small crosses unite together. Out of them grew a taller cross, uniting with her. She heard the words "riveted to the cross". This vision and a number of other religious visions completely changed Violet Tengberg's world. She started to compose poems in great number, a result of a sort of automatic writing. Her life and artistic work was suddenly imbued with meaning. But at the same time she felt a great need to integrate the visionary experience in an all-embracing world-view. One of the consequences of her intense religous experiences was that Violet Tengberg felt the urge to reveal glimpses of Divine Reality through the medium of her brush and pencil.

With this information about Violet Tengberg's inner, visionary world, which has not been made public before, we have a key which, in the words of William Blake, opens "the doors of perception" as far as Tengberg's artistic creations are concerned. In a chapter on symbolism in Violete Tengberg's art, the artistic symbols could easily be related to her own inner experiences. The symbolism of the cross, for example, was clearly related to her visionary experience of the crosses in Paris in 1969. In the years before this vision, the cross was a dominating motive in her paintings. We witness here a sort of cyclical process in which visual motives in art are related to a visionary experience of a similar motive, which in turn influences new artistic expressions. In other word: from picture to vision to new picture, etc.

About a hundred pages in my book about the artist are descriptive, alternating between her 'outer' and 'inner' world. In part two it was my task, I thought, to persue modern research on mental imagery and the psychology of creativity. Could this exciting research shed new light on the psychology of visionary experience? The result was a new theoretical perspective, regarding visions as perceptualizations of basic needs. The perceptualization implies a solution of an intrapsychic conflict concerning the meaning of life in general and artistic creation in particular. This process has probably been facilitated by a special disposition for mental imagery, a disposition which was stimulated through her life as an artist and her interest in aesthetics. The experience of the cross was partly prepared for by an intense artistic commitment in the cross as an artistic motive the years before the vision.

My conclusion was that Violet Tengberg's religious visions and artistic creations represent two sides of the same coin—the relation is one of mutual reinforcement of the basic motive to be a prophet or a messenger of divine truths in the service of God. Her symbolism actually circles around one main motive: the spiritual and the worldly, spiritual awakening as opposed to worldly interests. If her visions are the nucleus in this world-view, than her artistic symbolism, her poems and ideas represent concentric ripples around it.

This metaphor does not entirely do justice to the relation, because the dynamics of ripples in water are movements from the center outwards. But there is also a movement from the periphery inwards, a relation of reciprocity. From vision to image, poem and thought; from image, poem and thought to vision, etc. Violet Tengberg's artistic and poetical production can be regarded as an expression of creative mysticism.

This study helped me to formulate a new theoretical perspective on religious visions, an area in great need of renewal. Now was the time, I thought, to plan a more comprehensive nomothetic study of about a hundred persons having visions in contemporary Sweden.

By advertising in Swedish newspapers and with considerable aid of the media I came into contact with approximately 150 persons. About 100 of them decided to participate in the project which, as I explained to them, would take several years to accomplish. As a first step in our cooperation I asked them to write a short biography (about 6 pages), focusing on decisive positive and negative experiences during childhood, adolescence and, especially, at the time shortly prior to the religious vision. I call this part of my method a Critical Incident Biography (CIB). I also asked them to write down details about the contents of the vision, for example what Jesus or the angel looked like, and if he or she had seen something similar before.

I also sent the informants a questionnaire, focusing, among other items, on religious activity (church attendance, how often the informants pray, read the bible), their attitude towards the bible (for example fundamentalistic, hermeneutic), their concept of God (personal-impersonal, transcendent-immanent), and their religious orientation as defined by Batson & Ventis (1982), i.e. means, end and quest orientation.

A few months later I sent them the same questionnaire again, but now in the past tense. In an accompanying letter I asked the informants to sit down, relax, and to return, in their minds, to the time before the religious visions. I was interested in processes of change concerning religious activity, attitudes, concept of God, etc. I am well aware of the methodological complications involved in such a procedure. The alternative was to have nothing at all as a comparison.

The methodological considerations are the following. First of all there are time aspects and factors from the psychology of memory. Some of the experiences described by the informants refer to events of several decades ago. An old lady wrote the following words in her first letter to me: "Tears still run down my cheeks when I write this, although it happened 50 years ago." The quotation is a good example of the intense emotional factor involved in these experiences. In this connection I was reminded of the so-called 'intensity-of-affect-hypothesis', according to which there is a relation between the intense emotions at the time of the experience and the individual's memory of it.(See Holmes 1970; Pettersson 1975, p. 115 ff) An additional argument in favour of the above-mentioned procedure is that people who went through dramatic conversion experiences often divide their lives into a 'before' and an 'after', which often leads to a reinterpretation of the lives before the experience (Cp. Ullman 1989, p. 14). I have met the same phenomenon in my case studies. I would also like to add that people who have had intense religious experiences remember them very well and they usually know in which way their lives, attitudes, and values are being transformed. Bearing these considerations in mind I decided to send out the second questionnaire.

Almost all informants, 91 in all, returned both questionnaires. Their ages were relatively high. No less than 43 informants were between 50–70 years old. Nineteen informants were older than seventy, while only fourteen informants were younger than forty. One informant refused to reveal his age.[2]

The data were computarized with the aid of a program called StatView (MacIntosh). I chose to describe 35 cases in the form of short biographies (4–6 pages), integrating all the data gathered from letters, the CIB's and the questionnaires. All informants read my draft for approval. This way it was possible to study the visions in the biographical context. Inspired by the so-called 'grounded-theory approach' developed by Glaser & Strauss (1967), I continuously compared the data and continued to work with the following categories: the religious socialization, the parental relation and the degree of psychological stress during childhood, adolescence and the adult life. All categories were, in accordance with this method, further divided into dimensions and qualities. The category religious socialization, for example, was divided in the dimensions sunday-school, religious socialization in the parental home, at school, etc, dimensions which were further divided into the qualities weak, moderate, or strong religious socialization.

The method used is accordingly of an inductive nature. The starting point is the collected material, which has been compared over and over again, leading finally to a theory which aims at integrating the results. From another perspective the method chosen can be characterized as a combination of qualitative and quantitative methods: a content analysis of case-studies and statistical analysis of the questionnaires. In my opinion this type of combination offers a lot of promises for the future.

Some of the results of this comparative analysis are the following relations between a weak, moderate, or strong religious socialization and the type of vision. Ten out of thirty-five informants gave evidence of a strong religious socialization. Nine of them had visions of Jesus. Fourteen of the remaining informants exhibiting a weak or moderate religious socialization had more abstract visions of light, force, or unity in nature. The rest of the thirty-five cases, eleven in total, either had visions of angels (4) or of Jesus (7).

The comparative analysis also showed that the most striking common denominator of the visionaries was a life-crisis, not primarily during childhood, but shortly prior to the religious vision. Only four out of thirty-five cases re-

---

[2] With regard to the relatively high age, compare Hay 1982, p. 120f., where a similar result is shown.

ported a crisis in their early childhood, while twenty-six informants experienced a strong crisis and seven a moderate crisis during the time just prior to the vision. This strong relation between an acute life-crisis and the religious vision reminded me of a poem with the headline "Friend, in moments of devastation", written by the well-known Swedish poet Erik Axel Stagnelius:

> Therefore rejoice, o friend, and sing in the darkness of sorrow: The night is the mother of day, Chaos lives next to God.

This relation can easily be exemplified with summaries of a few case-studies. Let me present only one of them, the case of Reidar, born in Norway in 1930, where he grew up during the German occupation of the country. In the year 1944, when he was fourteen years old, the Germans put him in a concentration camp just outside Oslo. When the war ended he stole a bicycle in order to return home to his parents about a hundred miles to the north. He got caught by the police and from that time on he became criminal and spent many shorter and longer periods in prison. During the 60s he became involved in drugs, especially heroin, which he took for many years. During the summer of 1970 he reached the absolute bottom of his life. "The craving for heroin burnt in my body. I had blood in my urine and feces, and when I vomited there was blood." He finally came to a doctor who gave him one more month to live. Reidar decided to inject a final dose of heroin and then climbed up on the highest bridge in Gothenburg, Sweden, ready to jump. At this moment he both heard and saw Jesus:

> In front of me I saw the outline of a face. Was I hallucinating again? But the outline became more clear. I did not see clear features, but I saw that there was a crown of thorns on top of the head and that the hair was curly and shining gold. It sort of radiated light from it, and I saw two hands, the palms of which were wounded, stretched out to me. And I heard a voice, so soft and fatherly loving, as I have never heard before. "Reidar, Reidar", I heard. "You have tried everything in life. You have lost everything. There is nothing more left. The only thing you look forward to is to take your life. If you decide to do that, you will be lost eternally and there will be no memory of you. But you have forgotten to count with me. Put what is left of your life in my hands and I will heal and save you."

Reidar does not know how he managed to climb down from the bridge. From that moment on his life became organized. About one and a half year later he married and eventually the couple had two children. Reidar still visits prisons, but now as a pastor, preaching the gospel of Jesus.

In an attempt to integrate the data in accordance with the approach of Glaser & Strauss (1967) I presented a model of personality based on ego-psychology. The model focuses on perceptual-cognitive processes, without neglecting primary process mechanisms, belonging to depth-psychology. Below I will try to outline the main parts of the chosen model and the dynamic process which, according to my judgment, can be activated in religious visions.

Following Rothstein (1981), and in connection with developments in object relations theory, Epstein (1988) distinguishes between the representational and functional aspects of the ego. With the help of the former, the individual constructs a differentiated view of himself and the outside world. This subsystem can further be divided into object- and self-representations. The functional system consists of adaptive, defensive, mediating and synthetic functions.

The adaptive function is responsible for adaptation to reality. It has at its disposal a number of abilities or dispositions which are inherited, for example perception, memory, intelligence, and language. The ego psychologist of the forties and fifties spoke of the primary apparatus of the ego (Hartmann 1958).

The defensive function of the ego also in one way serves man's adaptation to his environment, more particularly to his psychological environment. In contrast to the former function, however, the ego's defense mechanisms are not inherited but acquired under the influence of the socio-cultural milieu. In previous ego psychology this function was called the ego's secondary apparatus.

The mediating function corresponds to the classic psychoanalytical view of the ego—acting as a mediator between the id and the super ego, or between the id and the environment. An interesting function is the synthetic one, that is an 'organ for equilibrium', which strives for balance in a constantly shifting psyche. We see here, in other words, that the psychoanalytical theorizing of Freud has been carried considerably further. Epstein's model, here rather simplified, integrates amongst other things post-war advances, including object relations theory.

It thus emerges that the "I" is not identical with the ego. The "I" is rather one component in a composite structure. The "I" is described as "the self-representation as agent" (Rothstein). It is an active subject since "it sees itself as the one capable of activity", comments Epstein. The I is developed from the ego's continuous sensation of itself.

I tried to relate this model of personality to Leuner's concept "autosymbolic representation of intrapsychic conflicts"(Leuner 1977,1978). According to Leuner, this psychological process is often activated in situations of extreme emotional stress. His results have been confirmed, amongst others, by Slade & Bentall in a recently published empirical study of hallucinations (1988).

Bearing these theoretical concepts in mind, I am now in a position to summarise some of the results of this study. The acute crisis prior to the vision leads to a situation of self-surrender or a cognitive shift to a receptive mode, through different situations of relaxation. Such a shift alters the normal balance or homeostasis within the complex ego-structure, which in its turn leads to an inhibition or partial inhibition of adaptive, defensive, and mediating functions, in favour of an activation of the synthetic function. An inhibition of these functions simultaneously leads to a partial or total inhibition of the 'self-representation', the experience of the I as an active subject. The synthetic function chooses that psychological process which is most suited for it's goal: homeostasis, equilibrium. Religious visions can be understood as autosymbolic representations of intrapsychic conflicts, a dynamic process 'chosen' by the synthetic function in order to establish homeostasis. It is striking that the content of the informants visions fit so well into their situations of chaos. The religious visions immediately establish order in chaos. In other words, religious visions, or object representations like Jesus or Angels are symbolic representations of order, as against chaos.

Evaluation of Data and Methodological Flexibility

A crucial part of the reconstruction phase is the evaluation of data. This brings us to the question of different types of data. Within behavioural science the hermeneutic approach is closely related to so called qualitative research, which is part of a 'quiet methodological revolution' in the social sciences.[3] Qualitative data can be grouped in three categories: documents, interview data, and data from participant observation.

Documents are mostly of a kind which Allport in a now classical study called 'personal documents', defined as "any self-revealing record that intentionally or unintentionally yields information regarding the structure, dynamics, and function of the author's mental life"[4] (1942, p. xii). Defined as such Allport distinguished between autobiographies, diaries, letters, as well as artistic and projective documents. The list could be made much longer.

In my study of Hjalmar Ekström, the basic type of documents consisted of letters, approximately four thousand letter pages of his hand, written at the best available paper and the best pen money could buy. In some cases the letters of the addressee were also preserved, which of course highly increases the value of the correspondence. The analysis of these documents involve different dimensions. First of all we have to learn about the addressee and the relation between this person and Hjalmar Ekström. For what purpose has the letter been written? On the basis of an analysis of this type it is perhaps possible to categorize the letters. In the case of Ekström I distinguished between personal letters, written to close friends and containing biographical information; letters which circulated in a small group, often having a dimension of pastoral care; and intellectual letters, containing discussions around intellectual topics. It goes without saying that a categorization of this type is a matter of emphasis; there are no sharp boundaries between types.

The study of the Swedish artist was also based on different kinds of personal documents, including her own paintings. At several occasions I interviewed her with the aid of a video camera, directed at her paintings. I simply asked her

---

[3] The quotation is from Denzin & Lincoln 1994: ix. The next two sentences in their preface are the following: 'A blurring of disciplinary boundaries has occurred. The social sciences and humanities have drawn closer together in a mutual focus on an interpretitive, qualitative approach to research and theory'.

[4] To the best of my knowledge, Allport's only study based on the use of personal documents is *Letters from Jenny* (1965).

to interpret her own motives. Other important data were all the printed sources like art reviews, articles, and books.

A qualitative approach is usually described as a flexible method. The researcher has to adapt to new situations all the time. Things do not always turn out the way they were planned at your desk. Again I would like to exemplify from my research in Istanbul. I had just finished my book about the Swedish woman artist and I was planning the nomothetic study of Swedish persons having visions and hearing voices, and their religious interpretations (See Geels 1991, 1992). So, when the Shaykh asked me about the purpose of my study of the Halveti-Jerrahi order of dervishes I told him about my study of visions and that I would be extremely interested to talk to dervishes about their experiences. This, I explained, was part of a third step in my study of visions—the cross-cultural part. The Shaykh acknowledged that many dervishes indeed had visionary experiences, but he wouldn't recommend the dervishes to tell me about them. So I had to change plans and ended up writing a description of the ritual. "Yes, that's us," the Shaykh told me later, adding that it is an appropirate, but exoteric description of a religious activity which has a deeper meaning to those willing to be initiated in the order.

Returning to the dissertation study of the Swedish mystic, I planned to *interview* three of Ekströms siblings. Out of methodological considerations I wanted to interview one at the time. They did not like my plan at all. After all, they lived in the same house and wanted to share memories together. Again I had to change plans. In order to secure the reliability of the data I chose to interview the siblings three times, rephrasing the questions all the time and putting them in another context. All the interviews were written down and the answers were compared with each other.

In my cross-cultural studies in India, Nepal, Turkey, and Indonesia I often used *participant observation* as a complementary data collecting technique. In some cases the rituals studied could be documented on video, as was the case in my study of repetitive prayer in Istanbul (Geels 1992a). This kind of visual information could be analysed in different ways. I asked a blind *Hafiz*, for example, a person who knows the Koran by heart, to listen to the videotape and identify recitations from the Book. It did not take him more than a few seconds to tell me which Sura he heard and how many verses were recited. Another example is to take down the 'hard' data of the tape, viz. how many minutes the dervishes devoted to a certain repetitive prayer, like *La ilaha illa-lah* ('There is no god but God') or *Hayy* ('Life', or 'always living') or *Hu* ('He'), and how many times they repeated the divine name in question. I then asked a physiologist what happens in the body when a person thrusts forth a word like *Hayy* for a hundred times or so a minute. A final example is a cooperation with a music-ethnologist, whom I asked to transfer the melodious repetitions of divine names into notifications. In a following-up study, which I am planning at the moment, the dervish repetitive prayer will be compared to a similar kind of prayer in Hinduism, Buddhism, and Christianity. This is an argument not only for a cross-cultural study but also for an interdisciplinary approach to religious experience.

Sometimes fieldwork is not only a question of observation but also of participation. Once I asked the Shaykh whether I could take part in the ritual. "Oh, I don't mind", he replied. "The only thing that matters is the unity of God; everything else is of less importance." Afterwards I wrote down a few words in my notebook: "I simultaneously felt deeply rooted and euphorically lifted". Then the Shaykh asked me: "What more do you want to know about our ritual?" I answered: "At the moment I do not feel like asking any question."

Cross-Cultural Studies

Every reconstruction is, as we have seen, in a sense an interpretation. Our ways of presenting data involve a structuring according to some sort of pre-conceived idea, adapted to the main research question. Grounded theory is also a way of structuring data. Now I would like to focus again on the importance of cross-cultural studies and other ways of structuring our data in an appropriate way. The model of structuring (and analysis) mentioned below has been applied, among other projects, on studies of the Sufi order in Istanbul and a Tibetan shaman in Nepal (Geels 1992 b).

Generally speaking, it is my conviction that intense religious experiences should be considered from different levels of understanding and analysis. Since about a decade ago I prefer to present the data at four different levels: the socio-cultural, social psychological, psychological, and somatic level. Let me present this multi-dimensional model of description (and analysis) in somewhat more detail.

The basic approach in this model can be described in the following way. The starting point is the interactionistic view, according to which man must be studied in relation to his social environment. The model I usually apply is in no way controversial in its general outline. It is relatively common, for example, within psychosomatic medicine. The first and broadest level in the model is concerned with society at large, with all its norms and values, in short—society's definition of reality. The scientific discipline on which I am building here is the sociology of knowledge, more precisely the kind represented by Berger & Luckmann (1966). Here we are concerned with religion as a legitimation of society at large and the life of the individual on a micro-level.

The next level in this model deals with social milieu. The scientific discipline is social psychology. Especially interesting is the type of reference group theory presented by Shibutani (1955, p. 569). A reference group is defined as "that group whose perspective is assumed by the actor as the frame of reference for the organization of his perceptual field". A perspective is "an ordered view of one's world—what is taken for granted about the attributes of various objects, events and human nature. It is an order of things remembered and expected as well as things actually perceived, an organized conception of what is plausible and possible; it constitutes the matrix through which one perceives his environment"(Ibid., p. 564). When studying for example religious experiences of a person within a certain group it is necessary to study "how a person defines the situation, which perspective he uses in arriving at such a definition, and who constitutes the audience whose responses provide the necessary confirmation and support for this position. This calls for focusing upon the expectations the actor imputes to others, the communication channels in which he participates, and his relations with those with whom he identifies himself"(Ibid., p. 569).

The third level in the model focuses on man as an individual, the study of intrapsychic processes. The scientific discipline used here is psychology, particularly ego psychology and its cognitive components. The fourth and final level is the somatic one. The scientific discipline here is physiology. What religious techniques are used to produce physiological changes? How are these changes interpreted by the individual within the frame of his conception of reality? We can see that, in the context of the somatic level, we also touch on the other levels of the model. We move from overall descriptions of reality via groups to the individual with his psychological and physiological capacities. The aim of this multi-dimensional model is a holistic description and analysis of human behaviour and experience, both in secular and religious spheres.

This multi-dimensional model can be related to the problem of text and context, mentioned in the introduction of the article. The term 'text' comprises all the documents available, as well as their critical evaluation. Probably no scholar of religion, independent of method, can do without an evaluation of data or documents. It is also one of my presuppositions that the documents have to be studied in their proper context. The model above includes this context, consisting of both the religious tradition to which the informant belongs, and the way this tradition is transmitted.

This means that the systematic reconstruction of a phenomenon can be the very basis for an analytical interpretation. If space permitted I could give an example from my analysis of the prayer ritual in Istanbul. At the descriptive level it is required to consider all levels involved. This includes questions concerning the transmittance of the Sufi tradition; social psychological issues like group dynamics, whether there is an hierarchy in the group, the role of the Shaykh, and so on; psychological questions related to the experiences and behaviours of the dervishes; and somatic issues about physical exercises and bodily movements.

Conclusion

The qualitative study of contemporary, intense religious experiences can be characterised as a flexible way of relating to data and theory, to reconstruction and interpretation. The relation between theory and data can be of different kinds. In my own research I pointed at the study of the Swedish mystic Hjalmar Ekström, where the theoretical perspective consisted of both the sociology of knowledge as defined by Berger & Luckmann (1967) and the theory of cognitive dissonance presented by Festinger (1957, 1964). The two perspectives, however, were not related to each other. They were applied merely *after* the descriptive analysis. Does that mean that we, so to speak, 'put the yeast after the dough?' No, this is probably a result of the so called 'hermeneutic spiral', rather than 'circle', that is the process of studying the phenomenon from some sort of preconceived idea, reconstruct the data from this viewpoint, and interpret with the aid of a theoretical perspective, having a heuristic value. The value of the interpretation is more or less limited, while the reconstruction is lasting. Interpretations can always be changed. Reconstructions can possibly be extended, but hardly altered.

Another aspect of the above mentioned study is that the theoretical perspectives chosen have been used in a number of other studies. This means that my interpretation only can add a little bit more to the credibility of the theoretical perspective. In the case of the Swedish artist, however, I ended up with an innovative perspective, which, I think, increases its value. This perspective turned out to be of interest also in the nomothetic study of visionaries in our time. The result of both of them is a new theory about religious visions.

As far as reconstruction is concerned, the following preliminary principles can be formulated.

1) It is necessary to search for all data relevant to the research problem.
2) All data should be critically evaluated.
3) All data should be used in the reconstruction, enabling the researcher, or other scholars, to present alternative theoretical interpretations.
4) It is recommended to present the reconstruction and interpretation separately. This will do justice to the phenomenon or persons studied. We tell their untold stories, and they probably do not like to encounter them in a framework of psychological terminology.
5) In the reconstruction we should consider problems of text and context, for example by gathering and structuring the data related to socio-cultural, social psychological, psychological, and somatic factors.
6) Theoretical or analytical interpretations can be mono-dimensional or multi-dimensional. In the latter case the internal relations of perspectives chosen should be discussed.
7) The value of the interpretation should be evaluated, including a discussion of important elements in the reconstruction which fail to be part of the interpretation.

Finally, let me mention that I think that the psychology of religion is in need of inductive research, possibly leading to new theoretical perspectives. In addition, I do believe in the value of a cross-cultural approach, not in the least because Western countries are multi-cultural. In Sweden, Islam is next to the

Evangelical-Lutheran Church the largest religion in the country. In all religions there is, besides belief, a practice, consisting of for example prayer and different techniques like meditation and isolation. Moreover, in multi-cultural countries conversions are becoming more common (see Josselson & Lieblich 1995).

The overall theoretical point of view I adhere to is what Bertalanffy (1969) called "a general systems approach". The methodological problem in this approach is to formulate problems of a general type, expressed in a search for isomorphisms, i.e. structural similarities in different fields. An example is repetitive prayer, which basically does not differ from other monotonous exercises as repeating one's own name, described by Alfred Tennyson (see James 1902). The result of this approach in my research is the permanent search for models with a potential to unite phenomena which from a content point of view are quite different, but from a process point of view exhibit similarities. The model of personality presented above can be applied on phenomena like meditation, visionary experience, shamanistic trance, and so on. This basic approach is perhaps an expression of my primary motive when starting my academic studies: to search for elements that unite rather than separate human beings in their ways of coping with fundamental existential issues.

Bibliography

Allport, G. W. (1942). *The Use of Personal Documents in Psychological Science*. New York: Social Science Research Council.
Allport, G. W. (1965). *Letters from Jenny*. New York.
Batson, C. D. & Ventis, W. L. (1982).*The Religious Experience. A Social-Psychological Perspective*. New York: Oxford University Press.
Berger, P. & Luckmann, T. (1967). *The Social Construction of Reality*. New York: Anchor Books.
Bertalanffy, L. von (1969). *General Systems Theory*. New York: International Universities Press.
Epstein, M. (1988) The Deconstruction of the Self: Ego and "Egolessness" in Buddhist Insight Meditation. *The Journal of Transpersonal Psychology,* Vol.20, No.1, pp.61–69.
Denzin, N.K. & Lincoln, Y.S., Eds. (1994). *Handbook of Qualitative Research*. Thousand Oaks: Sage Publications.
Festinger, L. (1957). *A Theory of Cognitive Dissonance*. Stanford: Stanford University Press.
Festinger, L. (1964). *Conflict, Decision, and Dissonance*. Stanford: Stanford University Press.
Geels, A. (1980). *Mystikern Hjalmar Ekström (1885–1962). En religionspsykologisk studie av hans religiösa utveckling*. [The Mystic Hjalmar Ekström (1885–1962). A study of his religious development from the perspective of the psychology of religion.] Malmö: Bokförlaget Doxa.
Geels, A. (1989). *Skapande mystik. En psykologisk studie av Violet Tengbergs religiösa visioner och konstnärliga skapande*. [Creative Mysticism. A Psychological Study of Violet Tengberg's Religious Visions and Artistic Creations]. Löberöd: Bokförlaget Plus Ultra.
Geels, A. (1990). *Extatisk religion. Ett bidrag till mystikens psykologi* [Extatic Religion. A

Contribution to the Psychology of Mysticism]. *Religio*, No. 33, published by the Department of Theology, Lund University.

Geels, A. (1991). *Att möta Gud i kaos. Religiösa visioner i dagens Sverige.* [Encounter with God in Chaos. Religious Visions in Contemporary Sweden]. Stockholm: Norstedts.

Geels, A. (1992). Chaos lives next to God. Religious Visions and the Integration of Personality. *Studies in Spirituality, 2,* pp. 223–236.

Geels, A. (1992a). A Note on the Psychology of Dhikr. The Halveti-Jerrahi Order of Dervishes in Istanbul. Ahlbäck, T. (Ed.), *The Problem of Ritual.* Stockholm: Almqvist & Wiksell International, pp. 53–82.

Geels, A. (1992b). Ego-Psychology and the Problem of Ecstasy. A Case-study of a Tibetan Shaman. *Tibetan Studies, Proceedings of the 5th Seminar of the International Association of Tibetan Studies, Narita 1989,* pp. 451–464.

Glaser, B & Strauss, A. L. (1967). *The discovery of Grounded Theory: Strategies for Qualitative Research.* Chicago: Aldine.

Hartman, H. (1958). *Ego Psychology and the Problem of Adaptation.* New York: International Universities Press.

Hay, D. (1982). *Exploring Inner Space.* Harmondsworth: Penguin Books.

Holmes, D. S. (1970). Differential Change in Affective Intensity and the Forgetting of Unpleasant Personal Experiences. *Journal of Personality and Social Psychology, 15,* pp. 234–239.

James, W. (1902). *The Varieties of Religious Experience: A Study in Human Nature.* New York: Longmans, Green, and Co.

Leuner, H. (1977). Guided Affective Imagery: An Account of its Development. *Journal of Mental Imagery, 1,* pp. 73–91.

Leuner, H. (1978). Basic Principles and Therapeutic Efficacy of Guided Affective Imagery (GAI). Singer, J. L. & Pope, K. S. (Eds.), *The Power of Human Imagination.* New York: Plenum Press, pp. 125–166.

Pettersson, T. (1975). *The Retention of Religious Experience.* Diss.Uppsala.

Rothstein, A. (1981).The Ego: An evolving construct. *International Journal of Psychoanalysis, Vol.62,* pp. 435–445.

Shibutani, T. (1955). Reference Groups as Perspectives. *The American Journal of Sociology, 60,* pp. 562–569.

Slade, P. D. & Bentall R. P. (1988). *Sensory Deception. A Scientific Analysis of Hallucination.* London & Sydney: Croom Helm.

Ullman, C. (1989). *The Transformed Self. The Psychology of Religious Conversion.* New York: Plenum Press.

Psychology of Religion
Towards a Synthesis for a Challenging Discipline

Nils G. Holm

Introduction

The scientific examination of religion is an ancient activity, the beginnings of which can be traced at least back to the ancient Greeks. Although the investigation of the psychology of religion goes back equally far, it does not make its appearance as a distinct scholarly discipline until the latter half of the 19th century.

In the 'pre-scientific' study of the psychology of religion several stages can be recognized. The earliest is represented by the Ancients' mythologically-oriented speculations about the soul; later comes Christian theology and mysticism, with its drive to comprehend the psychological sides of religion, followed by the rationalism and critical deism of the Enlightenment. By the beginning of the 19th century, however, we reach a stage where F. Schleiermacher within theology and L. Feuerbach in philosophy were laying the basis for the scrutiny of religion from an anthropological perspective; but it was the rise of experimental psychology and *Religionswissenschaft* which finally led to the emergence of psychology of religion as the scientific study of religion on the basis of psychological premises (Luoma 1965).

Since then, too, a number of distinct phases can be identified. As a result of major advances around the turn of the 20th century, many scholars (not least within mainstream *Religionswissenschaft*, such as N. Söderblom, R. Karsten, G. Mensching and R. Otto) became aware of what the new discipline could offer. In the period between the Wars, however, the dominant tendencies in mainstream psychology and those within psychology of religion developed in sharply diverging directions. Since then, for mainstream psychologists, religion has for the most part been a topic for investigation only in exceptional cases. Psychology of religion also came under attack from some theologians, who maintained the uniqueness of Christianity and dismissed its psychological dimensions.

Since the Second World War, psychology of religion has continued to develop, especially in the USA, Western Europe, Poland and Scandinavia. In some circles, however, the discipline is still not full acceptable, and it continues to struggle with problems of identity. Symptomatically, there are relatively few universities with professorial chairs in psychology of religion: in Scandinavia, only in Sweden (where there are two, one in Uppsala and one in Lund).

This fragmented picture is further disturbed by the tensions between competing schools of thought. Here I am thinking not only of the opposition between depth psychology and quantitative-empirical orientations, but also of the difference in approach between critical science and pastoral psychology.

As can be seen, therefore, despite its relatively recent emergence as a field of scientific enquiry, psychology of religion encompasses many angles of approach and problematical areas. Before I embark on outlining my own perspective on this field, I would like to consider this problematical situation further.

The Questioning of Religion

In one form or other, the phenomenon we call 'religion' has occurred in all known human cultures. Within the Western tradition, however, there has also long existed a critical line of thought which questions the validity of religion, or at any rate of Christianity. By the end of the last century, this point of view was very widely held by scientists and scholars of many different persuasions. Science was expected to provide a method for exposing religion's absurd pretensions, its non-rational functions and its at times pathological consequences. From this point of view, the task of psychology of religion was to demonstrate the flawed nature and inutility of the phenomenon of religion, which ideally, in the long run, would be totally eliminated. This (much debated) scientism can be traced, for example, in S. Freud or J. H. Leuba; they looked for the day when man would stand as a fully rational being, freed from the need for irrational, religious elements (cf. Holm 1987).

This hostility towards religion pushed many people, especially in the churches, to reject the claims for psychology of religion, which they identified as a threat to Christianity and therefore had no wish to share in the insights it offered. When it also became evident that (some) scholars saw religious phenomena as a pathological condition, it became even harder for many to see anything positive in psychology of religion.

A crucial question raised by this debate is the reliance on reductionism. Is it the case that psychology of religion *reduces* religious phenomena to an internal, psychological, even (at worst) to a sexual phenomenon? Does psychology of religion lead to the destruction of religious feeling, the authentic experience of contact with God? Many of these questions were raised in the debate around the turn of the century and coloured standpoints at that time.

At the VII International Psychologists' Conference in Geneva in August 1909, these questions were given prominence by two of the most distinguished scholars of the time, Théodore Flournoy and J. H. Leuba, but no solution was reached. In the aftermath, however, psychology of religion was advanced by moderate psychologists such as J. B. Pratt and R. H. Thouless, who took no stand on the facticity question, but instead worked empirically with human reports and experiences (Luoma 1965).

Psychology or Not?

Around the turn of the century, all the major psychologists (Hall, Starbuck and James in the USA, and Wundt and Flournoy in Europe) dealt with religion as one of the range of psychological phenomena. Psychological textbooks of that period usually devote attention to religion, whereas in later texts, sexuality appears to have taken its place, and in modern psychological manuals, religion is hardly mentioned at all. It is striking to observe how a phenomenon of such widespread distribution in human behaviour has failed to attract psychologists' attention in recent decades. What can be the reason?

It is worth noting that as long as an open approach to psychological methodology prevailed, its purview also extended to religion. When introspection and subjective reports were accepted as valid working materials for psychologists, religion had a place in their investigations. Narrow behaviourism, with its insistence upon strict methodology and objectivity, came to exclude important areas of human experience, for all which cannot be defined by objective methods was quite simply disqualified from the scope of enquiry. With the steady advance of behaviourism between the Wars, religion fell further and further into the background. At that time (and to some extent still today), scientific psychologists were expected to demonstrate their scientific acceptability by adopting as objective an approach to the phenomena under scrutiny as possible. Subjective input was proscribed as an erroneous source of information.

As the psychologists gradually abandoned the investigation of religion, however, the *Religionswissenschaftler* and theologians took over. This can be seen, for example, in the elaboration of a pastoral theology grounded in psychological approaches, especially depth psychology. This school of thinking became especially strong in the USA, partly as a result of the immigration of many psychologists from Europe during the Nazi period.

It is only in very recent years, it seems to me, associated perhaps with an increasing tendency for mainstream psychologists to distance themselves from strict behaviourism and display a greater concern with the total human personality, that one can once again detect an interest among them in religious phenomena. On the other hand, mainstream psychology has in the meantime ramified into a multitude of specialized subdisciplines, very few of which can be said to offer a holistic perspective on man; where should religion be allocated, then? Who is responsible for it? Surely this would be one obvious niche for the psychologists of religion—if only they were not disqualified as 'impossible theologians', with no grasp of true psychology. We are still today faced here with a serious gulf which needs to be bridged.

Psychology versus Theology

As I suggested earlier, psychology of religion at the beginning of this century was characterized by a somewhat critical stance towards religion. This provoked a counter-reaction among many theologians and students of religious questions, some of whom went so far as to argue that a true psychologist needed to have experienced conversion in order to be able to understand religion as a phenomenon (for example, the resolution passed at the Geneva Conference in 1909 which stated that conversion is as important a qualification for the psychologist of religion as test tubes are for the chemist). In the long run, however, this view failed to command assent, and most came to accept that researchers' status as human beings can equip them with the insight which will enable them to study religion. As Leuba pointed out, for example, in order to study criminals one does not need to be criminal oneself (Luoma 1965).

The critical attitude towards psychology of religion has been particularly characteristic of the school of "dialectic" theology elaborated by Karl Barth. Here, faith is seen as a divine gift, *senkrecht von oben*. Since human nature is seen as fallen, the scrutiny of religion as a psychological phenomenon within the individual is condemned as inappropriate. A similar reaction has also been very widespread among Christian revivalist movements, where it was felt that there was a clear theological model which explained the origin and function of religious experiences, so that no psychological interpretations were needed; indeed, many felt that these would merely undermine the authentic religious experience. Such attitudes can still be widely encountered.

Within German-speaking Europe, the new theological orientations to a large extent eliminated the former interest in a psychological understanding of religion. The theological programme outlined by Schleiermacher and Ritschl in the 19th century was now abandoned. Parallel with this tendency, the impact of Nazism also worked against psychology of religion, and it took a long time for the discipline to rehabilitate itself in the German-speaking countries. Indeed, even today it could be said that German-speaking psychology of religion has a long way to catch up, but it appears to start moving forward at the moment.

Elsewhere, recent decades have seen rapid advances in psychology of religion, as can be illustrated, for instance, from the handbooks published on the subject. In the USA, and to some extent in Western Europe, the discipline may be found affiliated to departments of psychology; in Scandinavia, on the other hand, it has largely been appropriated by *Religionswissenschaft* and theology. There is also a vast store of expertise relating to psychology of religion available within applied theology: pastoral psychology and therapy. The consequences of this inconsistency in the academic affiliation of the discipline have not so far been disentangled, but are not necessarily entirely negative. Apart from the differences in organizational status there seems to be agreement among scholars that psychology of religion as an interdisciplinary science can be studied in various ways.

The Fundamental Choice for Religion

One of the dilemmas faced by psychologists of religion is the choice of theory to apply in order to understand religiosity. On the one hand, we have post-Freudian depth psychology, which sees religion as the result of processes, incomplete or not, in the human individual's early years. This school of thought has provoked extensive discussion as to what is healthy and unhealthy religiosity. Is there some form of religion which should be aimed at, and what attitude should be adopted towards the questions of facticity? The debate around these questions is not finished (if indeed it ever can be), but most commentators would seem to agree at least that religion is a field of human experience which cannot be simply ignored, but needs to be examined and explored.

The other theories which have been applied have mainly been oriented towards social, personality, or developmental psychology. In many cases, this has been combined with strict empiricism in methodology (e.g. the use of statistics, etc.). Not infrequently, this has led to the adoption of a position opposed to depth psychology, which has opened up a wider range of approaches to the significance of religion in human life.

There are thus a wide range of questions which the psychologist of religion nowadays faces: for example, the question as to true and false religiosity. Can the psychologist recommend certain forms of piety? Can one perhaps identify therapeutic methods for helping individuals along their 'path of faith'? Can the psychologist of religion offer any statement as to the ideal form of religiosity (in practice, often, the ideal form of Christianity)? Are there harmful forms of piety, and when does piety become destructive? What can we say about sects and revivalist movements which demand the submission of their members' entire personality? And what indeed can one say about occultism, parapsychology, or superstition in general?

These are questions which the psychologist of religion is constantly faced with. The pursuit of totally objective research with strict methodological objectivity is difficult in a field where sooner or later one is inevitably drawn into moral questions and is faced with the demand to take a stand on what is recommendable and what is not. Psychology of religion, like *Religionswissenschaft* in general, is thus constantly confronted by the dilemma: should one proceed with research or manipulation where there is the danger that one's entire field of research might be radically affected? What are the most appropriate methods for investigation? How far can subjective approaches be adopted without compromising one's own objectivity?

The problems the psychologist of religion faces are thus manifold. Although these problems are by no means unique to *Religionswissenschaftler*, they do represent a special case, since religion so often carries a heavy emotional loading (not solely among ordinary laypeople, but equally among scholars, theologians and clergy). Psychology of religion, therefore, is by definition inter-disciplinary, and arouses feelings and throws up challenges. Is there any way out of this dilemma?

The Object of Psychology of Religion

The object with which psychology of religion is concerned is religion as a phenomenon. Religion is a social quantity, occurring in all societies known to us, which generates a comprehensive intellectual, moral and experiential system by means of which mankind expresses his relationship to a transcendent dimension: spirits, powers, gods, or whatever. For the psychologist of religion, perhaps the most important aspect for investigation is the experiential, but other aspects of religion, such as dogmas, rites, ethics and social institutions, are also relevant.

In most developed religious systems in the world, explicatory and behavioural models are available which address human life in its totality. There is typically no demarcation in practical life between specifically religious phenomena and cultural phenomena in general. In Western societies, on the other hand, over recent centuries a system has evolved in which it is possible to some extent to differentiate between (popular) culture and religion; but such a distinction is not viable in most societies around the world.

We might say that it is characteristic of religion to set out to provide comprehensive and acceptable 'explications' for mankind's intractable questions about life and death, about origins and destinations, about right and wrong, good and evil, etc. This means that believers are able to live within an entirely closed system, within which explications of some kind are available for all the experiences encountered in the course of one's life. A fully developed religious orientation thus provides (both for the individual and for the society at large) a firm foundation upon which to build one's life, one's ambitions, one's morality and one's expectations. Notwithstanding the inevitable occurrence within the system of doubts and questionings, religion is often able to justify a form of 'metabolism' in both individuals and groups.

It is precisely this metabolism which most profoundly interests the psychologist of religion. How does it occur? How is it transmitted between generations? How is it maintained through the course of the individual's life, and what significance does it have for life *in toto*? What problems and challenges today confront a traditional kind of religiosity? What is replacing it? How are changes, integration and innovations implemented?

Contemporary psychology of religion works with conceptual tools which include theories addressing various aspects of religious reality. We have a wide battery of theories available, oriented towards developmental psychology, personality psychology, social psychology, depth psychology, humanism, etc. Not all of these theories support each other, but nowadays considerable unanimity prevails concerning certain basic questions, such as the significance of childhood, early learning processes, the security-providing functions of religion, and the significance of positive emotional bonding.

The Necessity of Reductionism

As I mentioned earlier, religion often offers comprehensive explicatory models for important events and experiences in human life. The transcendental concept ascribes to gods, spirits, supernatural powers, etc., the power to bring about events in human life. In the religious experience (the intense forms of which we ascribe to mysticism), the cognitive transcendental dimension is realized and enters into a totality which forms an integral part of the personality. It thus takes on significance on all psychological levels of the personality: cognitive (doctrinal conceptions), behavioural (ritual), and ethical (moral norms). The religious experience can therefore be termed constitutive, an integral element in man's way of living.

In order to analyze and elucidate human religious experience from a scientific and scholarly perspective, therefore, it is often necessary to reformulate the way in which such experience has come about. One of the most fundamental principles of valid scientific enquiry is that reality must be analyzed on the basis of objective, empirically verifiable measures; the transcendental can be retained here, but as a conceptual category occurring within the individual under scrutiny. Experientially operating transcendental entities cannot be deployed as empirical variables, and this may well lead to conflict between the psychologist of religion and the believing individual. For the psychologist of religion, it goes without saying, the transcendental concepts represent crucial psychological entities which must be dealt with, but one cannot allow them to become active subjects of action, which is what they typically are for the believer. In the face of this dilemma, it is therefore inevitable that the psychologist of religion must 'reduce' the religious categories of experience. The scholar is compelled to deploy *methodological reductionism.*

Some, of course, will condemn this reductionism as totally unacceptable, but this stance is at risk of leading one into dogmatically-grounded explicatory models. Alternatively, one may declare scientific empiricism as the only valid approach, taken as given for modern man. It was precisely around such value judgements that much of the debate at the beginning of the century turned, and similar dilemmas continuously confront psychologists, social scientists and philosophers today. The fact that believers with no scientific training may cling to their conceptions and their judgements, however, is simply one of the points for which scholars must have respect and understanding.

The scientist who is at the same time also a believer, however, faces a serious quandary. It is obvious that at actual moments of revelation, epiphanies, believing scientists cannot apply scientific categorization to their experience. In this respect, such persons need to differentiate between different functions within their personalities, and recognize life's varied ways of approaching the same phenomenon.

Religion as a Life Category

Many a debate within philosophy, *Religionswissenschaft* and theology has turned around the status of religion as a fundamental category in human life. While some have talked about religion as 'false consciousness', or even as 'the opium of the people,' others see religion as the truly human element, which elevates mankind above animals and creates a moral awareness. Whichever view one may hold, however, it seems to me that the statement that religion forms a significant category in human life is well motivated common sense. It is not a relic from times past, nor is it merely a product of stressful situations. The religious stance towards existence is an authentically human characteristic; but this does not mean that all forms of religion are equally desirable or 'good'.

In Scandinavian theology, it has at least since the 1920s been argued that religion needs to be considered as a legitimate category, parallel to others such as ethics, the pure scientific, etc. I am thinking here in particular of the work of the Swedish theologian Anders Nygren in the field of the philosophy of religion.

In Uppsala in the 1950s, a less subtle debate around this topic was launched by Ingemar Hedenius' powerful critique against theology and the church. He was fond of demonstrating that many Biblical statements are cruel and inhuman pronouncements which demand submission under the sanction of eternal punishment. For modern critical philosophy, he argued, the whole system of Christian thinking was totally distorted and archaic. It is only in recent years that Swedish theology has recovered from these attacks, and begun to explore new paths (Thalén 1994): for example, examining religion — in the spirit of Ludwig Wittgenstein or D. Z. Phillips — as a 'language game', a life category with its own proper justification (Phillips 1991), and which expresses a profoundly human response to life and its conditions. One should not confuse this with other, different life categories. One should not dismiss all religiosity simply because there are also depraved forms. Once religion is recognized as an authentic category of human life, it can be seen how it follows its own 'laws' and structures. It has its inner 'logic' which needs to be identified and followed (cf. Kurtén 1995).

There are some similarities to the experience of falling in love: we can provide verbal descriptions of love, we can give it expression in art and poetry, but we cannot gain a true insight into it without our own personal experience. Only then do loving words take on their full meaning, and become capable of deepening and ennobling our own feelings. In a similar way, religious experience is something one can surrender to, something one can cultivate and refine, something that can provide joy and satisfaction.

The Capacity of Symbols to Create Reality

Fundamentally, man is a biological being, dependent upon physiological functions in nature and his own body. Nonetheless, around these functions man has constructed a culture, a 'refinement' which raises him above the merely materially and biologically given. He interacts with nature and his fellow humans, and even with the course of his life, in a manner which creates experiences of beauty, joy and significance but also sometimes of despair and chaos. Through the medium of his psychological and mental qualities, man creates for himself an experiential world which extends far beyond the merely physiological and material dimensions: he creates for himself a culture which can be transmitted to new generations in an unending sequence.

When man creates for himself a meaningful cultural experience, this typically occurs by endowing selected forms with a profound significance in cultural interaction between people. In other words, man has the capacity to 'capture' important life categories by means of constructs (intellectual and behavioural) which can be transmitted from one period to another; man can create interpretative models both for intellectual life and for behaviour, and by passing through a learning process, adopt them, thus enabling them to generate new experiences in one's own life. In this way, new generations are brought into kinship with earlier ones, and the authenticity of an individual's personal experience can be claimed on the analogy of cultural or mystic exemplars. Mankind thus acquires a capacity for meaningful communication which extends beyond categories of time and space. In other words, one's own reality is reinforced through the absorption of qualities from the accumulated experience and wisdom of the generations.

When this happens, human abilities find expression in varied available cultural forms. The most important are, perhaps, those in language (e.g. literary genres such as epics, poems, tales and novels) but equally important are also the corresponding religious genres: myths, legends, psalms, hymns and songs. Parallel to these are the many behavioural categories of the religious world: processions, services, prayers, baptism, the Eucharist, etc. Through the mediation of relatively stable forms, both of thinking and of action, culture, and with it the content and form of religion, are mediated from generation to generation. Notwithstanding the undeniable range of individual variation, the form is transmitted as a given basic structure where continuity can be recognized over the categories of time and space. Through this transmitted, condensed experience of generations, for those who assent to these models, reality takes on even more 'reality'.

When mankind creates cultural constructions which transmit important forms of experience, these take on the function of *symbols*. The distinctive feature of symbols is the fact that they comprise something significant in the culture, something which has achieved widespread recognition and in which, through a process of apprenticeship, the individual can partake. This apprenticeship process involves a surrender of personal feelings and memories, and learning to link the content of revelatory experience to forms transmitted by the tradition. Through the functioning of symbols (both cognitively and, often, behaviourally), a world of experience is opened up which has an individual foundation but also a deep cultural background. In this way, new individuals are constantly being initiated into the culture, gaining meaningful experience therefrom, and being enabled to enrich the received symbolic forms with their own individual nuances.

Religion as a Symbolic System

From the perspective set out here, the socially given forms of religion emerge as symbols in the sense outlined. Some of these are cognitive: gods, spirits, powers, creation, eschatology, heaven and hell, etc. In addition, however (often in combination with the cognitive forms), we have symbols on the behavioural plane: church services, prayers, baptism, the Eucharist, music, art, etc. Religion thus emerges as a comprehensive symbolic system with long traditions where specific forms (both intellectual and behavioural) are rendered absolute, sacred, and thus unchanging. In cases where this becomes linked with a reverential attitude which proscribes change, and the tradition must be followed slavishly, we easily find ourselves confronted with what is called fundamentalism. In the religious sphere this is indeed far from unusual, even if the more rigid forms are relatively rare.

For the individual, the socially given religious symbols are transmitted in conjunction with normal socialization. One learns forms and behaviours at the same time as other emotions and patterns of action. All of this is stored in the individual memory, and the individual's life history.

When one looks at religious symbols, one finds that they are often based on universal forms of experience, such as the perception of father and mother, of siblings and companions, of love and hate, of need and comfort, of suffering and punishment, etc. All of these are experiences in which people typically participate as part of their ordinary profane socialization.

This therefore means that in the culture, and specifically in the religious world, general human forms of experience take on the distinctive status symbols. The process of acquiring knowledge thus implies two sources: one in personal experience, in one's immediate family and peer group; and the other in the culturally shaped symbols which the culture makes available through linguistic forms and patterns of behaviour. The image of God as Father, for example, resonates both with personal experience, and with traditional teachings about God the Father. In personal experience, these sources are fused, to generate an individually modulated form which can be charged with very varied levels of energy and with widely varying feelings. In other words, we all acquire individually qualified variations of the culturally available symbolic forms.

Within the individual these mental processes take place within what I have termed the 'inner existence space', the scene where the mental functions man is capable of are played out. Here a struggle takes place between various components of experience, shifts in the memory, compressions and purifications, all of which contribute to the evolution and endowment of the symbols with affective power, so that they acquire both a purely individual, and simultaneously a socially given significance. When individuals perceive a correspondence between inner symbolic expressions and social circumstances, they experience meaning and identity in their social context. The religious symbols can in this manner create a meaningful relation to existence, and provide hope and trust in life, possibly through interior role-adoption. On the other hand, where the correspondence between one's own experiential material and the socially given models is infelicitous, the function can also be negative (Holm 1995).

The psychologist of religion is able to analyze and describe such conditions, to point to the symbols and their significance, both in the life of the individual and of the group. Symbols can sometimes shift into a destructive configurations, both on the social plane (nationalist ideas, ethnic cleansing, terrorism, etc.), or in the individual (negative blockings, affective anthropomorphism, etc.) In such cases, it is important for the psychologist of religion to be capable of ethical reflection and judgement, but this must be grounded in societally accepted values and patterns of thinking, and needs to be kept distinct from the scholarly analysis of the symbolic functions of religion. Inevitably, values promoted by interest groups such as churches, sects, political organizations, etc., may also play a role. There is thus a real task for pastoral psychology in a wide sense, provided that one remains aware of the value implications.

Conclusions

Psychology of religion thus has a long history, stretching from the 'pre-scientific' phases in antiquity through to the mid-19th century rise of a scientific approach. Ever since the beginnings of the scientific phase, this frame of thought has been exposed to polarizing tendencies. For some, psychology of religion has been offering an opportunity for a critique of religion, possibly even for the abolition of the entire phenomenon. For others, psychology of religion has been seen as enabling the achievement of what might be called a healthy and mature religiosity. The relations with mainstream psychology have been far from unproblematic. Whereas at the beginning of this century religion was still recognized as a valid object for serious psychological study, in the inter-Wars period it was virtually eliminated from the psychological horizon, and only in recent decades and in some quarters can a reapprochement with mainstream psychology be seen. Similarly, relations with theology have been difficult, since some theologians have been willing to recognize only transcendent realities, and have dismissed any link between these and the physical realm, thus creating a discontinuity between physical reality and that activity perceived as supernatural. These developments, and others like them, have made it difficult for psychology of religion to find its niche as an academic discipline in society or in academia. It has provoked challenges and been the object of challenges from other sides.

Nonetheless, in recent decades psychology of religion has made reasonable progress on several fronts, not least in the USA, Western Europe, Poland and Scandinavia. This is not to overlook the variety of schools of thought, sometimes pushing in different directions; nonetheless, it has now established itself as a discipline which no social scientist, theologian or *Religionswissenschaftler* can afford to ignore. In global terms, religious phenomena are certainly not on the retreat; rather, this is a dimension of human behaviour arousing increasing interest, often (unfortunately) in its extremist forms.

Within the circles of the philosophy of religion, in recent times religion has increasingly been recognized and assented to as a distinct, autonomous *life category*, rather than as a relic from times past or occurring solely in stressful situations. The recognition of the justification of religion as a distinct category of human experience is valuable, but this must not be confused either with assessments of specific forms of religiosity or with personal convictions. To evaluate religion and its details must be kept distinct from the scholarly investigation of the forms and functions of religiosity (a stipulation which applies equally both to the critics and the defenders of religion).

If one takes as the starting point the admission of religion as a distinct category of experience, it can be allocated a place in the total cultural context. This comprises the recognition that mankind shapes reality through the use of *symbols*, through which he creates 'spiritual' realities which extend far beyond a purely biological/physical frame of reference. Such symbols can be found both on the cognitive and the behavioural planes. Concepts such as God, the devil, spirits, powers, eternal life, the final judgement, etc., and rites such as baptism, the Eucharist, processions, religious services, prayer, etc., need therefore to be seen as symbolic forms which past generations have developed in order to express structures of experience and forms of life important for mankind. In mysticism and legendary form they are constantly transmitted onwards to new generations in the culture.

These socially given symbols also possess an individual foundation, however. In the course of one's life, especially while growing up, each individual acquires contact with significant others in one's immediate environment, who become exemplars for the construction of experience. It is in this way that concepts are formed of the significance of the father, mother, grandparents, siblings, and others in one's immediate milieu. This fuses with significant moments of experience of qualities such as forgiveness and mercy, punishment and condemnation, joy and sorrow, good and evil, etc. These personal experiential constructs are shaped into symbolic entities in the individual's *inner existence space*, often in conjunction with the symbols available from the cultural and religious context. When this happens, the individual acquires a sense of meaning and a place in life, and reality becomes more 'real'. Not all links are positive, however, and often the consequences can be destructive, both for individuals and for society.

When the psychologist of religion analyzes these symbols and their function and significance in the life of the individual and of society, he deploys, of necessity, *methodological reductionism*. Within the religious personality, through an internal role-taking process, the symbols became the active subject, something which they can never be for the objectively analytical and evaluative scholar. A division of a very fundamental nature is thus created; yet this must not be charged with negative feelings, at least on the part of the scholar.

Seen from the perspective outlined here, the task of psychology of religion is to expose the significant symbols in human life, investigate the socially available models in relation to individual patterns, establish when they lead to negative or destructive modes of thinking and action, and show when they endow the individual's life with meaningful and constructive experiences. As a psychologist of religion, one inevitably finds oneself sooner or later in a value discussion, and it is then vital that one is in the clear about the implications and consequences of these experiences. Unconsidered personal convictions must not be permitted to colour the discussion.

In other words, religion is a major symbolic system which can endow mankind with profound and pervasive experiences. The exposure through psychology of how these symbolic quantities operate, and take on significance in the life both of the individual and of the group, is a major and rewarding task. The task of psychology of religion, therefore, is a broad one.

Bibliography

Holm, N.G. (1987). *Scandinavian Psychology of Religion*. Religionsvetenskapliga skrifter nr 15. Åbo: Åbo Akademi, Religionsvetenskap.

Holm, N. G. (1995). Role Theory and Religious Experience. Hood, R.W. Jr. (Ed.): *Handbook of Religious Experience*. Alabama, Birmingham: Religious Education Press.

Kurtén, T. (1995). *Tillit, verklighet och värde*. [Faiths, Reality and Value]. Nora: Nya Doxa.

Luoma, M. (1965). *Uskonnonpsykologia eilen ja tänään*. [Psychology of Religion Yesterday and Today]. Acta Academiae Socialis ser. A vol. 1. Tampere: Yhteiskunnallinen Korkeakoulu.

Phillips, D. Z. (1991). *From Fantasy to Faith: The Philosophy of Religion and Twentieth-Century Literature*. London: Macmillan.

Thalén, P. (1994). *Den profana kulturens Gud: Perspektiv på Ingemar Hedenius' uppgörelse med den kristna traditionen*. [The God of the profane culture. Perspectives on the view of Ingemar Hedenius of the Christian culture]. Nora: Nya Doxa.

The Empirical Study of Mysticism

Retrospective and Prospective

Ralph W. Hood Jr.

The opportunity to be both "passionate and yet serious" in reflecting upon the psychology of religion is a bit too tempting. Science seems ill advised by bemoanings from those who would prescribe what it is that constitutes the proper subject matter of the psychology of religion or how it is that research ought to be done. I am encouraged by the more radical philosophies of science and by theorists whose sociology and psychology has anarchistic sympathies. So I shall resist the temptation of the editors to wax too personal. Still, I shall engage what I take to be the intent of the offer: to speak of the psychology of religion, past and future, in light of my own research interests. I have something to say, much of it prescriptive. However, my prescriptions are more in terms of things that *might* be done, not hings that *ought* to be done. I shall speak about mysticism, for it is the one topic I think that defines, for me, what ought to be central in any psychology of religion.

Two Strategies Define the Empirical Study of Mysticism

One can divide empirical research in the contemporary psychology of mysticism into two extreme camps. While such dichotomies always court a variety of dangers, including oversimplification, they also serve to more sharply focus upon strategies that guide research. This will become acutely evident as we discuss possibilities for empirical research in the psychology of mysticism that bridges both camps.

One camp argues for "getting respect" (Batson, 1986) by directing the psychology of religion into the mainstream of current academic psychology. Despite wide variations in interpretation of exactly what mainstream academic psychology is, the intent of this camp is clear: The psychology of religion can be enhanced and made both theoretically and empirically more meaningful insofar as its concepts and methods are derived from mainstream psychology. Current proponents of this view have focused upon attribution theory (Spilka

& McIntosh, 1995), attachment theory (Kirkpatrick, 1995) and helping behavior (Batson, Schoenrade & Ventis, 1993: 331–364). None have focused upon mysticism, probably for good reasons as we shall see.

In the other camp are those investigators, decidedly fewer in number, who find that at least some of the concepts central to the psychology of religion can most profitably be found within the academic study of religion. For these investigators, it is psychology that gains respect from incorporating into its discourse concepts and methods endemic to religion. Among these investigators one central thesis emerges: Social scientists have been unable to account for the totality of the sense of God within concepts once thought to be definitive as explanations of religion (Bowker, 1973). Furthermore, insofar as the Enlightenment project that drives the social sciences to take as a central goal the explanation of religion is concerned, it has decidedly failed (Preus, 1987). As such, a psychology of religion is enhanced, rather than diminished, to the extent it shares a common discourse with religious studies. This is the position I wish to argue in the presentation of a psychology of mysticism that is both empirically based and yet guided by discourse derived from religious studies as much as from mainstream psychology. As I develop this chapter, I shall first focus upon recent critical assessments of mainstream psychology that have served ultimately to broaden the horizon of what constitutes empirical study. I shall then focus upon the conceptualization and measurement of mystical experience, survey reports of mystical experience, the facilitation of mystical experience and finally upon the evidential value of mystical experience. While this review is limited in scope in each instance I will suggest empirical research that can lead investigation in a gradually escalating manner. I shall move from studies possible within mainstream social psychology to possibilities of empirical research legitimated and made meaningful by contemporary re-conceptualizations of methodology and theory construction influenced by postmodern discourse (Gergen, 1991; Parker, 1989; Parker & Shotter, 1990; Roseneau, 1992).

A Philosophical Caveat

A caveat is in order here to remind the skeptical reader that there exists a vast literature critical of mainstream psychology, especially mainstream social psychology. Whether one begins with forcefully argued conceptual critiques of a too narrow empirical social psychology (Harre & Secord, 1972) or one focuses upon the entrance of postmodern discourse into criticisms of social psychology (Gergen, 1991), the outcome is the same: Claims to methodological privileged avenues to scientific knowledge are indefensible. Within a postmodern perspective, mainstream social psychology is itself problematic (Parker 1989; Parker & Shotter, 1990). At a minimum, any appeal to absolute methodological criteria as normative for the social sciences in general, or social psychology in particular, is both suspect and ultimately question begging. Psychologists need not be unduly sensitive of this fact, for as Ravetz (1981) has noted, the claim that advancements in science are methodologically driven is less historical fact than cultural image:

> For, ever since the time of Galileo, Descartes and Bacon, the dominant image [of science] has involved their claim that there exists a correct Method that leads to Truth (p. 200).

Within postmodern discourse methodological claims to truths are themselves problematic. Neither measurement (Gorsuch, 1984), experimentation (Batson, 1986; Batson, Schoenrade, & Ventis, 1993: 379–386) nor indeed any single methodology (Roth, 1987) can be the criteria by which adequate social science is to be judged. Despite the fact that most journal articles are still written as if theories are in some sense tested as empirical hypotheses to be either verified in a classic positivist sense (Carnap, 1966), or falsified in a more contemporary Popperian sense (1959), advancements in the philosophy of science such as the Duhem-Quine thesis (Robinson, 1981:19) make it apparent that no single study nor set of studies falsify or verify a theory based empirical research program. Indeed, the debate from Kuhn on, centering on the omnipresent yet ever rejected notion of "paradigm" has raised to critical sensitivity the possibility of the incommensurability of evidence and the entirely suspicious nature of the social sciences (Hood, 1994; Kuhn, 1970, 1977; Lakatos & Musgrave, 1970; Laudan, 1977). Most striking is the growing appreciation of the irrational bases by which scientists select and choose among methodological and theoretical options. Feyerabend (1975), whom Jones (1986: 31) calls the "self-proclaimed Dadaist of epistemology", has made the philosophical case most forcefully, but his views are echoed in less extreme form in critical histories of psychology, particularly dynamic psychology (Ellenberger, 1970). The complex issues involved in this immense debate cannot be fairly explored in this chapter. However, they do provide a horizon that suggests a broader context within which I wish to place the empirical study of mysticism. I only wish this caveat to remind the reader that what constitutes empiricism, and an empirically derived theory, is in no sense resolved. As such, the proposal in this chapter regarding the empirical study of mysticism, utilizing concepts and ontological claims from the domain of religion is not as radical as it might appear to those unfamiliar with contemporary critical debates regarding the philosophical foundations of the social sciences. As empiricists, we must still gather and assess our data, but precisely what this process is must be evaluated with an open minded sense of discovery and an ecumenical spirit perhaps more characteristic of contemporary religious studies than the social sciences. And, in the true spirit of the anarchist undertones of radical science, proposals are not prescriptive but simply things one could do.

Empirical Identification of Mystical Experience

For purposes of this chapter I will define mysticism as a form or way of life that acknowledges the validity of personally experienced mystical states. Such acknowledgment may apply to one's own experience or to experiences of others. Nothing inherent in such mystical states requires religious interpretation. However, when mystical experience becomes part of one's ultimate concern, mysticism becomes religious mysticism (Jones, 1986: 42–47). It is important to note that mysticism need not be defined as the essential aspect of any religion. However, for those for whom mysticism is an ultimate concern, the claim to have experienced mystical states implies the centrality of mysticism to their understanding of religion (Katz, 1983). An empirical corollary of these claims is that mystical experience can occur both within and outside religious traditions. A second corollary is that mysticism within religious traditions can be expected to differentially effect lives as it is either defined or perceived to be an experience of reality about which one is ultimately concerned. A final corollary is that the nature of mystical experiences, particularly whether personal or impersonal ought to have identifiable empirical consequences. One example is that insofar as one experiences ultimate reality in personal terms, metaphors such as "love of God" become operative; reality experienced in impersonal terms suggests other metaphors, such as submission or acceptance of "what is." As we shall latter note, embedding the study of such experiences within a longitudinal context permits the empirical study of variations in interpretation over time as to the precise meaning of such experiences for an individual. Not untypically, such understandings are guided by the growth of knowledge within particular faith traditions (Katz, 1983). In my own terms, religious experience acknowledges a foundational reality that entails truth claims (Hood, 1995). It is unlikely that religious experience has any force outside of the beliefs that both constitute and derive from the experience. I view mysticism as the prime exemplar of this aspect of religious experience in general.

Conceptualizing and Measuring Mysticism

Consistent with operational definitions of concepts permitting measurement, it is possible to operationalize and measure the report of mystical experience. Operational definitions gain meaningfulness when they are conceptually or theoretically based. Our concern with mysticism is based upon the phenomenological work of Stace (1960) in which two forms of mysticism are delineated: introvertive and extrovertive.

While criticism of Stace abound (see Katz 1978), his analysis of mysticism remains central to the conceptual and philosophical literature. Furthermore, his distinctions are as often found to be supported in independent studies as they are criticized and found lacking (Hood, 1995; Jones 1986). In addition, Stace's phenomenological work is the basis for the most frequently cited scale to empirically measure the report of mystical experience, the M-Scale (Hood, 1975; Doblin, 1990). For purposes of this chapter I will emphasize two aspects of Stace's conceptualization of mysticism most relevant to measurement efforts.

First, Stace argues for a distinction between experience and its interpretation, a matter that has dominated the current conceptual debates of mysticism and religious experience (See Hood 1985; Proudfoot 1985; Spickard, 1993). Basically, this debate centers on the extent to which interpretation dominates any claim to minimally based mediated experience. The gist of these arguments is that any claim to experience is interpretive. Thus, mystical claims to unmediated experience are either wrong, meaningless, or seriously compromised. While the debate cannot be engendered here, an empirical corollary is that factor analyses of mysticism measures ought to identify an interpretative factor or factors relatively independent of a more fundamental experience factor. Various factor analyses of the M-Scale have all identified at least (1) a minimal interpretive phenomenological factor and (2) an interpretive factor. Several factor analytic studies of the M-Scale suggest the adequacy of a two factor solution readily identified as mystical experience and its interpretation (Caird, 1988; Hood, 1975; Reinert & Stifler, 1993). However, both Caird (1988) and Reinert & Stifler (1993) suggest the possibility of a three factor solution in which two interpretive factors emerge, one religious and the other not. At a minimum, factor analytic studies suggest a stable structure to the M-Scale, reflecting at least Stace's unity criteria of mysticism plus an interpretative factor or factors. However, all these studies lack sufficient subject to item ratios to be definitive (Tabachnick & Fidell, 1983: 379).

Second, the conceptual literature on mysticism identifies two discrete experiences of union as central to mystical, one sense based and the other not (Hood, 1985, 1989a; Stace, 1960). Measurement of mysticism ought to identify both these experiences. Stace (1960) refers to them as extrovertive and introvertive mysticism. Extrovertive mysticism refers to a perceptual identification of unity perceived among a multiplicity of objects. Introvertive mysticism refers to a non-sense awareness of unity devoid of all content. Stace (1960) suggests that extrovertive mysticism is a lower form of mysticism likely to lead to introvertive mysticism; I have suggested that introvertive mysticism is likely to lead to extrovertive mysticism (Hood, 1989a). Empirical investigation of the relationship of these two mysticisms requires longitudinal studies to identify possible developmental patterns. However, until recently factor analysis of the M-Scale failed to identify these two mysticisms as independent factors. Part of the problem is that in most analyses the ratio of subjects to items was too small for adequate analysis. Caird's (1988:123) sample was 115 while the Reinhart & Stifler (1993: 383) sample was only 87. Recently, a more adequate factor analysis based upon a sample size of 740 identified a three factor solution in which an introvertive, an extrovertive, and an interpretative factor were clearly identified with acceptable reliabilities (Hood, Morris & Watson, 1993). It is recommended that this three factor solution be employed in future empirical research concerned with both extrovertive and introvertive mysticism, as well as their interpretation.

Given the centrality of these two mysticisms in the conceptual literature, their differential empirical assessment is essential. For now we suggest several empirical corollaries based upon these measured distinctions. First, different processes are likely to be involved in each mysticism since one involves sense perception and the other either does not involve or minimally involves sense perception. Second, the intensity of extrovertive mysticism ought to be a function of the number of sense items integrated or seen as "one" in the experience. A more intense extrovertive mystical experience integrates more sense objects. The obverse of this should hold for introvertive mysticism—the more sense precepts abandoned the greater the intensity of the introvertive experience. Third, introvertive mysticism is traditionally cultivated within various meditative and religious traditions and hence is more likely to be susceptible to voluntary attainment. The rich literature of meditation supports this contention (Goleman, 1977; Naranjo & Ornstein, 1971). Fourth, extrovertive mysticism is more likely to be spontaneously reported. However, it also can be cultivated.

A suggestion for further empirical investigation is that extrovertive mysticism is similar in process to concept formation where discrete items are integrated under a broader term. The retort to one cannot compare apples and oranges" is to talk about fruits. However, extrovertive mysticism is more perceptual than conceptual. Still, to talk about it necessitates reflection. Thus, research on both language and perception is relevant to reports of extrovertive mysticism and has yet to influence the empirical studies in the psychology of religion. Fruitful suggestions and progress has been made in the related area of altered states and transpersonal psychology (Tart, 1969; 1975).

Survey Reports of Mystical Experience

Summaries of surveys of reports of mystical experience consistently report that this experience is not uncommon and clearly not restricted to pathological populations (see Hood, 1985; Spilka, Hood, & Gorsuch, 1985: 182–185; Yamane & Polzer, 1994). Furthermore, a third of randomly sampled populations in both America and Europe report this experience. Empirically, there are few studies intercorrelating various indices of mystical experience used in survey research and so precisely what is being measured is in question. However, at face value most survey questions relate to items relevant to the M-Scale (Spilka, Hood & Gorsuch, 1985:182–185). While some have demonstrated that the report of mystical experience correlates positively with socio-economic class, education, and age (Hardy, 1979; Hay & Morisy, 1978) the main consistent finding is that it relates to gender, females typically report higher and more frequent experiences. The precise role of language in the report of mystical experience is heavily conceptually debated but remains a limited focus of empirical investigation (Hood, 1995; Proudfoot, 1985; Spickard, 1993). Empirical studies suggest that a simple constructionist view relating language to the report of mystical experience is not totally adequate (Hood, 1994, Spickard, 1993). Three studies are particularly relevant.

First, Thomas & Cooper (1978) found that persons positively responding to a question commonly used in survey studies of the report of mystical experience revealed upon further content analysis of descriptions of their experiences a variety of identifiable experiences, predominantly psychic and faith and consolation experiences. Only 2% were codifiable as mystical in the sense of an experience of unity and other criteria compatible with Stace's analysis. This suggests that samples variously identify experiences as mystical. Without specific measurement criteria a variety of experiences are likely to be affirmed as mystical that have minimal conceptual relevance to the concept as developed by Stace and Hood. Yet further analysis cannot rule out even some psychic and faith experiences as also mystical (Hood, 1995). Different language may or may not reflect experiences similar within another context made relevant only by the investigator's interest and concerns.

Second, Hood & Morris (1981) have shown (using the widest possible criteria of mysticism employed in empirical measurement studies), that persons equally knowledgeable about the criteria for identifying mysticism nevertheless differentially report having this experience. Hence, persons do not simply equate knowledge about mysticism with a personal experience of mysticism.

Finally, using physiologically assessed voice stress analysis, it has been shown that among persons affirming or denying mystical experiences, stress can be used to differentiate persons. Some claim experience perhaps they in fact have not had, while others deny having experience which in fact perhaps they have had (Hood, 1978). Thus, no simple relationship between language and experience is adequate to handle the complexity of precisely what the referent is when descriptions of mystical experience are given or what roles language plays, other than descriptive, in the discourse of mysticism in particular, or religious experience in general (Keller, 1978; Ramsey, 1957).

These studies suggest several empirical propositions worthy of future investigation. Among them are the following: (1) Persons with appropriate language are more able, and hence more likely, to report mystical experiences, this can include both false positives and false negatives. (2) The report of mystical experience is not simply linguistically determined. Language may serve to identify an experience as an instance of mysticism rejected by others even though the experience is the "same." Measurement criteria can be used to identify "sameness" in these case, but such claims are bounded by the conceptualization that guides the measurement criteria used. Furthermore, experiences identified as identical in light of a given set of measurement criteria still leave unmeasured differences. Theory must guide what constitutes irrelevant differences. All English novels simply use the identical 26 letters of the English alphabet. However, this measurement identity is theoretically trivial in light of higher order criteria that distinguish literary works. (3) The role of language in experience links psychology to literary criticism (Parker & Shotter, 1990). Reports of mystical experience need not be descriptive. Reports of mysticism as with mystical literature can be aphoristic, biographical, performative, evocative, dialogical, or mere commentary, to cite but a few instances (Katz, 1992; Keller, 1978). What is being done when persons speak of mysticism needs sophisticated empirical investigation (Brown, 1994). As one example, studies failing to differentiate contemplative and institutionalized psychotic populations from normals on the M-Scale (Stifler, Greer, Sneck, & Dovenmuehle, 1993) indicate that further contextualization is needed to see why M-Scale scores do not differentiate psychotics from contemplatives. Nothing inherent in the report of mystical experience is the determinant of obviously different social psychological fates of groups reporting these experiences. The reaction to and exploration of a mystical experience determines its social psychological relevance. Hence, studies of mysticism must embed their measurements in longitudinal, developmental contexts, both for individuals and groups so that the wide variety of consequences of mystical experience can be fruitfully empirically explored.

The Facilitation of Mystical Experience

Mystical experience undoubtedly can be facilitated. While many reports of mystical experience identify them as sudden and unanticipated, many other reports follow upon specific practices whether within a religious tradition or not. Recently I have reviewed quasi-experimental studies in which psychedelic drugs, set and setting stress incongruities, and solitude have all been shown to facilitate mystical experience (Hood, 1995). Another vast literature on meditation suggests its role in facilitating mystical experience (Almond, 1982; Goleman, 1977; Naranjo & Ornstein, 1971). From these studies several empirical propositions are relevant. Among them are the following: (1) Cultivated mystical experiences are likely to follow upon belief commitments to traditions which value and legitimate such experiences and their cultivation. These traditions have beliefs and practices that both share and identify which experiences are legitimately mystical. The empirical investigation of how this is done is crucial and has just begun. Preston's (1988) work on Zen practice is a noteworthy example. (2) Mystical experience unattended to or not incorporated into meaningful belief systems is not likely to be influential in one's life. Mystical experience need not be seen as inherently meaningful (Rosegrant, 1976) and when not so interpreted is likely to be uneventful in one's life. (3) No particular belief or action consequences need follow from mystical experiences. The widest variety of beliefs and actions have followed from reports of mystical experience. How mystical experiences are contextualized in groups (if they are) and internalized in personal lives (if they are) is the empirical predictor of their effect. While mystical experience has often been identified in the conceptual literature as unanticipated and evocative of new beliefs (O'Brien, 1965), it may also be anticipated and confirming of one's prior beliefs as one empirical study has demonstrated (Spilka, Brown, & Cassidy 1992). Furthermore, it may lead to more esoteric interpretations of otherwise mundane doctrines among those who stay within traditions after personal mystical experiences (Katz, 1983; Tiryakian, 1974). This latter fact accounts for the vast literature within every tradition that suggest an inner, "esoteric" meaning to otherwise more "exoteric" and literal doctrines (Tiryakian, 1974). As Jacobs (1995) has emphasized, Judaism has both its rabbinical tradition rooted in the Torah and its mystical tradition rooted in the Kabbalah. It can safely be said that no faith tradition exists without esoteric interpretations of otherwise exoteric doctrines proffered by those claiming a deeper experiential understanding. The empirical study of how traditions shape such esoteric understandings is crucial.

The Evidential Value of Mystical Experience

A vast conceptual literature exists identifying mystical experience as having an ontological relevance that contributes to its psychological importance (see Burhenn, 1995; Copleston, 1982; Davis,1989; Hood, 1989b, 1994; Jones, 1986; Katz, 1978). While not denying constructionist claims to social reality, empirical research can benefit from hypotheses derived from the immense conceptual literature on the evidential value of religious experiences in general, and mystical experiences in particular. Clearly the language of mysticism, whether expressed as God or ultimate reality ,suggests that an ontological claim is made. Perhaps most instructive because so far removed from psychology is the large literature, both popular and critical, relating mysticism to ontological claims compatible with modern physics (Capra, 1983; Jones, 1986; LeShan, 1966; Talbot, 1980; Zukav, 1979). While we cannot engage this debate here, it parallels our own position that mystical experiences are evidential in an inductive sense (Berger, 1980: 114–142; Hood, 1995). If mystical experiences are accepted as empirically valid then the language of their expression may require broader considerations essentially metaphysical in nature as James noted (Hood, 1992; James 1902/1985: 382-408). Mystical experience is noetic and its ontological claims, while not privileged, must nevertheless be taken seriously. Furthermore, they are capable of empirical investigation analogous to scientific claims (Schoen, 1985). To refuse to confront mystical claims as descriptive of reality is to miss an important aspect of the empirical psychological investigation of mysticism. While we do not wish to debate metaphysical issues in this chapter, the philosophical caveat above suggests that an a priori refusal to admit the possibility of the descriptive validity of mystical experiences is unwarranted. Two additional points need to be made in this regard, both in terms of the noetic claims of those who report either extrovertive or introvertive mystical experiences.

First, insofar as extrovertive mystical experience is sense based, it makes claims to reality that must be taken seriously as perceptual experiences. That they may be about phenomena more conceptually legitimated within religious discourse is not to rule out their reality status for the psychologist. As Swinburne (1981) has succinctly put the issue:

> Unless we take perceptual claims seriously, whatever they are about, we shall find ourselves in an epistemological Queer Street. Religious perceptual claims deserve to be taken as seriously as perceptual claims of any other kind (p. 195).

Second, despite the appeal to a non sensory-experience, introvertive mysticism must be taken seriously as a reality claim. Whatever the troublesome nature of "matter" in contemporary science, the claim that it alone is real is no essential part of science. The effort to make it so is usually question begging. As Jones (1986) has noted:

> Invoking Occam's Razor to disallow reference to factors other than sensory observables ones is question-begging in favor of one metaphysics building up an ontology with material objects as basic (p. 225).

The inductive approach to the evidential value of religious and mystical experiences suggests a variety of empirical propositions certain to enliven empirical research in the study of mysticism. First and foremost it makes the study of mystical experience decidedly empirical but in a manner that requires the facts of the experience and not a priori metaphysical and ontological propositions (whether implicit or not) to rule out in advance relevant data. Second, despite wide variations in descriptions of mystical experience, the inductive strategy demands that we take seriously linguistic elaborations and seek to identify the experiences that make such elaborations meaningful. Such experiences are empirically identifiable either in the life of the describers or of those within their tradition upon which they are parasitic (James, 1902/1985). While the discourse of any tradition must be empirically appreciated, it is no more privileged than any other discourse. However, as Reich (in press) has recently shown, perhaps certain language common within religious discourse gains a meaningfulness only when certain forms or levels of thought are achieved which themselves can be empirically identified. Fourth, descriptions must be taken seriously as empirical reality claims with ontological and metaphysical relevance. That God exists, that one can be absorbed in the Void, that all is One, are claims to be investigated under the possibility that they are true and effect experience. Perhaps as Jones (1986) has concluded, mystical experiences reveal the "that-ness" of the world and not necessarily the "how-ness" of the world explored by science. But *that* the world is, is as empirical as *how* the world is. Religious reality claims are in principle analogous to scientific claims. The experiencer must be sensitive to reality, conceptually sophisticated in what is to be perceived, and committed to canons of truth that demand an openness to experience within which reality is revealed. As perceptions of the scientist are corrected and modified by conceptual concerns linked to reality, so too are mystical claims. Theories of the transcendent are no more "troublesome," to use Garret's (1974) term, than any other. One could argue that all scientific theories reference some aspect of transcendence. Kuhn's (1970, 1977) much maligned arguments concerning the role of paradigm in scientific knowledge affirm the necessity of tradition as a source of knowledge both of and about the transcendent. Advancements occur within traditions by those knowledgeable of how the tradition experiences reality, what it defines as problematic, and the nature of what is transcendent. Thus, as Ravetz (1981) has noted, a Kuhnian view of science affirms the link between tradition and knowledge. Thus, religion and science share in the affirmation of tradition based knowledge claims. Problems are as much defined by traditions as they are resolved within them. Perhaps this accounts for the historical fact that most mystics have stayed, however troubled, within a tradition (Katz, 1983). As with science, there is a craftsmanship within any tradition in which one knows more than one can say (Polyani, 1958). Empirical research is needed identifying the procedures within traditions by which mystical practices expand awareness of the ineffable as they articulate what it is that can be said. Ineffability is itself paradoxically capable of articulation (Scharfstein, 1993). Faith is a craft. Mystics must learn their craft and how it is their world is to be experienced as a form of life (Wittgenstein, 1967). To paraphrase, Wittgenstein (1971: 149), how mystical language games are played is empirical, not that they are played (see Sherry, 1977).

If psychologists would abandon the limited constraints of attempting to study mysticism only with concepts derived from its mainstream discourse, the empirical study of mysticism would be broadened as would the horizon of those who explore it. One may (but need not) follow Staal's (1975) recommendation that the investigators of mysticism themselves be mystics. The crucial point is that mystical experience be considered for what it claims in both psychologically and ontologically. The two are not independent. Mystical experiences carry inductive weight even for non mystics. As Swinburne (1981) notes:

> ... if it seems to me I have a glimpse of Nirvana, or a vision of God, that is good grounds for me to suppose that I do. And, more generally, the occurrence of religious experience is *prima facie* reason for all to believe in that of which the experience was purportedly an experience (p. 190).

However, introvertive mysticism, minimally sense based, cannot be fruitfully studied by analogy to discrete relationships between an object and its being sensed. The recovery of experience as a topic of empirical research requires recognition of an encounter between reality and a person capable of its apprehension. Such a person must be capable of both having and apprehending the encounter, of knowledge of feeling itself in the encounter and of linguistically engaging this awareness. This broader conceptualization of experience eschews the language of subject and object in favor of an intersubjectivity that incorporates both (Berger & Luckmann, 1966; Smith, 1968: 21–45).

Regardless, the reality claims of the mystic stand as authoritative as any other and as open to correction and extension as knowledge has always been within traditions, whether scientific or religious. The empirical study of these claims, including the linguistic realities constructed by those who believe from experience (first hand or otherwise) is part of what faith traditions are about and what a social psychology of religion must empirically be about as well. This terribly prescriptive sounding claim is really a vision of a path, of *a way* if you will, and not of *the way*.

A Concluding (Unscientific?) Postscript

My earliest recollection of anything "evidential" about religion came from my inability to understand a biblical phrase, one of many, carved into a newly built church (Unity) my mother attended (and hence, I too often was there). I came to learn the phrase that puzzled me from childhood on was from Habakkuk 2:20. It was the modern language translation that I recall (memories being what they are): "The Lord is in his holy temple; let all the earth keep silence before Him".

Habbakkuk speaks to me toady, in prophetic and evidential terms and guides my view of the psychology of *any* religion. I worry about a psychology of religion that is in Habbakkuk's (2: 18) terms, a "dumb idol" as much as I worry about religious psychologies that are religion in psychologist's clothing. Psychologists who study religion with a religious sensitivity seem crass and their often reductionistic theories, richly empirically documented, seem so much hubris. Religionists, of course, seem too secure and their psychology at best an adjunct to an agenda. Hubris too, they exhibit. How do we study silently?

So I end this chapter with passion and seriousness as requested. A simple image expresses both.

Think of religions as the spokes of a single wheel. The hub is what I think mysticism to be. The rim is the world. Religion are more the "same" near the hub; more distant as they near the rim. Yet as spokes all are equally distant from both the hub and the rim. Now think of the entire wheel expanding and contracting.

Bibliography

Almond, P. C. (1982). *Mystical experience and religious doctrine*. Berlin: Mouton.
Batson, C. D. (1986). An agenda item for psychology of religion: Getting respect. *Journal of Psychology and Christianity, 5:* 6–11.

Batson, C. D., Schoenrade, P. & Ventis, W. L. (1993). *Religion and the individual.* New York: Oxford University Press.
Berger, P. L. (1980). *The heretical imperative.* New York: Anchor.
Berger, P. L. & Luckmann, T. (1966). *The social construction of reality.* New York: Doubleday.
Bowker, J. (1973). *The sense of God.* London: Oxford University Press.
Brown, L. B.(1994). Talking and writing about experience: What can we tell? In R. W. Hood Jr. (Chair). The evidential value of reports of religious experience. Symposium presented at the Annual Convention of the American Psychological Association, Los Angeles, August.
Burhenn, H. (1995). Philosophy and religious experience. In R. W. Hood Jr. (Ed.), *Handbook of religious experience,* (pp. 144–160). Birmingham, Alabama: Religious Education Press.
Caird, D. (1988). The structure of Hood's Mysticism Scale: A factor analytic study. *Journal for the Scientific Study of Religion, 27:* 122–126.
Capra, F. (1983). *The Tao of physics* (2nd ed.). Boulder: Shambhala.
Carnap, R. (1966). *An introduction to the philosophy of science.* M. Gardner (Ed.), New York: basic Books.
Copleston, F. (1982). *Religion and the one.* New York: Crossroad.
Davis, C. F. (1989). *The evidential force of religious experience* Oxford: Clarendon Press.
Doblin, R. (1990). Pahnke's "Good Friday experiment": A long-term follow-up and methodological critique. *Journal of Transpersonal Psychology, 23:* 1–28.
Ellenberger, H. F. (1970). *The discovery of the unconscious.* New York: Basic Books.
Feyerabend, P. (1975). *Against method: An outline of an anarchist theory of knowledge.* London: NLB.
Garrett, W. R. (1974). Troublesome transcendence: The supernatural in the scientific study of religion. *Sociological Analysis, 35:* 167–180.
Gergen, K. J. (1991). *The saturated self.* New York: Basic Books.
Goleman, D. (1977). *Varieties of meditative experience.* New York: Irvington.
Gorsuch, R. L. (1984). Measurement: The boon and bane of investigating religion. *American Psychologist, 39:* 228–236.
Hardy, A. (1979). *The spiritual nature of man.* Oxford: Clarendon.
Harre, R. & Secord, P. (1972). *The explanation of social behavior.* Oxford: Basil Blackwell.
Hay, D. & Morisy, A. (1978). Reports of ecstatic, paranormal, or religious experience. *Journal for the Scientific Study of Religion, 17:* 255–268.
Hood Jr., R. W. (1975). The construction and preliminary validation of a measure of reported mystical experience. *Journal for the Scientific Study of Religion, 14:*29–4l.
Hood, R. W. Jr. (1978). The usefulness of the indiscriminately pro and anti categories of religious orientation, *Journal for the Scientific Study of Religion, 17:* 419–431.
Hood, R. W. Jr.(1985). Mysticism. In P. Hammond (Ed.). *The sacred in a secular society* (pp. 285–297). Berkeley, California: University of California Press.
Hood, R. W. Jr.(1989a) Mysticism, the unity thesis, and the paranormal. In G. K. Zollschan, J. F. Schumaker, & C. F. Walsh (Eds), *Exploring the paranormal* (pp. 117–130). USA: Avery publishing group.
Hood, R. W. Jr. (1989b) The relevance of theologies for religious experiencing. *Journal of Psychology and Theology, 17:* 336–342.
Hood, R. W. Jr.(1992). A Jamesean look at self and self loss in mystical experience. *The Journal of the Psychology of Religion, 1:* 1–14.
Hood, R. W. Jr. (1994). Psychology and religion. In V. S. Ramachandran (Ed.) *The Encyclopedia of Human Behavior Vol. 3* (pp. 619–629). New York: Academic Press.
Hood, R. W. Jr.(1995). The facilitation of religious experience. In R. W. Hood Jr. (Ed), *Handbook of religious experience* (pp. 568–597). Birmingham, Alabama: Religious Education Press.

Hood Jr., R. W.& Morris. R. J. (1981). Knowledge and experience criteria in the report of mystical experience. *Review of Religious Research, 23:* 76–84.

Hood, R. W. Jr., Morris, R. J. & Watson, P. J. (1993). Further factor analysis of Hood's Mysticism Scale. *Psychological Reports, 73:* 1176–1178.

James, W. (1902/1985). *The varieties of religious experience.* Cambridge, Mass: Harvard University Press.

Jacobs, J. (1995) Judaism and religious experience. In R. W. Hood Jr. (Ed), *Handbook of religious experience* (pp. 13–29). Birmingham, Alabama: Religious Education Press.

Jones, R. H. (1986). *Science and mysticism.* London and Toronto: Associated University Press.

Katz, S. T. (Ed.). (1978). *Mysticism and philosophical analysis.* New York: Oxford University Press.

Katz, S. T. (1983). *Mysticism and religious traditions.* New York: Oxford University Press.

Katz, S. T. (1992). *Mysticism and language.* New York: Oxford University Press.

Keller, C. A.(1978). Mystical literature. In S. T. Katz (Ed), *Mysticism and philosophical analysis* (pp. 75–100). New York: Oxford University Press.

Kirkpatrick, L. A.(1995). Attachment theory and religious experience. In R. W. Hood Jr. (Ed.), *Handbook of Religious Experience* (pp. 446–475). Birmingham, Alabama: Religious Education Press.

Kuhn, T. S. (1970). *The structure of scientific revolutions* (2nd. ed.). Chicago: The University of Chicago Press.

Kuhn, T. S. (1977). *The essential tension: Selected studies in scientific tradition and change.* Chicago: University of Chicago Press.

Lakatos, I. & Musgrave, A. (Eds.) (1970). *Criticism and the growth of knowledge.* Cambridge: Cambridge University Press.

Laudan, L. (1977). *Progress and its problems.* Berkeley: University of California Press.

LeShan, L. (1966). *The medium, the mystic, and the physicist.* New York: Random House.

Naranjo, C. & Ornstein, R. E. (1971). *On the psychology of meditation.* New York: Viking Press.

O'Brien, E. (Ed.) (1965). *The varieties of mystic experience.* New York: New American Library.

Parker, I. (1989). *The crisis in modern social psychology—and how to end it.* New York: Routledge.

Parker, I. & J. Shotter (Eds.) (1990). *Deconstructing social psychology.* New York: Routledge.

Polyani, M. (1958). *Personal knowledge.* New York: Harper & Row.

Popper, K. (1959). *The logic of scientific discovery.* New York: Basic Books.

Preston, D. (1988). *The social organization of Zen practice.* Cambridge, UK: Cambridge University Press.

Preus, J. S. (1987). *Explaining religion.* New Haven, Connecticut: Yale University Press.

Proudfoot, W. (1985). *Religious experience.* Berkeley, California: University of California press.

Ramsey, I. T. (1957). *Religious language.* New York: Macmillan.

Ravetz, F. R. (1981). The varieties of scientific experience. In A. R. Peacocke. (Ed.), *The Sciences and theology in the twentieth century* (pp. 197–206). Indiana: University of Notre Dame Press.

Reich, K. H. (in press). Can one rationally understand Christian doctrines? An empirical study. *British Journal of Religious Education.*

Reinert, D. & Stifler, K. R. (1993). Hood's Mysticism Scale revisited: A factor-analytic replication. *Journal for the Scientific Study of Religion, 32:* 383–388.

Robinson, D. N. (1981). *An intellectual history of psychology.* (Rev. ed.). New York: Macmillan.

Rosegrant, J. (1976). The impact of set and setting on religious experience in nature. *Journal for the Scientific Study of Religion, 15:* 301–310.

Roseneau, P. (1992). *Post-modernism and the social sciences.* Princeton, New Jersey: Princeton University Press.
Roth, P. A. (1987). *Meaning and method in the social sciences: The case for methodological pluralism.* Ithaca, New York: Cornell University Press.
Scharfstein, Ben-Ami (1993). *Ineffability.* New York: State University Press of New York.
Schoen, E. L. (1985). *Religious explanations.* Durham, North Carolina: Duke University Press.
Sherry, P. (1977). *Religion, truth. and language-games.* New York: Barnes & Noble.
Smith, J. E. (1968). *Experience and God.* New York: Oxford University Press.
Spickard, J. V. (1993). For a sociology of religious experience. In W. H. Swatos Jr. (Ed), *A future for religion? New paradigms for social analysis* (pp. 109–127). Newbury Park: Sage.
Spilka, B. & D. N. McIntosh (1995). Attribution theory and religious experience. In R. W. Hood Jr. (Ed), *Handbook of religious experience (*pp. 421–445). Birmingham, Alabama: Religious Education Press.
Spilka, B., Brown, G.. A. & Cassidy, S. A. (1992). The structure of mystical experience in relation to pre- and postexperience lifestyles. *The International Journal for the Psychology of Religion 2:* 241–257.
Spilka, B., Hood, R. W. Jr., & Gorsuch, R. L. (1985). *The psychology of religion.* Englewood Cliffs, New Jersey: Prentice Hall.
Staal, F. (1975). *Exploring mysticism: A methodological essay.* Berkeley: University of California Press.
Stace, W. T. (1960). *Mysticism and philosophy.* Philadelphia: J. P. Lippincott.
Stifler, K., Greer, J., Sneck, W. & Dovenmuehle, R. (1993). An empirical investigation of the discriminability of reported mystical experiences among religious contemplatives, psychotic inpatients, and normal adults. *Journal for the Scientific Study of Religion, 32:* 366–372.
Swinburne, R. (1981). The evidential value of religious experience. In A. R. Peacocke (Ed.) *The sciences and theology in the twentieth century* (pp. 182–196). Notre Dame, Indiana: University of Notre Dame Press.
Tabachnick, B. C. & Fidell, L. S. (1983). *Using multivariate statistics.* New York: Harper & Row.
Talbot, W. (1980). *Mysticism and the new physics.* New York: Bantam.
Tart, C. T. (Ed.). (1969). *Altered states of consciousness.* New York: John Wiley & Sons.
Tart, C. T. (Ed.). (1975). *Transpersonal psychologies.* New York: Harper & Row.
Thomas, L. E. & Cooper. P. E. (1978). Measurement and incidences of mystical experiences. *Journal for the Scientific Study of Religion 17:* 433–437.
Tiryakian, E. A. (Ed.). (1974). *On the margin of the visible.* New York: John Wiley.
Wittgenstein, L. (1967). *Lectures and conversations on aesthetics, psychology and religious belief.* (Compiled from notes by Y. Smythies, Rhees, R. & Taylor, J.). Berkeley: University of California Press.
Wittgenstein, L. (1971). *Tractatus logico-philosophicus.* (D. F. Pears and B. F. McGuinness, Trans.). London: Routledge & Kegan Paul.
Yamane, D. & Polzer, M. (1994). Ways of seeing ecstasy in modern society: Experiential-expressive and cultural-linguistic views. *Sociology of Religion, 55:* 1–25.
Zukav, G. (1979). *The dancing Wu Li masters.* New York: William Morrow.

A Proposal for a Psychology of Religious *Expression*

H. Newton Malony

The Psychology of Religion has come of age. It even has its own world-wide journal—*The International Journal for the Psychology of Religion*—but whether the Psychology of Religion is "ageless" is another question. As Van der Lans (1991) has noted, fewer and fewer persons meet William James' contention that religion is whatever persons do in relation to that which they consider divine (James, 1902). Thus, if it is to survive in the post-modern situation (Murphy, 1990), the Psychology of Religion may have to narrow its subject matter to sub-groups who still overtly believe in a transcendent reality or broaden its concerns to include ways of meeting religious needs in non-theistic ways. As will be seen, I prefer the former rather than the latter. While such an approach may limit the field, I am convinced that such an approach provides a socially acknowledged, recognizable subject for study plus avoids the pitfall of ascribing the label "religious" to those who would eschew the term. This essay gives my rationale for proposing such an approach. I have labeled it the Psychology of Religious *Expression*, in an attempt to avoid confusing this approach from religious *Experience*, the more common way to study religion.

As a prologue to the discussion, I should note that I have ceased to be interested in the "roots" of religion and intend to focus all my future attention on the "fruits" (cf. James, 1902). I have become disenchanted with psychoanalytic attempts to explore the origins of God representations (Rizzuto, 1981; McDargh, 1983), as well as with efforts to determine the Intrinsic or Extrinsic motives people have for being religious (Donahue, 1985). Further, I have become impatient with psycho-historical endeavors to understand the forces which shape individual faith (Erikson, 1958). I have even become bored with the types of out of-the-blue experiences reported by William James (1902) in his library and David Hay (1990) in the Alister Hardy survey in Great Britain. And, even though I have accepted Yinger's (1970) conclusions about what needs religion meets, I have lost interest in such theses as Jung's (1933) and Freud's (1928) regarding the psychodynamics of those who become religious. All of these seem to be ends in themselves and provoke only introspective ruminations about what was really happening. More than is helpful, these ruminations ignore the results of such experiences.

When I declare my interest to be directed toward religion's "fruits", I mean something more than religion's consequences (Lenski, 1963) in pro-social or ethical behavior, however. Although I retain some interest in these uniquely western forms of religion-based ethics, I also want to study religion's impact on such matters as coping styles (Pargament, Kennell, Hathaway, Grevengoed, Newman & Jones, 1988) and mental health (Malony, 1993).

Religion as State rather than Trait

More specifically, I have become invested in studying religion as a *state* more than religion as a *trait*. States of mind are immediate, self-conscious, and intentional. Traits of behavior are pre-conscious, habitual, unpremeditated.

For me, this concern for what eventuates from religious states, as opposed to religious traits, means that I have become much more interested in studying how people behave when they are trying to be religious rather than when they are just behaving in general.

Embree (1973) illustrates this distinction for me. He explored the difference in the way people behaved when they were told to be religious. On a word-association test he found a significant difference in the number of religious associations between administrations with and without instructions to see how many religious associations could be given to stimulus words. The intention to be religious in the task resulted in a greater number of religious word associations.

Far too often, in my opinion, research in the psychology of religion has been undertaken with the presumption that a religious *trait* would be evident in general behavior. According to this approach, religion, like other cognitive determinants, would presumably become part of the covert, subconscious motivational mass and show up as a one of significant influences on human action. Like a trace element in a chemical compound, religion was supposed to affect or color the mixture and reveal its impact.

In these trait, or trace, studies, typically religion has been assessed by ratings of activity, attendance, or importance and correlated with dependent measures of attitudes or actions. Using this general methodology of religion as sub-conscious influence or trait, it is not hard to understand why Batson, Ventis & Schoenrade (1993), found that religion accounted for less than five percent of the variance in predictions of mental health.

Rarely have associations between religion and behavior in such studies as these been explicit, in the sense that the participants in the studies were aware that the impact of their religion was being measured. An implicit, covert, or trait influence was assumed. Increasingly, I have become disillusioned with these presumed indirect associations with religion as some kind of pre-conscious trait and, instead, have become much more concerned with religion as a conscious, intentional, *state of mind*.

I am convinced that if religion is, as Yinger (1970) and Fowler (1981) have surmised, a search for meaning in the midst of the enigmas, tragedies, and mysteries of life, then religion is, indeed, a cognitive, conscious, deliberate and premeditated act. When people are being religious, they know it and intend it. And they know when they experience it and they know when they apply it. Religion, if it has impact, does not slip down into the apperceptive mass. It is at the forefront of thought and, as Allport (1950) suggested, it is encompassing and heuristic—it unifies life around a common theme and it spreads its effect to every aspect of existence. This point of view perceives religious behavior as deliberate, calculated, and purposeful.

Such reasoning as this has led me to conclude that if we truly want to study the impact of religion on life, we should focus on what persons do when they are seriously trying to be religious. In support of this approach, some recent theorists have distinguished between *moral* states and traits.

If one envisions religion à la Kant as the moral call, then it could be said that the essence of religion is that state of mind when persons are most aware that they are acting morally. I agree with this approach, especially when we consider the word "moral" in a more general sense. If by "moral" we mean those ideals which pull up toward the good and best, then to be religious means to try to live life in terms of these goals. And this only rarely occurs without conscious forethought and intention. Moral living can best be seen when one is in a moral state of mind. Only in saints does morality become habitual.

Morals function in yet another important way. The well known maxim states, "There is nothing more practical than a good theory". In human behavior, morals function like a good theory. They exert a pull on behaviors and give them meaning. There is determination both upward to and downward. Behavior is judged upwards by moral ideals when one says, "What happened on those days was not right" or "I think we did what was just and good". Behavior is planned downward by moral ideals when one says, "I will not do that because it is not right" or "Because I believe in being forgiving, I will do this". In all these actions, a moral state of mind, rather than a moral trait, determines behavior. Morals function like a good theory which can best be utilized self-consciously and intentionally.

Religion as Interest rather than Instinct

Taking this argument one step farther, I believe that religion should be perceived similarly to vocational interests. When vocational interests are strong and way above average, they will predict behavior. When vocational interests are weak or average, they will predict nothing. For example, if one is seeking to determine whether a person should become a biologist by scores on a vocational interest test, one should look for scores reflecting interest in science that are one to two standarddeviations above the average. Only such higher scores will predict that an individual will enjoy the work of a biologist enough to predict he or she will persist in the preparation such a vocation requires and, once in such a position, will continue to like the work after it become routine.

Religion is like that. Average belief, interest, and involvement in religion will predict nothing. In fact, one might question whether religion that predicts nothing should be called religion. It is this kind of average religion which has contaminated past research. Only the kind of religion that is way above average in strength and participation will predict behavior. If we want to study whether religion is a significant influence on behavior, we should look for the kind of scores that indicate relish for, satisfaction in, and passion toward religious activities that is in the top 20s of the population. It is here that we might expect to see the "fruits" of religious experience. That is my hypothesis.

In a recent presentation entitled "Religion as Interest rather than Instinct: Why religion has such little effect on mental health", I delineated this line of thinking and suggested that, while the urge to find meaning in life might be a universal "need", religious behavior could better be understood as a "culture-specific interest". It should be noted that religion is only one of the ways that persons assuage their need to find purpose and meaning. As Van der Lans (1991) has observed, in modern Europe, the religious option is only espoused by a small minority of people. Although there is much more overt participation in religious groups in the United States, there is still the possibility, even the probability, that a significant portion of the population handle their search for meaning and purpose in non-religious manners, just as they do in Europe. The presumption made by Fowler (1981), and others, that every one has a "religion" ignores the fact that most of those who meet their meaning and purpose needs in overtly non-, or a-religious manners would strongly deny that they were "religious".

Religion as Substance rather than Function

In light of the above discussion, I think it best to define religious behavior in substantive, rather than functional, ways. Religion is something people believe and do that has cultural substance or content. It can be identified as "religious" by the general public; i.e. by everyone, including the "man on the street". Berger (1974) contrasts this substantive viewpoint with a functional position which would emphasize the needs which prompt religious behavior. He noted that the functional point of view owed its origin to the thinking of the sociologist Emile Durkheim while the substantive point of view originated with Max Weber. Durkheim was interested in origins while Weber was concerned to study social realities. Fowler would be considered a functionalist; I would consider myself to be a substantivist.

The functional position emphasizes what religion does for persons, while the substantive position emphasizes what religion looks like in the real world. Participation in overt religious activity or giving an overt religious reason for one's behavior is based on a substantive view of religion. Going into a church would be recognized by everyone as a religious act. Saying, "I feel good because I know there is a God" is a religious statement. These behaviors are distinctly religious. They are unlike interpretations which might assert that persons use baseball as their "religion" because they say, "I attend every baseball game the LA Dodgers play and I know every player's batting average by heart". A passion for baseball would not be considered religious by either baseball fans or the public in general. I agree with Lemert (1975, p. 187), who asserted that we should avoid labeling activities as religious social phenomena which are not perceived to be religious by their *participants*.

From a substantive point of view, "religion" becomes a meaningless term if we say that everyone has a religion or that every passion, from baseball to English literature, is a religion. Fowler (1981) makes this error by equating the search for meaning with religion. I am not convinced that everyone has an "ultimate concern", as Tillich (1951) proposed, and I think it more than obvious that not everyone expresses such a concern, if they have it, in religiously recognizable ways. Thus, in stating that I want to focus on the fruits of religion, I mean that I want to study what people do that is acknowledged to be religious by their society and what they, themselves, claim to be religious acts.

I term this a "Substantive/Empirical" view of religion. In contrast to Van der Lans (1991) who opinioned that we would have to expand our understanding of religion to a variety of nontraditional expressions of the search for meaning, this approach would narrow the psychology of religion to "the study of personal and institutional behaviors which occur within the contexts of social groups based on trans-empirical realities". A diagram of this model follows:

A Substantive/Empirical View of Religion

COMPONENTS

	Cosmic Level Idea	Observable Social Group
E X P R E S S I O N S	Personal	
	Institutional	

The first panel, Personal Expression-Cosmic Level Idea, refers to all those individual thoughts, feelings, and actions which are based upon and stem from the basic transcendent conviction which is the essence of religion. Such expressions as faith statements, prayers, deeds of compassion, political judgments, readings of scriptures, etc. would be examples.

The second panel, Personal Expression-Observable Social, refers to individual involvement and identity with groups which reflect their corporate sense of faith in a cosmic level idea. Obviously, this refers to overt participation in worship in the mosque, the temple, or the church. It also reflects other outside-the-building identification with religious points of view espoused by the religious group of which one is a part.

The third panel, Institutional-Cosmic Level Idea, refers to statements, creeds, published positions, etc. produced by religious groups which explicitly reflect the position that they are grounded in a conviction about transcendent reality. This would include all the publications presented to the public by denominations and religious traditions which explained or promoted their basic beliefs.

The fourth panel, Institutional-Observable Social Group, refers to those gatherings of people which can be seen both on stated days of worship and at other times such as on pilgrimages and gatherings called to protest or support ideas central to the group's purpose.

Vivid examples could be given for each of the panels. It is crucial, however, to note how this model illustrates the substantive/empirical model of religion. Each of the four panels has substance, i.e. the central cosmic-level idea. This is the sufficient nucleus that makes a religion a religion. This idea does not have to be theistic, although most religion includes divine realities. Buddhism, however, is not theistic, but it is a religion because its central idea is transcendental. Such a central trans-empirical idea can be seen in both individual and institutional expressions; for example a person is obviously religious when she or he bows the head in prayer and a building is obviously religious when one sees a cross on the top of the steeple.

Then the model is empirical because it can be seen by all who are observing. While individual persons are critical to religion, it is their coming together that makes religion recognizable. A one-person religion is a non existent. The observable social group of like-minded persons is the necessary part of religion. It is only when two or more persons share a cosmic level idea and announce their conviction that a religion exists.

The Psychology of Religious Expression

Thus, I propose we rename our discipline to "The Psychology of Religious *Expression*" and leave to history "The Psychology of Religious *Experience*". Really, however, I should admit that I am being a bit too narrow in my thinking. Religious "experience", as I have defined it in an article entitled "An S-O-R Model of Religious Experience" (1985), is an encompassing term that includes a Stimulus, Organismic processing, and a Response. Understood in this manner, I have self-limited my interest to the R (response) in the formula and intentionally leave preoccupations with James/Hardy events to those who want to still ruminate about the S (stimulus) component. In actuality, both are part of the facets of experience; one simply precedes the other. I confess I intend to focus on the behavior that follows the organismic processing-behavior that is confessed or can be observed in overt action. Expressive religion is, indeed, "responsive" in the sense that it is a self-conscious, willful reaction to that which one has come to know or that which one has seen or heard.

The above phrase "behavior that is confessed or can be observed in overt action" is a way of saying that behavior encompasses thoughts, words, and feelings as well as acts that can be seen. Such a phrase does, however, exclude inferences. On the one hand, it excludes the type of inference which might conclude that underneath a passion for dog-breeding lay a religious impulse. I have indicated throughout this essay that I have no interest in this or any other inference about the motive or origin of religion. On the other hand, this understanding of behavior also excludes inferences about the motives behind religious acts, such as can be seen in the intrinsic/extrinsic literature. My definition of religious behavior emphasizes what people say about themselves and what they do out in the public world, not what we infer or think about their words or actions.

In a volume entitled *The Psychology of Religion for Ministry* (1995) I have indicated what I think is the logical progression from thoughts to actions in religious behavior. I believe that religious behavior begins with *insight* about the nature of the gods and their action in the world. Philosophically, this involves some sense of cosmology, anthropology, soteriology, and epistemology. It is this "Ah-Ha" or insight about the nature of reality and the function of transcendent reality in it that is the beginning of expressive religious behavior. When a person is converted, this is the type of insight that has occurred. That it has occurred can be heard by the words in a person's confession and, often, can be seen in some symbolic act such as standing before a congregation in public worship.

The next step in expressive religious behavior is *understanding*. Understanding is the application of insight to the affairs of life. Understanding could be conceived as a pair of spectacles one puts on through which to perceive the inner meaning of life experiences. This is what Yinger (1970) meant when he said that religion is the way people handle enigmas, tragedies, and mysteries in life. Understanding is a way of looking at life through the eyes of faith. Enigmas, or fateful circumstance which one cannot change, tragedies, or unplanned disruptions of wishes and plans, and mysteries, or yearnings to find purpose in the midst of chance and destiny—these are the life events to which faith understanding brings perspective and meaning. Faith understanding can be heard in confession and seen in the way people adjust to experience.

Understanding leads to *feelings* in this progression toward overt religious behavior. Feelings are those inward emotions that result from the practice of understanding. They are affections, inclinations, tendencies that build up at the subconscious level. They resemble the poise of the runner or the diver as they get set to race or dive. At choice points in life, feelings reflect the automatic bias to go one way or another. In the case of expressive religious behavior, religious feelings could be observed in the willingness of persons to look at life through faith eyes or become engaged in worship or witness. Feelings can be observed in the quickness with which people respond or their confessions of satisfaction and attraction to faith involvement.

The final aspect of religious behavior *is overt action.* Of course, this is the behavior that is most commonly observed. Overt action is that which can be seen by all who are looking at what is happening. Here religious feelings lead to religious action. Whatever a given culture or tradition determines is religious is where religious action occurs. It can be readily observed and reported. Religious persons are involved in religious action—church worship, religious witness, private devotions, etc. The important thing, however, is *to note that overt action is only one of four types of expressive religious behavior.* As I stated, religious behavior is that which can be confessed or observed. What people think, feel, and say is just as important as that which they do. Any and all of these behaviors will be taken at their face value and no inferences will be made as to their "real" meaning or function.

A Religious Psychology, Not a Psychology of Religion

I would like to conclude by asserting that I now see myself more as religious psychologist than a psychologist of religion. For many years, Benjamin Beit-Hallahmi (1974, 1991) has decried the infiltration of religious psychologists into the psychology of religion. I confess that I may be one of the worst offenders. Beit-Hallahmi and I are the best of friends. We have visited each other in Haifa, in Paris and in Pasadena. I respect his writing and have included him in both books of readings I have published (1977, 1991). Nevertheless, I have long been convinced that only psychologists who are religious could ask the questions that made sense to the theologians and/or ultimately made sense to devotees. My opinion has not changed in spite of Beit-Hallahmi's observation that one of the prime reason the psychology of religion lost the respect of main-line psychology in the 1930s was that religious educators took over the field.

I have decided to forthrightly and boldly come out and assert that I am a religious psychologist. I claim this trademark less because I am an ordained clergy person within the Christian tradition and more because I have become strongly convinced that psychology must be recognizable to those it claims to study and that every religious tradition affirms an implicit, if not explicit, psychology embedded within it. I believe we owe it to religious traditions to study them from within in a manner that will be acknowledged and respected. I have become weary of having my colleagues in the theological seminary where I work discount my research as trivial. I agree with Spilka and Mullin (1977) that what we need is a "theological" psychology of religion. What I have decided to do in the future I will call either "theopsychology" or "psychotheology".

As testimony to my "coming out," I confess that for the last decade-and-a-half my research has been directed toward the construction and validation of a scale to measure Christian religious maturity, or, better said "optimal religious functioning within the Christian tradition (Malony 1985b, 1988, 1991, 1992, 1993). The Religious Status *Interview* and *Inventory* are based on the implications of Christian theology for daily living. They attempt to assess the religious expressive behavior which lies in between creeds and motivations. These measures are content filled but go far beyond confessions of orthodoxy or simple worship attendance. These reflect my effort to produce a psychology of religion that can be respected both by the discipline of psychology and by theologians. I hope I am succeeding.

Conclusion

This essay has been my effort to step back and reflect on the psychology of religion. It has turned out to be a very personal document. While I did not intend its effect on me to be so pervasive, stating these ideas in print, has helped me clarify what kind of psychologist of religion I want to be in the years ahead. I regret that this clarification has come as late as it has for I am past retirement age. However, "grey in the hair does not mean the loss of fire in the breast", as the old saying goes. I still have much to say and do. I hope that those who evaluate my work when all is said and done will find that I have been faithful to this diatribe about my focus and my intention. I would even be so bold as to hope that others might join me in this approach. Maybe I am right in saying that the psychology of religion, which has come of age, will only prove to be "ageless" if it focuses its attention on such forms of religious *expression* as I have described.

Bibliography

Allport, G.W. (1950). *The Individual and his Religion.* New York: MacMillan.
Batson, C.D., Schoenrade, P., & Ventis, W.L. (1993). *Religion and the individual: A social-psychological perspective.* New York: Oxford University Press.
Beit-Hallahmi, B. (1974). Psychology of religion 1880–1930: The rise and fall of a psychological movement. *Journal of the History of the Behavioral Sciences 10,* 84–90.

Beit-Hallahmi, B. (1991, 1995). Goring the sacred ox: Towards a psychology of religion. In H.N. Malony (Ed.) *Psychology of religion: Personalities. Problems. Possibilities* (pp.169–194). Grand Rapids, MI: Baker Book House.

Berger, P.L (1974). Second thoughts on defining religion. *Journal for the Scientific Study of Religion. 13,* 125–133.

Donahue, M. (1985). Intrinsic and extrinsic religiosity: Review and meta-analysis. *Journal of Personality and Social psychology. 48,* 400–419.

Embree, R.A. (1973). The Religious Association Scale: A preliminary validation study. *Journal for the Scientific Study of Religion. 12,* 223– 226.

Erikson, E.H. (1958). *Young man Luther: A study in psychoanalysis and history.* New York: Norton.

Fowler, J.W. (1981). *Stages of faith: The psychology of human development and the quest for meaning.* San Fransico: Harper and Row.

Freud, S. (1928). *The future of an illusion.* Trans. by W.D. Robson-Scott. New York: Horace Livewright and The Institute of Psychoanalysis.

Hay, D. (1990). *Religious experience today: Studying the facts.* London: Mowbray.

James, W. (1902). *The varieties of religious experience. A Study in human nature.* New York: Longmans.

Jung, C.G. (1933). *Modern man in search of a soul,* Trans. by W.S. Dell and C.F. Boynes. New York: Harcourt, Brace & World, Inc.

Lans, J. van der (1991). What is the psychology of religion about? Some considerations concerning its subject matter. In H. N. Malony (ed.) *Psychology of religion: Personalities. Problems. Possibilities* (pp. 313–322). Grand Rapids, MI: Baker Book Integration Press).

Lemert, C.C. (1975). Defining non-church religion. *Review of Religious Research. 16,* 186–197.

Lenski, G.E. (1963). *The religious factor.* Garden City, NY: Doubleday.

Malony, H.N. (1985a). An S-O-R model of religious experience. In L.B. Brown (Ed.) *Advances in the psychology of religion* (pp.113–126). New York: Pergamon Press.

Malony, H.N. (1985b). Assessing religious maturity. In E.M. Stern (Ed.) *Psychotherapy and the religiously committed patient* (pp. 25–33). New York: Haworth.

Malony, H.N. (1988). The clinical assessment of optimal religious functioning. *Review of religious research. 30,* 3–15.

Malony, H.N. (Ed.) (1991). *Psychology of religion: Personalities. Problems Possibilities.* Grand Rapids, MI: Baker Book House (republished by Integration Press, Pasadena, CA.).

Malony, H.N. (1992). Religious diagnosis in evaluations of mental health. In J.F. Schumaker (Ed.) *Religion and mental health* (pp. 245–256). New York: Oxford University Press.

Malony, H.N. (1993). The uses of religious assessment in counseling. In L.B. Brown (Ed.) *Religion personality and mental health* (pp. 1–14). New York: Springer.

Malony, H.N. (1995). *The psychology of religion for ministry.* Mahwah, NJ: Paulist Press.

McDargh, J. (1983). *Psychoanalytic object relations theory and the study of religion.* Lanham, MD: University Press of America.

Murphy, N. (1990). *Theology in the age of scientific reasoning.* Ithaca, NY: Cornell University Press.

Pargament, K.I., Kennell, J., Hathaway, W., Grevengoed, N., Newman, J., & Jones, W. (1988). Religion and the problem solving process: Three styles of coping. *Journal for the Scientific Study of Religion 27,* 90–104.

Rizutto, A. (1981). *The birth of the living God: a psychoanalytic study.* Chicago: University of Chicago Press.

Spilka, B., and Mullin, M. (1977). Personal religion and psychological schemata: A research approach to a theological psychology of religion. *Character Potential 8,* 57–66.

Tillich, P. (1951). *Systematic theology vol. 1.* Chicago: University of Chicago Press.

Yinger, J.M. (1970). *The scientific study of religion.* London: The Macmillan Company.

The Confessions of a Theologian Interested in Religious Experience

Troels Nørager

Let me begin by making a confession: I came into psychology of religion by chance.

In 1985 the department of Theology and Religious Studies at Aarhus University decided to create a four-year position in psychology of religion. At that time I was a young theologian who had just spent a two-year research grant on writing a book on Habermas' theory of modernity. Prior to that I had done my Ph.D. on the concept of socialization and 'inner nature' within so-called critical theory. In other words, I had been working within that sub-department of theology which in Denmark is labelled 'philosophy of religion'. Since I liked to think then (and still do) that philosophy of religion and psychology of religion are members of one and the same family, I gave it a shot and have since held the position of psychology of religion (from 1989 transformed into a permanent tenure) with teaching obligations both in religious studies and in theology (practical theology and pastoral care).

The Question of Professional Identity

Today, 'taking a step back', I have every reason to be happy about the change of direction which my career took ten years ago. And yet, time and again I have been unsure about, and not entirely comfortable with, my new professional identity. In other words, I have sometimes wondered whether or not I may count as a 'real' psychologist of religion (whatever that is)? Not that it matters much to me anymore, but back then, hoping to find an answer to that question, I went to the SSSR-meeting at Louisville, KY in 1987. For me the most positive thing about that meeting (apart from the weather which was fine) was that I met Don Capps who later became a good friend and colleague. Other than that I have to confess that the dominance of correlation studies was downright depressing. Please, don't get me wrong here: it's not that I hate correlation studies, I just happen to think that there must be more fruitful ways of dealing with the reality we all have in common: the varieties of religious experience.

I have taken the issue of professional identity as my point of departure in this essay, because I believe that this is probably the decisive factor with regard to our 'investment' in and commitment to the ongoing 'project' of psychology of religion. But who, we may want to ask, decides what this project is all about? The answer is simple: the majority of the discipline's practitioners together with the official meetings and journals of psychology of religion. And even if history will eventually judge the objectivist, correlational approach as being primarily an American disease, this (or a similar) approach will always to some extent be backed by the popular notion that a psychologist of religion is 'out there', in the streets, asking people questions about their attitudes towards religion.

As far as my own professional identity is concerned, I have to make a second confession: Probably for the simple reason that I was trained as a theologian, 'theology' is a more important element in my professional identity than 'psychology of religion'. In other words, I consider myself a theologian studying psychology of religion (the subject of religious experience, in particular) and the relation between psychology and theology. And in this respect it is certainly a source of great comfort to know that one is part of a distinguished Scandinavian tradition of theologians writing on psychology of religion: Berggrav in Norway, Söderblom and Sundén in Sweden, and Høffding and Grønbæk in Denmark. These men have, quite correctly I believe, chosen to regard our aporetic discipline as being first and foremost psychology of *religion* and only secondarily *psychology* of religion.

What Kind of Discipline is Psychology of Religion?

How, then, does a theologian like myself conceive of the enterprise referred to as 'psychology of religion'? To my mind, psychology of religion is a 'science of religion' discipline with deep, historical roots in theology and the Christian tradition. Or, to give my point a slightly more provocative twist, I regard the last hundred years of 'modern' psychology of religion as a continuation (and translation into another tongue) of the experiential theology of Christian heart-language. This may sound as a preposterous claim, but its truth will become evident to anyone who (like I have done) studies the history of psychology of religion from Jonathan Edwards to contemporary psychoanalysis.[1] At the same time this perspective serves to explain, why modern psychology has had a perfectly good reason to exclude the study of religious experience from its curricula as well as its textbooks: Studying the subject of religious experience would bring back the repressed past of psychology, i.e. the fact that 'psychology', in the modern sense, came into

---

[1] This is the topic of my post-doctoral thesis entitled *Hjerte og Psyke: Studier i den Religiøse Oplevens Metapsykologi og Diskurs* [Heart and Psyche: The Metapsychology and Discourse of Religious Experiencing], Aarhus University, 1996.

being only by a process of painfully disentangling itself from the contexts of philosophy and theology. Further, the continuing influence of this repressed past is, albeit paradoxically, implicitly acknowledged when some of our objectivist colleagues indulge in the phantasm of being able, once and for all, to draw a line of demarcation between 'religious psychology' and 'psychology of religion' (proper).

The consequences of the point which I have briefly developed here, become clear in relation to the often raised question whether or not psychology of religion should be considered a *psychological* discipline. Simple as it may seem, there are at least three different answers to this question: 1) No, psychology of religion is not a psychological discipline, since the psychology departments will have nothing to do with it; 2) yes, of course it's a psychological discipline, since it shares major parts of the history and subject matter of psychology; 3) no, it's not a psychological discipline, since its purpose is to enhance our understanding of the religious life, and not to contribute to the development of psychology. These different answers are relatively common, but they are not necessarily adequate. In fact, it seems to me that the best way to answer the question 'What kind of enterprise is psychology of religion?' would be to make the seemingly paradoxical point that only by developing a strong, independent identity will psychology of religion be able to inspire the course of general psychology. But an independent identity is not developed in splendid isolation; only by constantly sharpening its interdisciplinary awareness of what goes on in psychology, theology, anthropology, philosophy, and religious studies will psychology of religion be able to adequately perform its task. Thus, psychology of religion is, first and foremost, a dialogue discipline.

It is customary among psychologists of religion to feel that they should make excuses for their discipline's intimate ties to Christianity. Accordingly, it is considered good taste to refer to the 'Christian bias' of modern psychology of religion. The implicit stupidity of this view is part and parcel of the relativistic premise that all cultures are equal and that (if we only gave up on our Christian bias) we could just as well study the religious experience of Australian aboriginals. But, as the hermeneutic philosophy of Gadamer and others have taught some of us, 'bias' and 'prejudice' are not something we can just emancipate ourselves from. On the contrary, 'bias', when forming part of our necessary preconceptions, is not something to be avoided, but rather something which we must 'throw into' (and eventually correct in) the dialogical process of understanding.

My point here is that if we do not want psychology of religion to be subsumed under the heading of 'cultural anthropology' (a perfectly legitimate and valuable enterprise, by the way), we should at least be honest enough to admit that in the western world Christianity is probably the only religion we know well enough to be able to analyze it 'psychologically', i.e. focusing on what the religious individuals consider the essential thing: the element of inner experience (not thereby denying its relation to behavior, interaction, and surrounding culture).[2] I am aware, of course, that many psychologists of religion shy away from drawing this conclusion, because they suspect the inevitable consequence being psychology of religion transformed into an uncritical, perhaps even apologetic, handmaiden of theology. Why, then, one may well ask, is this not the case? Because Christianity is unique in being the only religion we know of which has (almost sado-masochistically, as it were) since the Enlightenment institutionalized and celebrated its own critical reflection.

The Lack of an Adequate Philosophy of Science

In what I have said above, the word 'objectivist' has turned up a couple of times. What do I (and others) mean by objectivism? I am referring here to a methodological self-understanding dominated by the idea that theoretical concepts and models accurately 'mirror' an objective reality. I think everybody will agree that this is a beautiful idea guaranteeing the unhindered progress of objective, value-free science. The only problem with it is that it is false, a dream, a phantasm. Things do not work according to the objectivist myth. Not just because elements of subjectivism cannot be excluded, but more importantly because of *language* and its pervasively metaphorical character (Lakoff & Johnson, 1980).

Why is it necessary to make this excursion into philosophy of science in an essay on psychology of religion? Because psychology of religion is unique in its 'backwardness' with regard to methodology and philosophy of science. Far too many of the studies published appear to be almost totally ignorant of (or at least untouched by) the last three decades of philosophy of science. There is a bitter irony at play here, because psychology of religion is in this respect lagging far behind the 'general' psychology which many of its practitioners are trying so hard to imitate. In fact during the last ten years a stream of publications in psychology has demonstrated the extent to which this discipline has begun to struggle seriously with the philosophic issues which are inevitably part and parcel of any attempt to study something as complicated as 'man'.[3] And perhaps one should add here that this complexity is dramatically heightened, when one wants to focus on the *religious* aspects of man.

We will have to wait and see what the contemporary debates on philosophy of science will mean to future psychology of religion, provided that the two will ever meet (which I sometimes doubt). Let me just make one thing clear: it

---

[2] This whole issue of the positive and negative aspects of 'Christian bias' naturally deserves a much more elaborate discussion than is possible here. Also, it goes without saying that we may make valuable contributions to the study of 'other religions' by way of methods like 'field-study' and 'participant observation'. But my point here is that if we agree with Capps (see his contribution in this volume) that something like 'introspection' is at the heart of what psychology of religion is about, we would do well to rethink the common charge of 'Christian bias'.

[3] Among many others, I am thinking here of the works of Gergen (1985), Leary (1990), and Danziger (1990).

is not that I entertain any naïve assumptions about philosophy of science being able to produce a 'paradigm shift' within psychology of religion prompting its practitioners to suddenly agreeing on basic issues like goals and methods. Far from it! In fact, the lesson one may learn from psychology seems to point in the opposite direction. At any rate, the vigorous debates on philosophy of science have not made previously existing disagreements disappear. Now as before, psychologists are probably the most internally disagreeing profession in the world, and something similar will most likely be true for psychologists of religion. Still, I believe it possible to predict that two major trends will come to play a more prominent role in future psychology of religion:

1) Social constructionism as a 'third way' between the untenable positions of objectivism and subjectivism.
2) A more conscious realization of the importance of language, reflected in a growing interest for discourse analysis, and studies of the pervasive role of metaphors in scientific as well as 'folk' models of the religious mind.

A New Perspective on the Connection between 'Experience' and 'Language'

In the process of 'shaping up' to the realities of contemporary philosophy of science there is, however, one danger that psychology of religion should try to avoid, namely the danger of subscribing to a 'linguistic imperialism' stating that language or 'discourse' is 'everything'. The pitfalls and aporias of such a view are reflected in the proposal for a 'new' psychology presented by Harré & Gillett (1994). My point here is that there are aspects of man (the notion of 'experience' in particular) which (social) psychologists may choose to neglect, but this is a step which psychologists of *religion* cannot afford to take. Rather, psychologists of religion could make a unique contribution to its neighbouring cultural and social sciences, as well as to theology, by utilizing the new focus on language and discourse to reopen the classic problem of the relation between 'experience' and 'language'. For this problem is the heart and soul of any psychology of religion with theoretical ambitions aiming beyond the majority of empirical studies of religious behaviour or religious 'orientations'.

In the history of psychology of religion the relation between experience and 'language' (description, interpretation) has been analyzed by my compatriots Høffding (1918) and Grønbæk (1935). But, as one might expect, the heroic attempts of these men only serve to demonstrate that this problem cannot be solved within the confinements of the 'consciousness concept' which both Høffding and Grønbæk adhered to. On the other hand, in more recent times we have the somewhat reductionistic, wittgensteinian solution to the problem outlined in Proudfoot (1985). What is needed, however, is a much more dialectical approach, striking the right balance between experience and language and thus preventing the object of psychology to evaporate into the alleged ubiquity of 'language' or (in some deconstructivist circles) 'literature'.

In the context of the present essay, all I can do is to sketch very briefly what this solution would look like. First of all, I believe with Gendlin (1962) that there may be good reasons for drawing a distinction between 'experiencing' (the process) and 'experience' (the result). Obviously, it is no longer possible to adhere (like Høffding and Grønbæk) to a view of 'experiencing' as something 'pure' and uniquely 'inner' totally untouched by language and surrounding culture. But the crucial point is still to make sure that the difference between 'experiencing' and 'experience' does not collapse. How then should we conceive of this internal relation? I believe that we should see them as occupying different areas in a *continuum* delineated by the dialectically related poles of *metapsychology* and *discourse*. To illustrate, we would get a model like the following:

CONTINUUM	METAPSYCHOLOGY ...	DISCOURSE
Level:		
Level of religious individual	Religious experiencing (A)	Relegious experience (1)
Theoretical level of researcher	Religious experiencing (B)	Religious experience (2)
Model:		
Folk model	'HEART'	
Scientific model	'PSYCHE'	

Thinking along the lines of this model would result in a new perspective on the research process of psychology of religion: From discursive accounts of religious experience (= religious experience 1) the researcher aims to describe phenomenological and (meta)psychological aspects of religious experiencing (A). From here, theoretical reflection and analysis of a representative sample of experiences would lead us to a more general conception of religious experiencing (B) which must in turn be discursively formulated as a theory of religious experience (= religious experience 2). At the same time, an important point in this model is its ability to distinguish between the two levels of the 'folk' model of the religious individual, and the scientific model (a theoretical construct utilizing metapsychological reflection as well as metaphoric discourse) of the psychologist of religion. Furthermore, I believe it possible to adequately emcompass the double task of 'interpretation' and 'reconstruction' (see Geels in this volume) in the proposed model.

Conclusion

Have tried in this essay to see psychology of religion as a discipline rooted in Western religious tradition (Christianity), and with an obligation to enhance our understanding of the varieties of religious experience. From a contemporary perspective this means that psychology of religion is both an autonomous and a dependent discipline. It may be said to be autonomous in the sense that it has its own perspective and contribution to make, but in the actual research process it proves to be highly dependent on insights from many other disciplines (psychology, philosophy, linguistics, theology, sociology, etc.) and thus a decidedly *interdisciplinary* enterprise.

Furthermore, I have tried to show from which direction we may expect a future methodological breakthrough in psychology of religion. My pointing to the continuum delineated by *metapsychology* and *discourse* as a useful theoretical model has at least two important perspectives: First of all, it points to a future where psychologists of religion have relinquished the infantile wish to gain the respect and acclaim of the 'father' (psychology 'proper'), and instead strive to develop an independent identity by integrating insights from neighbouring disciplines. Second, it prompts us to develop a sorely neglected area, namely the study of religious experience as 'discourse' and as an important aspect of the *texts* of different religious traditions (cf. Nørager, 1996).

It is hard to give a direct answer to the undisputably relevant question as to what psychology of religion 'is good for'. I think we would be able to answer it more easily (and probably also with a better conscience), if in the future our discipline would move in the direction proposed above. One thing, however, is certain: if psychology of religion did not already exist, we would have to invent it for the simple (but important) reason that it is part and parcel of the religious life itself. And I, for one, would still be—if not a 'real' psychologist of religion—then something more modest, namely a theologian interested in understanding religious experience.

Bibliography

Danziger, K. (1990). *Constructing the Subject: Historical Origins of Psychological Research.* Cambridge: Cambridge University Press.

Gendlin, E. T. (1962). *Experiencing and the Creation of Meaning. A Philosophical Approach to the Subjective.* New York: The Free Press of Glencoe.

Gergen, K. J. (1985). The Social Constructionist Movement in Modern Psychology. *American Psychologist,* 40, 266–275.

Grønbæk, V. (1935). *Om Beskrivelsen af Religiøse Oplevelser* [On Describing Religious Experiences]. København: Gads Forlag.

Harré, R. & Gillett, G. (1994). *The Discursive Mind.* London: Sage Publications.

Høffding, H. (1918). *Oplevelse og Tydning* [Experience and Interpretation]. København: Nyt Nordisk Forlag.

Lakoff, G. & M. Johnson (1980). *Metaphors We Live By.* Chicago: University of Chicago Press.

Leary, D. E. (ed.), (1990). *Metaphors in the History of Psychology.* Cambridge: Cambridge University Press.

Nørager, T. (1996). Metapsychology and Discourse: A Note on Some Neglected Issues in Psychology of Religion. *The International Journal for the Psychology of Religion* (forthcoming).

Proudfoot, W. (1985). *Religious Experience.* Berkeley: University of California Press.

On Second Thoughts

Personal Retrospect and Prospect

Conrad A.J. van Ouwerkerk

Invited to compose an essay on the psychology of religion from a personal, professional perspective, I think it to be neither meaningful nor interesting to present a bare catalogue of whatever views or positions I happened to hold in the course of about thirty years of professional engagement in the field. I think it more intriguing to recall the underlying interests, preferences and especially recurrent, unanswered questions which qualified and coloured the psychology of religion I envisioned. Moreover, such an approach seems appropriate in the case of a discipline more than ever in search of its bearings.

Professional progress and one's autobiography prove to always be interwoven; from both 'histories' I will mention some data, where helpful to clarify a certain idea, a critical stand, a recurring question. The profound Lacanian question: 'out of which desire is one acting and speaking' may suggest the thrust of this essay, without fully answering to its challenge.

Looking back on more than 30 years of professional occupation in the field (Catholic Theological Institutes, Wittem and Heerlen, The Netherlands [1956–1967], Williams College, Williamstown, USA [1967–1973], State University, Leiden The Netherlands [1973–1993]) I see emerging five areas of persistent personal interest and recurrent questioning; areas which I consider should be central to a psychology of religion. These areas will form the space, in which I will freely wander about, selecting from the confusing abundance of experiences and ideas which memory evokes, mentioning some only in passing, discussing others more fully.

The areas are: The multiform, hardly definable phenomenon of religion(s) with, at its controversial centre (at least to me), the idea of 'transcendence' ('the transcendent'); Faith and its alternative (?): religious experience; The tension between 'high' religion and everyday *Lebenswelt;* The psychological implications of religious narrative and metaphor; The distinction, with respect to religion, between central and peripheral issues, between core and surface.

These themes suggest a marked interest, on my part, in more general, fundamental and theoretical questions within the field. This interest has run parallel with a progressive move into the border region between philosophical anthropology and empirical psychology, a move not alien to the initial schooling (partly in Rome) as an catholic theologian and ethicist, and to the subsequent university training as a clinical psychologist, in a department of psychology (University of Nijmegen, The Netherlands) in that time (mid fifties) strongly influenced by phenomenology. This initial phenomenological orientation has received support, enrichment and correction from Ricoeur's hermeneutic philosophy, with which I felt and feel great affinity. The way in which Ricoeur assumed Freud's hermeneutics of desire as a subversive criticism of autonomous and transparent consciousness re-introduced me, in a new, critical way, to some basic Freudian analyses of the human condition. Antoine Vergote (Louvain, Belgium) confirmed my search for a dynamic psychology of religion, in which religion is seen as inserted in the complex, conflictual economy and vicissitudes of the psyche. To these influential names should be added an eclectic, unbalanced list of some other names: Cl. Geertz, H.-G. Gadamer, E. Husserl—via Theunissen (1965)—A. Schuetz, S. Strasser and Ph. Rieff.

Throughout this essay, one will notice a growing estrangement from a dominantly empirical-*experimental* psychology of religion. Valuing and using its relevant contributions, I have been impatient with the disparity and spread of its results. The following analyses (which will throughout the argument imply and suppose the 'empirical', be it in an larger sense of what is open to observation and reflective interpretation), may hopefully compensate for a limitation.

A Regional Psychology of Religion

Let me begin by confessing, that I have reluctantly resigned myself to the insurmountable problem of the chaotic multiformity of religion(s), each particular religion again being complicated by inner diversification and subject to frequent socio-cultural and inner evolution. The sheer mass of disparate data unsettles individual research and professional communication.

Seeking an adequate object of a psychology of religion, I have been forced in the end to admit and accept the *regional* character of religion and consequently of the psychology of religion, in contrast with contemporary intercultural and inter-religious ethos. Religion is not an ontological entity to be unfolded by the way of reflection on self and world; it is a cultural phenomenon, relative to time and place. Religions, like all cultural phenomena, are in all their expressions marked by *contingency*. A trivial statement, pertinent however in view of its implications. One of these implications is, that one should speak of *a* rather than of *the* psychology of religion.

The choice of a regional psychology of religion has been motivated by an unease over the ways in which psychology of religion often handles its object. Surprising is for instance the ease with which a general, abstract and vague definition of 'religion' (with or without a summary paraphrase) is sometimes used as a basis of research. It is as if there be a widespread uncertainty in the area of religious studies (especially within the psychology of religion?) about their object, what gives occasion to reformulations of religion which are in no way adequate to the concrete complexity of religions as they are *found* in actual culture. But perhaps religion is not any longer 'found', is not any longer open to observation, because traditional religions, which have a sufficiently determined cultural *Gestalt*, are waning, while modern, new religious trends and movements have not yet acquired a clearly defined shape. These new religions exemplify a situation of uncertainty and of lack of clarity, in which religion and the study of religion find themselves.

A psychology of religion is confronted, not for the first time but more urgently now, with the pressing question, wether it *finds* its object, trying to understand it in psychological terms, or 'constructs', 'create' religion in terms of a psychological system, risking to indeed pursue an illusion?

To mention an other occasion of unease: does one not have the recurrent sense of *déjà vu*, when coming across, within the mainstream of academic psychology of religion, the umpteenth functional (existentialist) definition of religion or description of religious experience? How many times does an extensive research ends up, proposing self-evident conclusions? For instance it seems evident (without extensive research) that religiosity as a human, cultural phenomenon will exhibit 'intrinsic' and 'extrinsic' modes, literalistic and symbolic-metaphoric ways of appropriation. It is also evident, that religion will follow the structural make-up and the developmental course of all affective and cognitive psychic processes. The question is, in how far such self-evident statements touch specifically religious phenomena.

I am not underestimating the significance of research that draws attention to general and unspecific, but forgotten or neglected elements, operative in the process of religion. This type of research however has, as far as I see, fulfilled its task, providing an inventory of basic information. At the moment more urgent problems present themselves, some of which we will address in the course of this essay.

As a counterweight to abstraction and generality, threatening *the* psychology of religion, the complexity of religion should be given a chance to assert itself. Complexity suggests richness, first in a religious sense, but consequently—for our purpose only of interest—in psychological respect. By psychological richness I mean the range and variance of *concrete* visions, feelings, emotions, perceptions, tensions, conflicts, with respect to *concrete, factual* religious issues, tenets and percepts, as far as they present *reality* for a religious subject, however 'reality' may be qualified. In my view only a *regional* psychology of religion is able to address the varieties of religion in their also psychic significance.

The diversity of religions can not be psychologically neutralized by passing this diversity simply onto religious 'content' (doctrine, ritual, organisation), as a *context*, external to the religious person, who is conceived as endued with a set of universal, invariable psychological characteristics, immune to religious varieties. On the contrary, a religious subject develops a specific lifestyle, mentality, mental and affective habits, and passes through conflicts, in dialogue with the religion he adheres to. Surely, as long as a psychology of religion performs below the level of 'higher' psychic complexes, like e.g. mentality, lifestyle, relational patterns, and exclusively operates on the level of basic psychic functions (e.g. perception, affect, imagination) and of structural orientations (e.g. attitude, motive, experience in general), the illusion of a universal psychology can be maintained, but at the expense of the religious factor itself and certainly to the detriment of the relevance and adequacy of a psychology of religion itself.

One may object, that a regional psychology, stressing the disparity of religions and rejecting a thin universalism, seems to be in flagrant opposition to the modern thesis, that inter-cultural exchange is possible, at least to a certain extent, in analogy with the translatability of foreign languages. Without objecting to this thesis in geneneral, I would stress, that in the case of religion, when communication between cultures reaches out to deeper, existential levels of mutual understanding, a long and intimate familiarity is required to meet the challenge of understanding or adopting a 'foreing' religious way of life. Only experts in the field and those, who *live* in personal and vital commerce with an alien culture, may adventure in comparative psychological studies. It seems to me inadmissable to construct *the* psychology of religion in assembling for convenience elements from diverse religious-cultural settings.

The situation of an inter-religious psychology is, however, to be valued differently, when authors, on the basis of broad learning, adventure—in the form of an *essay*—to explore new territories and dare to open new vistas. The essayistic genre allows for a freedom of suggesting and trying out new combinations and interpretations, not arbitrarily, but neither hindered by strict scientific conventions. James' *Varieties,* Freud's *The Future of an Illusion*, Otto's *The Idea of the Holy*, Erikson's *Young Man Luther*, Eliade's *The Sacred and the Profane,*—all represent classic essays, their richness largely compensating for the lack of scientific rigor. With this essayistic style of research I have always felt affinity.

Christian Religion and the Psychological Impact of Transcendence

The foregoing paragraphs were enlarging on the contingency of religion, and on the regional character of a psychology of religion. In my case one and the other have led me, first rather uncritically, later as a well considered choice, to select christian religion as a central object of study. I am aware, that so whole areas of exciting religious phenomena have been excluded from my attention or relegated to its periphery.

Legitimate reasons of personal and professional convenience may be advanced; I feel at home, not without critical reservation, in a authentic catholic tradition of major religious figures and classical religious texts (theological, liturgical, spiritual), marking one's idea and one's life. But the choice of christian religion as object of study asks for a justification of principle.

Christian religion presents, in my view, what is a marked element of many religions, namely 'radical' transcendence, qualifying and elaborating it in their own characteristic way. Transcendence as a psychological theme holds the prospect of being a testcase of the resourcefulness of a psychology of religion, but also of being a point of departure of a broader purview, in as far as radical transcendence pursues central religious themes to extremes. One such 'extreme', which has intensively occupied me, is the tension between the presence and absence of God; an intriguing theme of a psychology of religion.

Introducing the term 'transcendence' will invite severe criticism from certain quarters. The term (in the strict sense of 'radical' transcendence) may suggest a privilege, accorded to a certain (traditional) form of religion as if presenting the ideal and prototypical *Gestalt* of religion, excluding for instance certain non-western religions and specifically the multitude of upcoming groups, movements and trends which claim to be religious, without any reference to a so-called radically transcendent reality. Moreover, even alluding to the term transcendence touches psychology of religion on a sour spot, because transcendence is felt to threathen its scientific status, its methodical a-theism. When in addition transcendence proves to be an abstract and highly ambiguous term, covering a whole range of 'beyonds', why then venture on such a risky issue?

The issue, however, can not be avoided, because it touches upon certain basic options and will determine, which subjects of study are excluded or admitted and in what way they will be interpreted. So, one may object that religions which centre in faith in a transcendent God are waning, not any longer standing up to modernity; consequently faith in (or experience of?) a transcendent reality should and could not be taken seriously, asking for psychological exposure. Furthermore, in the issue of religious transcendence certain preconceptions about for instance so central a subject as religious experience comes up for questioning.

It is my conviction, that a psychology of religion would wrong itself, when it would evade the confrontation with transcendence *as the core* of (certain) religions. It is precisely psychology that has grown into the competence and generosity of studying the whole range of human experience and conduct. The openness and generosity of a psychology of religion should equal the plasticity of the psyche. Apart from the fact of the still impressive presence of christian faith in some individuals, groups, and cultures, there is in modern religiosity, at least in Western cultures, always also a moment of confrontation with traditional religion, be it in the manner of disappointment, rejection, revolt, deconstruction. On the other hand, there is no contemporary psychology of faith in transcendent reality that could avoid entering in discussion of alternative, modern modes of religiosity, because the faith it studies undoubtedly is affected by its modern alternatives.

Let us return to the discussion of religious transcendence. In its most simple use the term refers to a beyond, to an (also psychic) act of 'moving beyond'. But there appear to be so many 'beyonds', some religious, some non-religious (ethical, esthetic, existential). But what characterizes a 'beyond' as religious? An *ultimate*, all encompassing (?) value, meaning or reality, in which one is deeply, totally involved (a person, a relationship, nature, an occupation, a task, science, art)? To be religious, does the ultimate have to refer to what is radically withdrawn from man's disposition, what is a gift beyond merit or effort, what is fulfilment beyond expectation? Does it pertain to human and mundane reality without however coinciding with it?

Uncertainty how to define 'beyond' and its religious variety haunts a modern psychology of religion especially because it is not evident how to define religious transcendence in specifically psychological terms, distinct from philosophical or theological terms. There is for a psychology of religion only one, difficult way to clarify the issue: the way back to what in concrete existence is experienced, lived and expressed as being religious and religion. But what are the criteria to discriminate between serious, probed, authentic experience and its utterances and, on the other hand, its adulterations?

For the moment we must proceed and what ever the outcome may be of the ongoing process of definition, in any case christian religion confronts us in a peculiar, provocative manner with what may be called transcendence. It introduces the elements of exteriority (Levinas), of alterity, of contingency (a 'sacred' history of events), of a 'coming from elsewhere', of initiative (*adventus Dei*). It may be here the place to convert the anonymous term transcendence into a name: God. To this name is attached a series of conceptions (ideas, images, symbols) like redemption, salvation, election, convenant, grace; all refering to the dynamic, relational nature of this beyond.

Christian religion represents the dramatic and dynamic aspects of religion and its life-historic moments, with all their inherent oppositions, frictions and desillusions; with loss and absence, but also with its happy incidents of acceptance, dedication and trust, of relations, lost and restored. In this religion psychic activity and passivity thus center in the vicissitudes of the *relation* with God.

Is all this accessible to psychological interpretation, especially when the interpretation admits the christological concentration of this religion? In any case, it is not psychology which decides what will be included in or excluded from its field of study, as it likewise does not determine the *Gestalt* of a concrete religion. Its task is to study the make-up of given religion, its psychological implications, complications and effects. Is there a psychological alternative for the frequent psychologizing of christian tenets?

In this context I will deal with a more common issue, which from the beginning has occupied a psychology of religion: *religious experience*. The idea of radical transcendence, as presented in the foregoing paragraphs, questions a too easy acceptance or introduction of constructs like religious experience, experience of the sacred etc., if these constructs pretend to locate not only the subjective act, but also the *locus* of origin of the relation to transcendence. An experience being conditioned by a subject is not to be identified with an experience being produced, created by a subject. Where the origin of religion and religious experience is exclusively located within the confines of an autonomous subject and is attributed to its competence, religious immanence prevails.

Religious Experience and Faith

A discourse on religious experience in general and vague terms is trivial. Why not give religious experience its proper name? There is no religious experience in general; it always is a particural, specific occurrence. Informed by so many excellent, sometimes discutable analyses of religious experience, I have, in the context of my idea of radical transcendence, tried to more clarify its implications, and have come to favour a distinction between (at least?) three different basic modes of religious experience, corresponding to three basic 'ways of being religious'.

There is a form of 'religious' experience, which originates in the disturbing sense of the finitude, the contingency, the fundamental disharmony of man and his world. This acute awareness of human predicament can set in motion a search for something, which would, on an alternate level, ultimately solve, soulage, bring to completion the disparities of life, or, for that matter, would guarantee and consolidate man's fragile happiness. I think this situation should be taken seriously; it is unfortunate, that functional theories of religion have arrogated it to construe an explanatory model of (all) religion(s), with utilitarian and egoistic overtones. The sense of existential predicament can evoke various reactions, such as indifference, resignation, revolt. The *search* however, which it can provoke, for a corresponding transcendence—if authentic—can be a religious *experience,* but of a particular nature. It is a dynamic experience, in the way of tending towards, of expectation, of inclination and desire, of moving towards what does not clearly present itself and can not be named or defined, but what may be expressed in various forms: narratives, images and imaginative representations. Certainly the quest can loose its open, dynamic character and degenerate into illusion. It is a task of a psychology to exercise here its power of discernment without preconceptions.

In any case this form of religious experience, because its character of tendency, of moving towards, does not exhibit the directness, the empirical self-evidence, so often attributed to it. It is not that easy point of departure, which an empirical psychology of religion often wants and pretends it to be.

There is an other way of potentially religious experience, that originates in the awe and fascination with respect to the profound mystery of self, of the cosmos, of the highest exaltation or deepest dejection of human existence. It is an experience, which apparently can not recognize and realize itself, unless appealing to the solemn and exalted categories of the sacred, the numinous, the marvelous, the sublime, expressing them in a plethora of symbols, myths, narratives and rites. This mode of experience also lacks the empirical clarity and transparency a psychology is often pretending to find in it, thereby neglecting the nature of 'beyond', characteristic of the sacred and its concomitant categories.

There is finally the sense of radical transcendence (as we tried to characterize it by the sigle *adventus Dei*). What however does here mean 'a sense of'?; is it an experience?; should here not preferably be used the term 'faith', in order to set this sense of transcendence against religious experience?

The sense of radical transcendence presents a complexe character. In its concrete practice faith is composed of a whole complex of 'ordinary' realistic experiences, inner and outer, culminating in the celebration of the liturgy. They are all concrete experiences, however refering, pointing to God. What does this act of 'refering to' constitute in psychological terms?; certainly a question which still occupies me. Where theology may speak of *attingere Deum*, a psychology sees a movement, not its end.

Faith can be analyzed in a series of acts like hope, confidence, devotion, expectation, desire, love. But all these acts and attitudes, rightly called experiences, become, at least in psychological perspective, problematic, in as far as their 'referent' God is not experienced. A too easy answer to the problem would be to contend, that the believer is relating to representations, images, ideas of God (as presented by a religious tradition). But the psychological crux of the problem is, that the believer does not want or intend to relate to representations, but to the *reality* of God. Sense of transcendence in faith is a sense of reality; this sense of reality constitutes the psychological problem of faith. Taking seriously the deep conviction of religious realism on the part of religious men requires at least a serious attempt at pychological clarification, which is different from a socio-cultural, contextual one.

Religion: Reality Imaginatively Remade?

In my study on the absence of God, searching for a psychological approximation of the experiential nature of faith and its realism, I compare the 'experience' of faith with the peculiar nature of experience, evoked by reading a fictional narrative (van Ouwerkerk 1986). Ricoeur (1984, p. 150 ff) argues, that in reading a fictive narrrative the reader undergoes experiences, but of a peculiar nature; they are *fictive experiences* induced by the artistic, imaginative composition of the literary work (e.g. the not-realistic emotions of fear and pity evoked in the the spectator of a theatrical tragedy; emotions fundamentally different from those one is undergoing, when assisting a real tragedy).

Fictive experiences don't occur, unless the reader or spectator attaches credence to the authority of the narrative, and let himself be transferred to the fictional world. This fictive experience is a *virtual experience,* in as far as it invites to be transformed into a 'vivid experience'*(une expérience vive)*, which occurs, when the reader and his life are existentially transformed by the impact of the fictive narrative.

Religious faith is not simply to be identified with fiction. Nevertheless, the religious text, by means of its imaginative composition, of its kerugmatic style, of its rethoric of metaphor, paradox and hyperbole, tries to present a reality *sui generis* with chacteristics of a virtual reality. In this way a *virtual* experience of the transcendent reality can be evoked, which only will come to its existential fulfilment by the factual religious transformation of existence. In the religious text itself are virtually present traces and indications of God as referent. Faith, however, becomes and is only vivid experience, 'real' experience in the experiential biography of a real life. All this presupposes an orginal act of credence in the text, which constitutes a seperate psychological issue.

In his way Thomas O'Dea reformulates the foregoing ideas as follows: "...religion is related to crucial breaking points in human experience...the question arises: Is not *religion itself* an experience of some kind of fundamental breaking point?" (1955, p. 19).

We mentioned above the rethoric of metaphor, paradox and hyperbole as linguistic strategies of the religious text. In order to corroborate the foregoing argument, I may express my interest in an analysis of the most important linguistic strategy of refering to a non directly accessible reality: the metaphor. In some new theories of metaphor (Ricoeur 1968) it is not a purely rethoric, stylistic ornament, but constitutes a complex linguistic process, in which by means of a tension between two significations (literal and figurative; e.g. mountain-spirit) a secondary reference is created, which deploys itself on the ruins of a primary referential relation (of literal language). A new referent is called for, because the linguistic tension, causing anomaly and absurdity, can not be solved, unless in an other (dimension of) reality. An imaginative *world*, is projected, revealing otherwise undetected dimensions of reality; a 'habitable' world, transcending every day reality: 'reality remade'.

The importance of a theory of metaphore is again, that it widens and lengthens the concept of reality in general, which makes it possible to *understand* the factor 'reality', which religious men attribute to a relation with a transcendent God. With Ricoeur, I am convinced, that a metaphor is not purely language-immanent, but like all language has a non-linguistic referent; a referent, however, of a particular nature. The metaphoric referent in poetry is the grandeur and mystery of the 'world', figuratively becoming manifest; in narrative fiction it is a life imaginatively transformed.

However enlightening the dynamics of narrative and metaphor are in qualifying the proper cognitive, affective and behavioral (ritual) modes of religion, being ways of discovering and opening up modalities of reality, the expression 'reality remade' must not tempt us into the idea, that religious language or ritual 'makes God present' in a realistic (literal) way. Nevertheless, narrative and metaphorical varieties of reality may at least widen the perspective of a psychology of religion, less sure of its positivistic proclivities and less suspicious of the far reaching claims of religious faith.

A Dramatic Psychology of Religion

The distinction between the various forms of religious experience we described, presses upon a psychology of religion the problem of the relation between these three forms. When transcendence implies or causes the rupture between realms of experience, living religiously in a transcendent perspective would be in danger of becoming desintegrated. When the first two ways of 'religious' experience we described, are common, human, mundane and undeniable experiences, how to integrate these experiences in a faith in a transcendent God? In fact, this problem of integration is not alien to the crisis of the relation between traditional religion and modern ways of being religious; in my opinion modern forms of religiosity have clear affinity with the first two modes of religious experience we discussed.

I have taken the view, that in an expressively transcendent religion the basic psychic dynamics, with which a psychology of religion is confronted, present themselves in a radical and enlarged mode. This view is in line with the assumption, that the *central riddle* of religion is: why does one feel urged to reach beyond a reality, which in principle is familiar, accessible, visible and comprehensible? The psychology of religion of its first classical representatives had its origin in this intriguing question.

This central religious riddle suggests an intriguing object of investigation, namely the psychological predicament, in which the believer places himself or is placed, when confronted with a radically transcendent reality. O'Dea (1955, p. 116) describes this predicament as follows: "Religious men must live in relationship with two incompatible and heterogeneous realms of experience; they must maintain relations with both the sacred and the profane; and they must live concerned with both the ultimate and the mundane." One may call this situation a dramatic one (not *per se* a tragic one); 'dramatic' meaning here, that confrontation with the transcendent is a critical event, provoking decisive activity, with consequences, extending beyond a particular place or moment, and thus re-orienting the course of a life.

For a psychology of religion the study of this predicament appears to be an interesting and adequate object in view of its own psychological performance. The relation to radical transcendence asks for a *dramatic, dynamic* psychology which, as a specific psychological approach, finds in religion elements, which are equally psychic and dramatic. Transcendence evokes dynamic tensions, which can not be dealt with on the level of basic psychological categories, which are the basic presuppositions of *all* experience and conduct. It requires a higher level of categories, borrowed from concrete, everyday experience and language; such as, for instance, confidence, jealousy, love, disappointment, resignation, despair, hope etc. Besides these categories there is the level of specifically dramatic complexes (mostly with relational connotations) like co-operation, opposition, misunderstanding, estrangement, defiance, loneliness, illusion, the sense of absence.

Elements of such a dramatic psychology are found in the work of James (the sick soul, the twice born), of Freud (Eros and Thanatos), of Erik Erikson (the polarity of basic trust versus mistrust etc.), of Antoine Vergote (tension in religion between autonomy and dependance; the vicissitudes of religious guilt and desire).

For me, an inspiring example of a dramatic socio-psychology of religion is Lucien Goldmann's essay *Le Dieu caché* (1959), in which the author analyzes the tragic religious vision of certain aristocratic milieus in 17th century France. Under influence of a dramatic social decline of influence and status, the faith of the aristocratic class of civil servants (*noblesse de robe*) undergoes a crisis. Its socio-cultural world is loosing its attractiveness and meaning, while God, in their experience, is moving away into intolerable absence, not expressing his will or concern. There is a feeling of man living in the world as in a theatre, exposed as he is to the all-seeing, scrutinizing eye of a God-spectator. The exemplary significance of Goldmann's study is its combined interest in and reciprocal clarification of individual religious predicament and its wider cultural expressions, as exemplified in the writings of Pascal and in the theatre of Racine.

Such a dramatic (in this case tragic) religious vision, as analyzed by Goldmann, with its clearly psychological implications, could function as a heuristic model in that it may draw attention to analogical personal or socio-cultural situations and their religious and psychic consequences. I see Goldmann's study (in spite of its marxist-dialectical drift) as an inspiring example of a dramatic psychology of religion.

The choice of christian religion, with at its centre the relation with radical transcendance has been corroborated by my fascination of its dramatics, which urges a psychology to explore new ways and test unconventional categories. I my self have investigated the theoretical preliminaries of such a dramatic psychology of religion in a study expectantly initiated as part of a larger project, only partly completed (van Ouwerkerk 1986).

Methodological Severity and Generosity

A dramatic psychology of religion does not necessarily meet with methodical problems like 'the exclusion of transcendence', as long as such a psychology restricts it self to the religious subject and its inner and outer vicissitudes as an object of study. As long as a psychology approaches religion in an attempt to understand psychologically the believer and his world as an meaningful whole, with the *reality* of God as its central *significance*, religion retains its own intentionality. At the moment, however, that a psychology of religion attempts to assimilate religion into its own pursuit, methodical problems do arise. At that moment, namely, religion is not any longer recognized as a phenomon *sui generis*, which can be studied from a psychological point of view; religion is then taken, pure and simple, as a psychic phenomenon. The insertion of religion into a psychological theoretical *system* transforms religion in an ambiguous phenomenon; it then means something different from what it intends to be in its own terms. The situation of double meaning (real and pretended) does occur in religion and has to be taken into account; assuming, however, it to be the normative situation, is a personal or cultural prejudice.

When religion is completely absorbed into psychology, psychological factors, explaining religion, are not *applied* to a given phenomenon, but constructed as the intrinsic, constituting and organizing principles of religion. In the process of analysis the phenomenon itself gets lost; religion becomes a raw 'material', not any longer a scientific object. Psychology has then fabricated its own alternative religion, suggesting new purely psychological solutions to solve man's existential predicament. No one would deny psychology in general such a therapeutic orientation, but when adopted by a psychology of religion, a title, a name is retained, a cause lost.

One might speculate, that the position of religion as psychologically a lost object parallels the contemporary situation of religion as culturally an *objet perdu* (Certeau 1987, p. 192–198). One might, on the contrary, expect from the study of religion to disclose and make intelligible what presents itself as the other *vis-a-vis* mundane culture, as its alterity. I myself have proposed in this context the thesis, that religion within the psychology of religion does not only undergo the fate of a 'lost object', but also shares the predicament of faith itself, namely the situation of the absence of God. For a psychology God's absence means, that psychology of religion always has to operate in an atmosphere of uncertainty, of recurrent apology and legitimation, being unable to get its object clearly in focus (see the above cited study on the absence of God: van Ouwerkerk 1986).

The foregoing methodical position does not reject the task of a psychology of religion to be a critical instance. But its critique can only be one in inner-psychological terms, and not one based on non-psychological preconceptions.

Challenges to a Contemporary Psychology of Religion

Concluding I may briefly present some tentative, unpretending ideas on the modern situation of religion, as a challenge to a contemporary psychology of religion.

For personal and professional reasons, I have in this essay concentrated my attention to radically transcendent religion and to some of its implications. I am, however, acutely aware, that such a religion cannot avoid the confrontation with modern religious movements and with modern religous agnosticism.

Religious tolerance is not in question; at stake is, wether the definition of religion can be overstreched to the point of religion being arbitrarily defined and consequently becoming irrelevant. A psychology of religion which evolves in the direction of a psychology about philosophies of life takes a too easy way out, while by speaking of functional equivalents of religion and of implicit religion one undermines all serious discussion. As far as a psychology of religion is concerned, I see it as urgent to inquire, in how far and in what way various forms of 'beyond' (which still deserve the qualification 'beyond') present themselves at the moment. The area of art and aesthetic experience (with their imaginative 'beyond'), which at the moment for many is of such central significance, deserves the special attention of a psychology of religion. Here as in other cultural areas, one gets the impression, that religion (religiosity) becomes a quality of culture rather than a distinct cultural domain.

The religious confusion in modern culture with its repercussions on a psychology of religion appears in a new light, when one dicovers the actual impoverishment of language, in which an experience of transcendence could be expressed. To many people there is not any longer a language available, in which a vague sense of transcendence could (for themselves in he first place) come to the surface of consciousness, to the clarity and reflexivity of a vivid experience.

Religious language is in large part formulated and dominated by religious experts and professionals, among them church representatives and theologians, but also the large class of scientists of religion. There exists a 'high' religion, which goes its own way at great distance from the *Lebenswelt* of not only the so called uncultivated and simple-hearted.

What is more: contemporary a-religious culture has lost or suppressed a whole range of religious expressions and does not present any longer a religious or at least 'sacred' imagery, which would offer expression and actualisation of what otherwise will remain virtual and underdeveloped. Is a psychology of religion, as psychology, able and willing to adress this for a large part *terra incognita* ?

From an open and serious discussion on various ways of being religious, in which a religion of radical transcendence should be a critical participant, no one of the participants will emerge untouched, unaltered, perhaps even not undamaged. I myself will follow the discussion and its outcome with the passionate and loyal interest of an observer.

Bibliography

Certeau, M. (1987). *La faiblesse de croire.* Paris: Le Seuil.
Dea, Th. O´(1955). *The Sociology of Religion.* Englewood Cliff N.J: Prentice-Hall Inc.
Goldmann, L. (1959) *Le Dieu caché.* Paris: Gallimard.
Ouwerkerk, C.A.J. van (1979). Psychology of Religion from the Point of View of Psycho-Biography. *Proceedings of the Colloquium of European Psychologists of Religion.* Nijmegen. 208–217.
Ouwerkerk, C.A.J. van (1983). The Absence of God. In Search of its Pychological Implications. *Proceedings of the Second European Symposium of the Psychology of Religion* Nijmegen. 25l–255
Ouwerkerk, C.A.J. van (1985).Religious Experience, Religious Language, and Biography. *Bijdragen.* 270–288.
Ouwerkerk, C.A.J. van (1986). *In afwezigeid van God. Voorstudies tot een psychologie van het geloof.* Den Haag: Boekencentrum.
Ouwerkerk, C..A.J. van (1989). Psychology of Religion and the Symbolic Structure of Religion. *Fourth Symposium on the Psychology of Religion in Europe.* Nijmegen. 242–250.
Ouwerkerk, C.A.J. van (1991). Mystiek en de reikwijdte van de psyche. *Blad van de Faculteit der Godgeleerdheid van de Rijks Universiteit te Leiden.* 75–94.
Ouwerkerk, C.A.J.van (1993).Religie in het netwerk van alledag. *Geloven tussen waan en werkelijkheid.* Nijmegen: De Ploeg.71–98.
Ricoeur, P. (1984). *Temps et récit*, Paris: Le Seuil.
Ricoeur, P. (1968). *La métaphore vive.* Paris: Le Seuil.
Theunissen, M.(1965). *Der Andere.* Berlin: Walter de Gruyter & Co.

Neither Masterly nor Ancillary

Antoine Vergote

Psychology of religion captured me rather unexpectedly. In 1954 Professor Josef Nuttin senior, the czar of the Institute of Psychology at the University of Leuven-Louvain, was in the process of gradually organizing and completing lectures, seminars and training-practices in psychology. He asked me to set up a program in psychology of religion, in both Dutch and French. I had completed a doctorate in theology, with a dissertation in New Testament exegesis, and another in philosophy, with a dissertation on desire and will in Aristotle and Thomas Aquinas, but had no degree in psychology. However, as Professor Nuttin knew, I had, solely out of private interest, read some major works in philosophy and psychology of religion, including works by Freud, Jung, Heiler, Otto, James, Eliade, and Janet. I accepted the proposal and set out after what had thus captured me unexpectedly. I am still searching, but in the meantime have acquired some convictions about the nature and competence of the psychology of religion. My convictions are stronger with respect to what it is not than to what it is. As I see it, the field is still in the process of emerging. Moreover, I consider this way of thinking to be in accordance with what we know from the history of science in general. It is only by differentiating among viewpoints and breaking down overly general theoretical concepts that the sciences have established their identity. It was with this in mind that I entitled a recent essay on this question "What the psychology of religion is and what it is not" (Vergote, 1993 and 1995a). Reacting to this, a non-European colleague made the sympathetic remark that it expresses a typically European way of thinking. I am not sure that this is so, but it does call for an account of that question, and of why it has preoccupied me throughout my career.

With many years of university studies already behind me, I thus began to search for training in the psychology of religion. At that time, more than 40 years ago, I could not find a center offering quite what I was seeking. In Europe, there was the German group of psychologists of religion gathered around the *Archiv für Religionspsychologie*. They continued the trend established by Heiler and Otto, restricting themselves to the observation, description and analysis of what they thought to be the specific structure of what was called religious experience. What they took to be psychology was actually phenomenological psychology. The implicit conception guiding these studies was, and probably still is, that there is a core of religious predisposition in human nature, with favourable circumstances permitting it to be expressed. Psychology of religion, then, is the discipline that observes and identifies these expressions. This phenomenological psychology can be compared with the religious psychology of William James, but with at least one major difference. James thought that psychology could find the source of religion in human emotion. However, he did have to admit that feeling is only religious when applied to "a religious object". James never clarified or overcame this theoretical ambiguity. I think that a combination of positivistic pragmatism and apologetic humanistic reaction against the materialism of his scholarly milieu may explain both James' project and that ambiguity. In contrast, the German group was committed from the beginning to the typically phenomenological idea of the structural unity of religious object and experience. What is common to both currents is a philosophical intention to study the essence of the religious person. On this view, psychology is a kind of empirical philosophy, and it is thoroughly consistent with that psychology's scope and peconceptions to focus on the individual's "religious experience".

I had received some training in phenomenological thought in Louvain, the well known international center of phenomenology and of the archives of Husserl and his collaborators. In 1943, I had completed a masters thesis in philosophy there, on the philosophy of Martin Heidegger. I could thus appreciate the principle of the structural intentional unity of (emotional) consciousness and its specific object. But my philosophical and theological training made me reticent about the fundamental philosophical preconceptions of German phenomenological psychology. I also thought that they had remained isolated from psychology as it had since developed. Their ignorance of psychoanalysis gave them the appearance of a surviving parochial group. Later on, in a congress of the *European Psychologists of Religion,* Sundén proposed to engage in organizational collaboration with the group of the *Archiv für Religionspsychologie*. I told my friend Sundén that this would be time lost, an assertion which he vehemently rejected. I did not then and still do not deny the usefulness and even necessity of practicing some phenomenological analysis within the psychology of religion. But it was and remains my contention that the basic phenomenological principles of the Archiv-group, as well as the basic concepts of William James are indefensible, and that they sterilize research. I have since been able to explain this conviction more fully, in the chapter on religious experience in a book on psychology of religion (Vergote, 1996).

Psychology was an important part of my philosophical training in Louvain. It had been the conviction of Mercier, the founder of Louvain's Higher Institute of Philosophy, that philosophy should be conducted in contact with modern psychology or/and with biology and mathematics. For me, this meant following the lectures and seminars of Michotte (Gestaltpsychology, perception of causality) and of Nuttin. The latter was concerned chiefly with the theme of motivation, and tried to integrate some Freudian conceptions into both his theory and his empirical research. This was an important experience for me, for it was there that I became convinced that psychology of religion must study religious phenomena with proper psychological categories and instruments. Psychology takes an exterior view of religion. This means viewing from the outside the ideas, emotions, expressions, and behaviour of the person who himself considers these ideas, etc., to relate to the religious object (God, the divine...). Psychology takes over from phenomenology the conception of structural intentional unity (idea-object; emotion-object...), but abstains from the scope of a philosophical anthropology which would illustrate an intimate correlation between man's deep being and the effectuation thereof in religious experience. Psychology of religion thus dissociates psychology from philosophy of religion.

I had neither theoretical nor religious problems with the project of a neutral psychology of religion taking religious beliefs, behaviour and experiences as its object. In both philosophy and theology I had been trained in the tradition of what has been called Neo-Thomism. At least in Louvain, this consisted in much more than redressing old philosophies in modern clothes. We studied Plato, Aristotle, Descartes, Kant, Hegel and so forth as much and with the same objectivity as we did Thomas Aquinas. For us, Neo-Thomism meant essentially the acceptance of the autonomy of human reason in philosophy and science, and the conviction that this autonomy is in harmony with the biblical faith in God's creation. That stress on the autonomy of reason in philosophy, science and also psychology goes together with a recognition of the differences between different domains of reality. Science neither proves nor contests God. As Mgr. Lemaître, inventor of the "Big-Bang" theory always said: cosmological theory and biblical faith in creation belong to independent intellectual comprehensions.

In some Protestant milieus the status of the psychology of religion has been contentious. Karl Barth contested its value forcefully. In doing so, he obviously had in mind the form of psychology with ontological and theological pretensions, which would of course also reduce biblical religion to a cultural expression of the naturally religious man. This context reminds one of liberal Protestantism as well as, in Catholicism, the "modernistic" crisis. The Protestant view that original sin rendered human nature fundamentally corrupt does not allow for the idea of a science of religion independent from theological intellectual authority. According to the theological conviction of my milieu, whatever may be the negative effects of sin on the collective and individual mind and affective disposition, these latter remain essentially undisturbed. I myself have not had to deal with the idea, still present in some Protestant contexts, that psychiatry and psychopathology should take into account Christian belief and elaborate a properly Christian science and practice (Belzen, 1989).

My theological training has not been time lost for my work in the psychology of religion. At the very least, it has made me keenly aware of the complexity of the religious phenomenon, "the most complex cultural fact" says Freud (1927). Time and again, I have been stunned by studies—often correlational—appearing in the psychology of religion. The items are of poor quality, and frequently there is a pronounced ambivalence or overt denominational bias. And the tendency to attribute to correlations the value of unilinear causal explanation is manifest.

What theology had also taught me is an awareness of the great variety of ways of living the same Christian faith throughout the changing history of our culture and even among individuals belonging to the same cultural period. Some introductory courses in the comparative study of religions intensified this sense of cultural and religious relativity. My philosophical and theological studies have greatly enhanced my conviction that religion is indeed a most complex phenomenon. When reading psychologists who, on the basis of some empirical research, pretend to explain religion, which invariably means explain its origin, I always think: more pretention than competence.

Not having found a place to go for a systematic training in psychology of religion, I decided to go to Paris for free research and a serious training in psychoanalysis. What I did know about Freud was sufficient to convince me that it was necessary to become thoroughly acquainted with his theoretical concepts. Only in this way could I hope to work out a truly dynamic psychology of religion.

At that time, psychology of religion was practically non-existent in Paris. When later I expressed my wonder at this to Paul Ricoeur, he replied that for a psychological understanding of religion, Kierkegaard is far more interesting than most empirical psychology of religion. I could not disagree with him, but hope that the situation has since changed somewhat. However, it did not change very much in France, which probably explains why the *Institut Catholique de Paris* invited me to give yearly lectures in the discipline as extraordinary professor, beginning in 1972. Even today, it is very rare for a French psychologist to attend the meetings of the *European Psychologists of Religion*. This absence of psychologists of religion in France stands in interesting contrast with their plethora in the U.S.A. And yet, neither scientific studies of religion nor valuable psychology are lacking in France. I surmise that the lack of interest in psychology of religion has to do with a dominant (mis)conception of psychology of religion as a kind of empirically-based theory of religion, its origin and its value. I may be wrong, but I often have the impression that this is still the explicit conception even of many American psychologists. Such a conception is incompatible with the culture of France, where the religious writings of great thinkers like Pascal and brilliant studies on medieval civilization are widely known among anyone with a reasonable education. To be sure, explanatory theories of religion sometimes adapted to ideological enthusiasm do exist, but they resort to complex systems with a tenor of cultural anthropology, sociology and philosophy, such as is the case with the theories of Marx, Durkheim or Freud.

If ever I might have been tempted by the conception of psychology of religion as an empirical philosophy of religion, the scholarly milieu I inhabited and the events I attended in Paris would certainly have rid me of it definitively. Everything I studied there reinforced my sense of the abyssal mystery of language, civilisation and religion. This was true equally of seminars in the linguistics of time structures, Claude Lévi-Strauss' seminars in cultural anthropology, and Maurice Merleau-Ponty's lectures on the concept of nature. Piaget, for his part, was at that time meticulously analyzing the formal structures and rules of the mind as it developed and coped with objects and their properties. I was impressed by his demonstration of the self-structuring process of the mind as it established itself while also coping with the conflict regularly disturbing its equilibrium. But I also regretted that Piaget pursued moral and even religious development no further than what had been determined in previous analyses. He probably wished to make of developmental psychology a strictly scientific work, and knew that moral and religious development does not proceed according to clear, uniform and lawful regularities. And there is a striking lack of any reference to the unconscious in Piaget's psychology.

I got my psychoanalytic training in the—at that time—newly founded *Société Française de Psychanalyse.* Brilliant and highly educated psychoanalysts had for different reasons separated from the *International Society of Psychoanalysis* and its Parisian branch, and had organized this new society. Some of the more well known members included Jacques Lacan, Daniel Lagache, Françoise Dolto, Jean Laplanche, and Jean-Bertrand Pontalis. They organized seminars where Freudian texts were read anew and with painstaking commentary, confronted with clinical experience and illumined with data from modern linguistics, cultural anthropology or philosophy. The contrast was great between this kind of psychoanalysis and the advice a psychologist-psychoanalyst friend from Brussels had given me: "Don't waste your time with reading Freud's theoretical texts. Today these have no more than historical interest. Read only the technical writings of Freud." Yet I myself have regularly commented on Freud's theoretical texts for advanced students and also for practising analysts, and both I and the others have always enjoyed their challenging insights and difficulties. They make one conscious of the complexity of the matters treated, and oblige one to question common psychological conceptions. They are as inexhaustible as the great philosophers.

It seems to me that my studies crystallized in some basic principles orienting my research in the psychology of religion from the beginning. However suspect it may be to trust memories reaching so far back, I think that my first book in the field (Vergote 1969) attests to the convictions I had then, and in fact still have. Am I incapable of change? Only God is immutable, but I was far from a novice in the field when I started lecturing and conducting research into the psychology of religion! I do think, however, that I now have better insight into my own essential convictions, especially after having been compelled by my empirical work to verify them and try to make them operational. Let me try to express those principles somewhat axiomatically:

1) The limited competence of psychology of religion prevents it from explaining the origin of religion. I have developed my arguments extensively in the essay and debate in the *International Journal for the Psychology of Religion* (Vergote 1993 and 1995a). The philosophical pretention of psychologists to explain religion—its origin, truth or error or illusion, value or menace—has been the most harmful factor and too often made this discipline into a confidence game. I have never understood the poor Enlightenment rationalism of psychologists who ignore even Ernst Cassirer, the great Enlightenment philosopher of religion. The methodological neutrality of psychology of religion is a principal of elementary epistemology of science. Perhaps it is difficult to grasp for psychologists without sufficient training in hermeneutics or phenomenological "bracketing". More than once, I have heard psychologists say that they should substitute religious categories for those of psychology. Is this not an astonishing confusion? Psychology addresses religion with its specific psychological categories, but religion expresses its identity with its own categories. "I believe in God, I confess my sin..." constitute the field of behaviour and attitudes which are religious. Motivation, experience, conflict, feelings of guilt and anxiety, etc., are categories belonging to human psychic reality and consequently to the psychology of religion.

2) Religion has a recognizable identity within the wider field of cultural phenomena in general. In a first step, phenomenology must define religion as distinct from surrounding data or imitations. Such a definition, of course, does not imply an evaluative judgment. Recognition of the identity of religion must also be accompanied by an awareness of the great variety of religions, each of which may be linked in different ways with a variety of cultures. A psychologist of religion takes into account the specificity of the religion he is studying. No serious examination of the Christian religion can act as if it is not fundamentally different from the religion of Australian aborigines, primitive natives of the Amazon, clan-religions surviving in Africa, or Japanese Shintoism. The psychology of a healing-religion is quite different from that of the Christian belief-religion.

3) Psychology of religion necessarily presupposes a philosophical anthropology, a conception of the person that is the basis for the aforementioned two principles. As an empirical science, psychology lacks the competence to make a judgment about the existence or non-existence of supernatural beings such as God, the gods, the devil, or spirits. Consequently, psychology should consider the human as *capable* of believing in the gods, God, etc., but without assuming that it is his natural destiny to do so. And, since this belief occurs in different

modalities—experience, faith, relation expressed in rituals—psychology of religion should keep an eye out for philosophical anthropologies promising to help in the elaboration of adequate psychological concepts and working hypotheses. A weak underlying philosophical anthropology is as debilitating for psychology of religion as is ignorance of historical and cultural varieties of religion. The hypotheses proposed by Skinner's behaviourism for studying religion are a caricatured illustration of this, as Wulff (1991) has shown. Ricoeur's disparaging remark about empirical psychology acquires its full significance only when one realizes how tenaciously and acutely he himself analyzed the dimensions and expressions of man, using the vast resources of the major philosophical authors. In this context, I like to recall an experience from my Parisian time. At a meeting of the *Société Française de Psychanalyse*, L. Festinger presented his dissonance theory, during the course of which he repeated his famous observation of sect-members waiting for the artificial satellite to come to pick them up and save them from the earth that would soon be destroyed. He concluded his presentation by linking this observation to a hypothetical explanation of biblical eschatological religious belief. Afterwards Lacan commented only: "These people know nothing." Indeed. For whatever the interest of the dissonance-theory in its own right, it is already massively present in Freud's psychology. And as for the explanation of eschatological belief, I would not insult the intelligence of my readers by spelling out the comic absurdity of Festinger's idea.

Jung's theory is a striking example of a philosophical anthropology which endeavours to introduce into man's nature what man actually achieved in his cultural creative activities. This kind of philosophy of man I would call psychologism. It is the most dangerous snare of a psychology of religion which begins by positively evaluating religion and then explains and guarantees its value by stating that it is inherent to the psychological nature of humanity. Religious beliefs, symbols, etc., are then "expressions" in the same sense that biologists call the effect of genes their expressions. Jung wanted to save the spiritual dimension of man; in fact, he reduces it to what I consider a psychological naturalism. He calls the expressions "projections", which ultimately means that religious people state as outside reality what belongs to their inner psychological reality (the archetypes of God, spirits...). Such a psychologism reinterprets religion in such a way that religious persons themselves would no longer recognize it as their religion. And is such a theory still a psychology? It completely assimilates religion and psychology with one another. Not even the metaphysics which stated that the human being is, by his ontological structure, dynamically finalized toward God, identified itself with religion. When a psychological theory states that it observes "scientifically" the religious disposition of man and God within man, it also necessarily makes of God an observable psychological entity. This is what Jung did. His psychology is literally a religious psychology, which of course is also a psychological religion, a new form of gnosis.

4) The object of psychology of religion is to a very large extent the becoming religious of man. Man is not by his psychological nature religious, but can be addressed by religion present in his cultural environment. Psychology should examine what this religious call awakens in man—its moments and processes of transformation. From reading accounts of religious conversions occurring throughout the history of Christianity from Saint Paul and Saint Augustine to some famous converts of our century, I had already come to the idea that the becoming of religious man is a major object of the psychology of religion. The study of psychoanalysis convinced me that all psychological facts are processes, made of conflicting tendencies and the process of (happily or unhappily) resolving conflicts. Reflecting on the essence of Christian religion, it became evident to me that in our civilization becoming religious occurs between the dynamic opposition of belief and unbelief. Attending seminars in cultural anthropology and reading of studies in this field showed me that in "primitive" cultures the initiation-rite is a condensed form of the process of human and religious becoming. For this reason, I have always stressed that the psychology of religion, at least in the western civilisation so profoundly influenced by Christian religion, is the study of belief and of unbelief. This thesis did not meet with much understanding, except among Christians who feel that it corresponds to what they observe in themselves. Does the uneasiness of psychologists of religion with this conception have its source in their lack of acquaintance with religion—and therefore with a conception of it which does not permit a dynamic psychology? Or is the reason to be found in some basic theoretical concepts of psychology? It would be interesting to study the ideas of psychologists of religion themselves.

In this connection, I have been struck by the reticence self-proclaimed nonbelievers often express in the face of a psychological study of unbelief. Apparently they think—and like to think—that religious belief can be explained by psychology, while unbelief is merely rational and "mature".

5) Developmental psychology of religion should, I think, examine how the different factors in religion evolve. My experience with this type of research has convinced me that imagination, different feelings (trust, guilt), the understanding of religious language, and identification with models, interests, and so on, do not follow the same pace, can interact conflictually, are transformed in different ways, and sometimes regress. The expression "development of religion" is deceptive. A number of unfortunate preconceptions too often lead to the idea of a linear development. The Piagetian model taken from the development of the mind has been harmful to the study of religion. In this context, the uncritical idea of "religious maturity" is in fact the effect of a very rationalistic idea of man. On occasion, it also resorts to apologetics that merely play to the sentiments of its listeners.

6) It is essential for psychology of religion to constantly bear in mind the fact that important issues in existence, such as religion, love or ethics, have their

roots in motives, drives and ideas which are partly beyond the grasp of consciousness; i.e., are unconscious in the broad sense of the term. Linguistics of metaphorization, phenomenology of icons and symbols, cultural anthropology of symbolic systems, philosophical and psychological analyses of emotions—in short, all human sciences—concur in stressing the large pre- or unconscious content of the major factors in religion: emotion, valuation, symbolic expression, metaphors, attachment and love. Considering the instruments used in psychology of religion, one cannot say that psychologists working in this field are posing with sufficient acuity the question of what comprises psychic reality. In the research I have done myself or conducted, I have always tried to get beyond the explicit consciousness of the subjects. Thus, instead of asking questions about the God-idea, I have spent days talking with different and differently believing religious persons. The result has been the conviction that the God-idea is composed of a set of relational representations and dispositions. We therefore had to construct and regularly revalidate a scale formulating these relational contents and dispositions. And when I started examining the religious relational disposition as it may be structured by the fundamental dynamic relationships of the family, I observed that in order to study this topic, psychologists had openly directed the subjects to compare God with father and mother. My contention is that for various reasons this is an erroneous procedure. In response to these considerations, I constructed for this project semantic scales composing symbolic parental figures (Vergote & Tamayo, 1980).

7) Clinical religious psychology is enlightening for the general psychology of religion in three ways.

7.1. Deep analysis of pathological cases shows that psychological causes are (co-)responsible for a wide range of psychopathologies. Now, a psychological cause consists of unconscious conflicts which, for very complex reasons, the person could not solve, and which have consequently been repressed (repressed unconscious, or unconscious in the narrow sense). These conflicts repeat themselves endlessly and in a hidden way. We arrive at a better understanding of normal conflict-solving though comparing it with neurotic (psychotic) conflict-repetition and morbid resolution.

7.2. Clinical studies manifest how religious signifiers are used by an unconscious intention. This fills them with meaning not fitting within the referred to symbolic system of religion, but helping the person to maintain himself. In this way, psychology explains some forms of religion. However, one must be very careful to take into account the specific culture and religion of the person in question.

7.3. Certain clinical entities, such as some depressions or paranoia, clearly display what prevents some persons from even being capable of religious disposition.

This brief overview of clinical religious psychology makes it clear that already on the basis of psychopathology alone I firmly oppose the introduction of religion into the service of psychotherapy—except, of course, in the context of a healing religion such as exist in non-western civilizations (Vergote, 1988 and 1995b). To this clinical argument, I add a religious one: to make Christian or Jewish religion subservient to therapy distorts their meaning. And this, in turn, is itself a supplementary clinical counter-indication.

Readers coming upon my foregoing remarks are likely to see that I continue to expect from psychology of religion still more penetrating observations and analyses of the components of religion, their interactions, conflicts or harmonization. We have had enough short studies which are more sociographical than psychological, or which naively pretend to explain. Sciences like biology, biochemistry, physics, and physiology progress by constantly sharpening their capacity to observing the processes in question. I would like psychologists of religion to focus their attention on the processes at work in the fundamental factors of religion: attachment, love, guilt, fear, doubt, trust, the dialectics of belief and experience, trust and self-confidence, unbelief, etc. A rather naive conception of science pushed too forcefully for statistically valid populations, rather than first attempting to refine the working hypotheses and instruments of observation. For instance, Allport's dichotomy of extrinsic and intrinsic religion was an excellent reversal of brutally elementary conceptions, but anyone who has read the analyses of some mystical authors of John of the Cross or Ruisbroeck is aware of the complexity and process-character of Allport's dichotomy. However, it must be asked: is it possible that, as in other sciences, a group of psychologists of religion would collaborate in the attempt to articulate more adequate concepts and instruments?

Neither *masterly*: psychology of religion lacks the competence to either explain religion or judge its truth. It can only come to judge peculiar religious conceptions (Vergote 1996). Nor *ancillary*: it is not dependent on religious, philosophical or clinical authority. It has its own autonomy and proper scope. It is neither theopsychology nor religious educational psychology. But, to the degree that it has its own consistent capacity to enlighten psychological structures and processes in religion (and unbelief), its insights are of help to religious educationists, psychotherapists who have to deal with clinical cases involving religion, and theologians. I myself have written some theological studies making recourse to psychology; these have included examinations of possession, visions and apparitions, mental health, etc. In Christian religion, God and man are existentially involved in a reciprocal relationship. Now, man is partly a psychological being! However, I always stress the necessity of distinguishing among the procedures and expertises of the different disciplines coming together within theology.

Reflecting on the proposal Professor Nuttin made to me a long time ago, I like to recall a phrase from an old poem: *Et ignotas animum dimittit in artes* (Ovid, *Metamorphoses* VIII, 18). "He gives his mind to arts unknown to him." Arts meaning here: constructive works requiring skills, bridges, literature, etc., and including psychology. But I also like to remind myself of what I have read in Husserl's *Krisis der Europaïschen Wissenschaften*: we are all eternal beginners.

Bibliography

Belzen, J.A. van (1989). *Psychopathologie en religie*. Kampen: Kok.
Freud, S. (1927) Die Zukunft einer Illusion. In: *Gesammelte Werke: Band XIV Werke aus der Jahren 1925–1931* pp 325–380. (Eds. A. Freud et al.). London: Imago 1938.
Vergote, A. (1969). *The Religious Man. A Psychological Study of Religious Attitudes*. Dublin: Gill & MacMillan. (Original work published in French 1966).
Vergote, A. (1988). *Guilt and Desire. Religious Attitudes and their Pathological Derivatives*. New Haven-London: Yale Univ. Press. (Original work published in French 1978).
Vergote, A. & Tamayo, A. (1980). *The Parental Figures and the Representation of God. A Psychological and Cross-Cultural Study*. Leuven-The Hague: Leuven Univ. Press-Mouton.
Vergote, A. (1993). What the Psychology of Religion is and what it is not. *The International Journal for the Psychology of Religion, 3,* 73–86.
Vergote, A. (1995a). Debate Concerning the Psychology of Religion. *The International Journal for the Psychology of Religion, 5,* 119–123.
Vergote, A. (1995b). Religion, pathologie, guérison. *Revue théologique de Louvain, 26,* 3–30.
Vergote, A. (1996). *Religion, Belief, Unbelief. A Psychological Study*. Leuven-Amsterdam-Atlanta: Leuven Univ. Press & Rodopi. (Original work published in French 1983).
Wulff, D. (1991). *Psychology of Religion. Classic and Contemporary Views*. New York: Willy.

From 'Facts' to 'Fiction'
On the Fragility of the Scholarly Glasses
Owe Wikström

As professionals we use to claim that the representation of God is colored by early relations and interactions. But also our mental representation of what we label science—in our case the psychology of religion—seems just partly related to thinking, research socialization or empirical findings. The glasses we wear—i.e. the theoretical models that are decisive for our way to raise questions and interpret our data—are in turn built by building blocks of personal experiences and relations as much as they are formed by the language games we label 'religious studies' or 'psychology'.

What will happen if one "takes a step back" and tries to find the personal and institutional patterns that can explain an ongoing ambivalence to the possibility of a psychological study of religion? As always we are hiding something when we tell the story of ourselves. To construct a memory immediately creates a filter that hides other parts of our history.

Nevertheless, my essay has three parts. In the first part I present some baselines of what I—so far—have seen as the most fertile ground for the psychology of religion. In the second part I look into a quite new sphere which may be of interest for one of the future studies of contemporary religious experience. Finally I give some personal clues to how it all started.

Social and Cultural

My basic approach as a teacher and as a scholar has been to look at religion through hermeneutical glasses. It has also been my continuing effort to find out what can be seen with which type of spectacle-glasses. The part of my spectacle-glasses that is formed through academic socialization, is stemming from both social psychology and the psychoanalytic tradition. On the one hand I have always found it necessary to stress the importance of the societal or socio-psychological genesis, function and maintenance of religious symbol systems, rituals and mythologies. On the other hand, it is as essential to understand the individual's psychodynamic/emotional and cognitive needs or motives that—from the individual's point of view—make these mythologies (worldviews, symbolic universes) personal, authentic and 'living'.

This means that the works of theorists like G.H. Mead, C. Geertz, P.Berger, T. Luckmann and J. Bruner always have been placed in the bookshelves close to my chair in my office. Their perspectives underline the role of language in a religious person's self understanding and in his way of giving internal and external factors a significant metaphysical interpretation. My mentor, Hjalmar Sundén, tries in his role-theory to understand the internalization of mythologies in terms of how their role system works as perceptual filters. Such sociocultural perspectives stress the role of languages transferred by a body of individuals. But they also underline the collective and individual ritual behaviours and the need to maintain the culturally-provided symbol system (Holm & Belzen 1995).

If examined through the combined perspective both my spectacle-glasses it is thus possible to understand religious experiences in terms of a *mutual* interaction between *social* and *intra-psychological* dynamics. And religiosity is seen as a way to make sense, to look for a general sense of coherence, to perceive reality through worldviews formed out of narratives. This pragmatically taken social-constructivistic approach has partly linked my way of understanding to terms from attributional and cognitive psychology.

The cultural or rather anthropological approach has made me aware that we have to elaborate and understand psychologically intra-theological terms and concepts for 'inner feelings of an ultimate concern' etc. of separate religions—i.e. we need a kind of phenomenologically-oriented psychology of religion more close to the works of R. Otto and of F. Heiler than to modern academic psychology. During the last years I have tried to scrutinize the way spiritual experiences are formed through rituals and languages of different religions and world-views (Wikström 1993). In my opinion one of the future directions of psychology of religion must be to re-explore the necessary bridge between psychology on the one hand and phenomenology of religion and comparative religion on the other. This seems to be especially important when one comes to questions of cross-cultural and clinical implications of our scientific endeavours. Theorists like M. Eliade, W. C. Smith are as important as comparative studies of prayer, fate, dreams, meditation and ASC (Altered States of Consciousness), visions etc. The functional perspective on religion must then be related to more substantial ones (Wikström 1994).

More and more I see our research strategies as psycholog*ies* of religion*s*. I even think that the term "psychology of religion" (especially the measuring operationalizing methods or a too rigid understanding of psychodynamic concepts) *in singularis* can create theoretical and methodological artefacts that we 'see' or 'find' in 'reality'. It reificates or rather projects on data or a case the religiosity of the scholar, often far away from the ordinary person's multidimensional and unstructured way of expressing her or his relation to the Unseen. After many shorter visits to India I recently spent a few months in Banaras, India. There I interviewed ricksha drivers as to their experiences of Lord Shiva when they went 'to take Darsán' in the small sites of temples close to the river Ganges. I found an interesting visual theology. The word *Darsán,* which means simultaneously "to see" and "to be seen", is of interest. It can, of course, be understood in terms of our Western theories of reciprocal interaction, attachment or object-relations. But the opposite can also be the case: these theories applied to folk Hindu religiosity are far too narrow-minded. My all too short periods in Asia clearly have indicated a western bias in our main models and instruments of research. The hidden agenda—an epistemological ethnocentrism due to our instruments, scales and designs—makes me feel more and more uncomfortable. At the same time, without theories and methods there is no research. A paradox to be kept in mind.

Individual

From an individual's perspective the questions arise why, how and to what extent the individual selects interpretative schemes from his or her mythological context. Here I have found it fruitful to select the basics from psychodynamic—neo-freudian—traditions. The intrapsychological forces—in terms of emotion, defence, transference, cathexis, projection, object-relation, transitional space, etc. are important when it comes to the exploration and hermeneutical investigations of the individual (Scharfenberg & Kämpfer 1980). During the last years our doctoral students have used religious object-relation theory from A.M. Rizutto and her followers. These psychoanalytical models, however, must be completed by cultural or socio-psychological perspectives, especially when it comes to cross-cultural psychological hermeneutics.

The tricky question of the relation between social, cognitive and emotional levels comes especially at the surface when elaborating two fields of research, of which it is important in my opinion to keep them apart: the clinical psychology of religion and the psychology of pastoral care (a name I prefer instead of 'pastoral psychology').

As to clinical psychology of religion, alongside my work as a therapist with patients with religious problems, I have tried to do research on the role of transference and countertransference. In some papers, chapters and books (for further references see Wikström 1993) I have discussed general themes, investigated psychotic religious delusions in terms of their intra-psychological function and collected data on neurotic religiosity. Through this I have tried to build models for a psychotherapist's responsible dealing with existential and religious themes in therapy.

As to the field of pastoral care, I have stressed the experienced knowledge of the Christian language for 'the inner spiritual life' and the ability to combine that language with a skilled use of psycho-dynamic terms and insights. For a long time I have observed a 'secularization from inside' in the mainline churches due to an uncritical admiration and a sometimes too diffuse use of psychotherapeutic theory. Now the pendulum seems to swing a bit too much to the other side. Some seem to love St. John of the Cross, the patristic fathers and want to idealize the mediaeval period. Simultaneously they have become unaware of or even suspicious towards psycho-dynamic or social scientific thinking. I struggle for a more balanced perspective and I support our students—at least the future pastors among them—to take courses in Christian spirituality.

In clinical psychology of religion, I have described cases where religion has played a decisive role in genesis and/or expression of a pathological behaviour. I have seen how patients 'use' religious mythologies just in order to have a framework that makes their inner turmoil understandable (i.e. in paranoic or delusional periods). Some 'use' religious symbols functionally but without accepting the theological truthclaims and without former or later socializing in a religious group. These religious mythologies seem to provide fertile symbol systems for grandiosity, self-denial etc.

In the psychology of pastoral care, on the other hand, I have tried to elaborate the cognitive dilemmas of the therapist/believer who simultaneously works with God as god and God as God, i.e. who both understand God as an early object-relation projected on a celestial screen and understand God as an independent force, a transcendent Thou. How is it possible for the counsellor to switch from a psychodynamic to a theological legitimation or the other way round, without committing intellectual suicide? Quite a number of ministers are for some years lost in a psychologistic trap and are not aware of its hidden meta-psychological presumptions. The ontological apriori behind a pure rationalistic understanding of reality—even the psychological reality—has to be problematized in my opinion. On the other hand, I am reluctant towards the other trap: a metaphysical baseline of a psychological study of religion. At least one has to search for an agnostic methodology, intersubjective norms and theories not laden by theological overtones.

To Destabilize One's Own Perspectives

Now to some critical questions. My training is the common one in Europe: history of religion, comparative religion, theology, psychology, psychiatry, sociology and finally a doctorate in psychology of religion in 1975. And in spite of this socialisation into the language games of authors like W. James, J. B. Pratt, G. W. Allport, K. Girgensohn, P. Janet, J.M. Charcot, S. Freud, C.G. Jung, J. Fowler, I. E. scales etc. up to the last years' thinkers, I have become more and more doubtful whether we really can see any progress in what we are doing. Sometimes I am convinced that our theoretical concepts ('mean'-'end'-'quest', 'transitional space', or 'significant Others' etc.) are kinds of reificators that create a reality of their own rather than mirroring the experiential side of a religious person. But even if I agree with the statement that our research is a kind of socially-constructed (scientific) reality that we need in order to be able to communicate to others in psychological or anthropological branches, I am rather dissatisfied. What kind of insight is psychology of religion really offering?

For myself and for my students it used to be a dangerous but a necessary experience to understand our own faith and/or lack of faith and/or ambivalence to faith in terms of early objects, projections, illusionistic states, social constructions, or attributions. But slowly it has become more and more necessary for me to even de-stabilize or de-reificate the models provided by the psychoanalytical or the social scientific socialization. Of course, I see clearly a need for myself and for the students to cling to one type of 'stable ground'. But can psychology of religion ever provide any baseline ? All it can offer are different models, or mental maps that one can use in order to see a little more of the function of religion for the individual. Therefore, during the last years I have begun to label myself a 'perspectivist'. I doubt that we, as social scientists, working on the domain of religion ever will find any constructs that are overarching, interreligiously or transculturally valid. The necessity to formulate contextualistic theories is now recognized by a growing number of psychologist. Maybe, in the light of the essentialistic ideals of the past, I am rather pessimistic when I say that any psychological effort to understand the religious world of human beings has to be *ad hoc,* a provisorium.

For some parts of our scholarly identity this is hard stuff to take. But we are often talking about data, validity, reliability, stages, chi-square, inductive phenomenological strategies etc., as if there were something 'out there' that could be observed and scrutinized. All we have, are (clever) tellings about tellings, narratives about narratives, questionnaries in the spiral galaxy we label research.

Novel Reading as a Religious Act

The situation in secularized Sweden is that most people do not know the Judaic or Christian history. They are also not acquainted any more with the main figures of the Bible. They have no relation what so ever to Abraham, Peter, Thomas, Mary or even to Christ. In terms of Ana-Maria Rizutto the inner representation of 'the living God', is not framed around stories that are taken from a self-evident Christian framework. The knowledge of the basic religious texts is minimal.

At the same time we can see an increasing 'use' of other transitional spaces or limenal arenas: novels, dramas, TV and films. Especially films whose main characters are actualizing existential dilemmas seem more than ever to be dialogue-partners in a secularized society. This stream coincides with another main trait in modern Sweden, individualism and a critical attitude towards organized and institutionalized forms of the "signals of transcendence" (Luckman 1990, Wikström 1997b). For many Swedes there is a highly 'selective theology', functioning out from religious *smörgåsbord* principles: the individuals seem to built pragmatically their own arcs. The content of this inner arc is not taken from traditional religious texts but from other 'texts' that help them to "come to grips personally with the questions that confront us because we are aware that we and others like us are alive and that we will die" (Batson & Ventis 1993, p. 22).

In this privatization process, the religious role of the humanities and especially literature and novel-reading must be taken more seriously, at least for one segment of the society. Fiction provides material for the individual. Novel-reading as a 'private' working with existential questions is not linked to religious rituals or classic Christian theology. It seems to fit well into a postmodern and individualized society.

But what happens when certain characters from culture, art and film become vehicles for individuals in their existential struggle and on their journey to a spiritual maturity? Reading and relating to literary figures as 'real' is structurally close to the role-taking process of the pious man who knows his Bible. According to Hjalmar Sundén religion is a way to perceive reality by means of provided roles taken from the myths.

Thus, my old literary interest has created a dilemma. It is both problematic and creative. I have found that my own novel-reading has shifted. Before, reading a good book was just something I did for fun, or in professional terms: an escape from scholarly thinking to a private transitional space. Today I am convinced that the reading process as well as the content of those particular epic universes we are invited into when we open a good book, are relevant to understand for the psychologists of religon.

As many of my collegues I have read the great Russian writers. Or rather, I return more or less regularily to scenes from their books. In certain periods I am maybe more involved with epic figurers than I am with my own friends. In condensed form good literature seems to illustrate or even deepen the understanding of the themes the psychologist of religion is dealing with. Nowadays in every reading list I select some novels or films that I ask the students to reflect on in their written or oral examinations.

But what to do with those insights about the psychological function of God, doubt, faith, trust etc. that one finds in the product of artists. In the works of modern writers, but even in those of classical authors like August Strindberg, Hermann Hesse, Marcel Proust, and John Cowper Powys, and also in movie pictures made by film-makers like Woody Allen, Ingmar Bergman, and Andrej Tarkovskij there are reference persons which we have found to be existentially very important identification figures, especially for the not formally religious individuals. Modern epic universes seem to have taken the place of the Christian and Biblical meta-narratives. The reading of modern (popular) novels that explicitly deal with subjects like suffering, evil, goodness or death seems to be particularly important for those who are critical towards the traditional churches and their sometimes all too trivial answers. This reading is something that you can 'do yourself'—without professional theologians who want you to become dedicated to this or that specific faith. The conversation partners that are hiding inside a text, are supporting, clarifying and interpreting reality as much as are biblical persons for the religious man. But of course, these epic figures are neither involved in rituals nor part of a social contract, as are the biblical figures who are 'living' in the liturgy or in the collective consciousness of a community.

My point is that we are in a transitional space when we visit the fantasy or illusory worlds of our classical writers. Their characters are struggling with existential problems and clearly demonstrate that doubt and faith can not be placed in a pure "real" or pure "autistic" world, but in an illusory reality, the "third world" according to Pruyser. Nearly every student around the globe has some kind of relationship to Dostoevsky's famous figures. They are parts of our common cultural heritage.

When I analyze literary texts, I try to be very close to the main characters. Hermeneutical tools are then mainly taken from psycho-dynamic theories. Through them I have been able to see the psychological role of faith in a God 'inside' a particular epic universe.

But in this endeavour, it is also possible to inductively understand the implicit psychological 'theory' that is working in the author's effort to give authentically *Gestalt* to his different figures. This theory, emanating from the literary domain, can in its turn function like a critical or sceptical discutant in relation to the all too well established models of our psychology of religion.

Doubts

But what should the psychologist of religion do with these observations? For a long time I tried to ignore the question. I said to myself that I am not working in the department of literature studies, my focus is not to study the content of a novel but to highten the psychological understanding of the religious person. The academic ambivalence is still inside me. What is one actually doing when one—as a psychologist of religion—enters into a symbolic and metaphoric space and gets access to a fantasized person's actions, thoughts, dreams and struggles with God and the meaning of life? Can this be psychology, and if so, what kind of psychological knowledge is generated?

Well read in models like Winnicott's transtititional space, Turner's liminal sphere and the sociological theories of play (*homo ludens*), I looked upon literature-reading as a way to rest from academic efforts, a way to let go off the rationalistic filters of my working days. I left the theorizing to the department of literature. My research socialization said that imaginative *Gestalts* can not provide data as to man's religiosity. Psychologists—i.e. psychologists of religion—are using (quasi)experiments, interviews, scales, tests, diaries, observations etc.

During the last years, however, I have not been able to suppress my research attitude, when reading literatur. When I read and reread the great classical writers—especially Dostoevsky—I think that through them one can get access to material that is much more multifarious than what we find in scales, interviews or in our notes after observations. But not only that. In novels sometimes one finds insights that seem to go directly against or at least problematize the 'knowledge' we claim is stemming from the psychology of religion. In other words, novelists and fictive figures do not only illustrate but also criticize theories. But in what sense are fictive worlds, created by a well known author, *wellsprings* to and not only *illustrations* of psychological theories?

My personal odyssey—from reading just for fun to investigating fictive figures inside a particular epic universe—raises a bunch of basic questions. There are methodological questions (how to investigate an epic universe) and epistemological problems (fictive figures evidently do not exist; but aren't they sometimes psychically experienced as more 'living' than biblical figures like Peter, James or Paul?) There are problems as to the theory of science (where 'is' the new knowledge one gets acess to, is it in the literature—the text—or is it in the psyche of man? (And maybe most, it is a question for sociology of science—where does this academic work belong, in humanities, in behavioral sciences, in theology, philosophy or in literature?) (Wikström 1982, 1997).

Novels, especially novels that are seen and understood as good literature, psychologically credible and dealing with existential themes, thus also provide important material for insights into religious experience. Authors are often able to express human conditions in a condensed form. But how about validity? Are not these novels just private explorations of the inner world of the genius or the artist? Artistic guessings of how ordinary men and women experience their world?

The great classics by Dostoevsky, Strindberg, Proust etc. are yearly read by thousands and thousands of people. New generations take part in Raskolnikov's fate in *Crime and Punishment*, in the mystical consciousness in Proust's *A la recherche du temps perdu*, or in Strindberg's struggle with his God in *Inferno*.

I see that recurring process as a kind of validation. Many seem to identify themself with literary figures. Reading in itself can be understood as a 'working-through' process. Unconsciously it provides possibilities to projective identification. The figures then become symbolic personifications of latent longing, doubts or trust. The figures verbalize, avoid, act out and live through religious conflicts (Detweiler 1989; Smith 1995). To describe and understand such fictive but nevertheless 'real' cases, is to work just on the border between the reader's inner transitional sphere and the socially constructed reality.

Oceans of material can be seen in the future. I have published a book on *The Brothers Karamazov* (Wikström 1997) in which I investigate Dostoevsky's psychological way of casting two main figures (Aljosja and Ivan) and their opposite relations to the Christian truthclaims. This novel challenges and fertilizes my own field of science. I am deeply convinced that the most fertile soil is to be found in the valleys between the traditional research arenas. New insight can be found also in the academic valleys, i. e. in those fields of reality that often fall between our ordinary mountain disciplines.

To label a novel writer a "psychologist of religion" is of course both a simplification and a provocation. A writer—as an artist—has no scientific claims. Especially the author Dostoevsky hides himself effectively behind a myriad of different voices. Nevertheless, regardless of his theological or ideological positions, in his casting of his main characters, the implicit or explicit author discloses tremendous insights into religio-psychological themes. My effort, however, was not to write just another essay on Dostoevsky to be put on the top of the pile on the desks of the Slavic scholar's table, or to offer something new in the realm of literature or literare criticism. Instead I hope that literary perspectives will provide some new and maybe provocative phenomenological material both for the fields of religious studies as well as for the psychology of religion.

Personal

"Taking a step back" means also to look upon the more personal dynamics for my choice of academic training. Therefore these ending remarks. Stemming from a lowchurch tradition of northern Sweden, Luther was my childhood's "Significant Other". Activities in the local church however were followed by serious doubts. In my gymnasium's blue period I was riding a Vespa, saw all the 'ought-to films' like Fellini, Bergman and Pasolini and cultivated the existential questions in the cafés close to the Seine in Paris. More and more I found myself caught in a philosophical or rather theological trap. The classical themes from Sartre, Camus and Russell made my childhood's 'first naiveté' erode. I played in a jazz orchestra in the weekends and read excessively, especially the Russians. My faith faded slowly. My father, a political activist on the left wing, was a bright and provocative thinker, kind and permissive. At the same time he was a pious man influenced by the mystics. With no formal academic training, he worked as a train driver. Our everlasting discussions still remain in my inner space. The arguments for either/or claimings of the belief statemens were constantly confronted with statements of both/and. The questions of "god" or of "God" are still fighting inside me. Maybe that's one of the reasons why I later became a professional psychologist of religion, whatever that means.

Thus my basic ambivalence has remained. I turned out to be someone living on a border: the border between the land of believers and that of the researchers, between psychology and *Religionswissenschaft,* between psychology of religion and spirituality, between humanities and social sciences, between fictive universes and 'reality', between the role of an artist/author and that of a scientist, and between aesthetical expressions and scholarly work. However, I feel rather comfortable living in this transitional space, border, limen or whatever we name it. Nowadays I am quite used to being a scientific nomad.

When I studied theology, psychology and history of art at the University of Uppsala, I worked extra in a mental hospital. There I met psychotic patients with highly religious visions. It led me to reading Eliade, Arieti, Jaspers and Winnicott. I became fascinated by the 'holy insanity' in the Russian tradition. Months of hitchhiking all over Europe during the formative student years brought me also to father Georgios Demetriades, an orthodox priest in Perama, outside Athens. I presume that this period in Greece started an interest in eastern theology, a thinking not influenced by the Reformation and the Renaissance. Later reading Gregorius of Palamas and having experiences of the Divine liturgy brought psychoanalytical concepts in fruitful confrontation with terms from Byzantine spirituality. Psychological models like primary processes, transitional spaces and object-relations were confronted in a fruitful de- and re-construction with the theology of the icons and the divine energy according to the patristic fathers.

Of course, it is not a pure academic curiosity that keeps my interest in psychology of religion going. To make the study of mathematics, biology or linguistics one's main topic as a scholar seems to me less existentially threatening than the continuing and serious study of the forms, functions and consequenses of the human being's struggling with his or her fate and with God. Many hours as a psychotherapist as well as personal crises have laid the emotional foundations in my effort to understand the individual and his religion.

One of these founding experiences was that one of our five children was born with cancer (now completely recovered). His birth and the problems around that period made me more aware of the fragility of this world. But, scientifically more important, it made me suspicious of all theological or psychological theories of man and of their claimings to be able to cope with life or make the mystery of man's condition understandable. The unbearable burden of the existence remains inspite theories. So, I'm very reluctant toward the all-too-embracing-scientific models presented now and then.

Thus, the admission of the relative and interremistic character of any theory is in my opinion a must. Rather recent research on the rituals of Lord Shiva in Banares, India (Wikström 1996) has made me aware of the narrow perspectives of psychology of religion and the huge risk of reification due to our basic western-born concepts. However, this epistemological pessimism does not have to lead to solipsism, to a naive theoretical or ontological anarchy, but rather to humility.

Theologically speaking, I am now and then returning to the 'second naiveté'. God then seems to be a personal Thou rather than a 'cognitive framework' to understand the existence, or an 'introject of some early objects glued around a mythological content' or another clever scientific solution. He/she/it seems to be (or at least to be able to be experienced as) a personal will: *Deus (et homo) semper maior.*

Bibliography

Batson, C. D. & Ventis, W. L. (1993). *The Religious Experience. A Social-Psychological Perspective.* New York: Oxford University Press.

Berger, P. (1992). *A Far Glory. The Quest for Faith in an Age of Credulity.* New York: The Free Press.

Detweiler, R. (1989). *Breaking the Fall. Religious Readings of Contemporary Fiction.* London: The MacMillan Press.

Luckmann, T. (1990). Shrinking Transcendence. Expanding Religion. *Sociological Analysis. 50:2* 127–138.

Scharfenberg, J. & Kämpfer, H. (1980). *Mit Symbolen leben. Soziologische, psychologische und religiöse Konfliktbearbeitung.* Olten: Walter.

Smith, M. (1995). *Engaging Characters. Fiction, Emotion, and the Cinema.* Oxford: Oxford University Press.

Wikström, O. (1982). *Raskolnikov. Den kluvnes väg till helhet.* [Raskolnikov—a psychological interpretation]. Lund: Doxa.

Wikström, O. (1993). The Psychology of Religion in Scandinavia. *The International Journal for the Psychology of Religion, 3,* 1, 47–66.

Wikström, O. (1994). Psychology in the Phenomenology of Religion. A Critical Essay. In Brown, L. B. (Ed.). *Religion, Personality and Mental Health.* New York: Springer. pp 29–42.

Wikström, O. (1995). Soul Recovery through Remystification. Dostoevsky as a Challenger of Modern Psychology. In Fenn, D. & Capps, D. (Eds.) *On Losing the Soul. Essays in the Social Psychology of Religion.* New York: State University of New York Press. pp 119–137.

Wikström, O. (1996). Darsan (to see) Lord Shiva in Varanasi. Visual Processes and the Representation of God by Seven Ricksha-Drivers. In *Åbo University Scripta Instituti Donneriani.* Åbo: Finland, pp 357–369.

Wikström, O. (1997). *Aljosjas leende. Om gudsfrånvaro, mystik och skönlitteratur.* [The smile of Aljosja. On the abscence of God, mysticism in literature]. Stockholm: Natur och Kultur.

Wikström, O. (in press). The Centripetal Journey. Individualized Religion in Sweden as a Defence against Plurality. In Bar-Lev, M. & Sharif, W. *Leaving Patterns of Religious Life. Cross Cultural Dimension.* Haifa: Bar Ilan.

A Century of Psychology of Religion
Where Does It Leave Us Today?[1]

David M. Wulff

In 1979, the American Psychological Association celebrated with considerable fanfare the centenary of the birth of scientific psychology. A hundred years earlier, as everyone attending that year's annual convention was reminded again and again, Wilhelm Wundt founded his famous laboratory for psychological experimentation at Leipzig University—"the very first formal psychological laboratory in the world," in the words of historian of psychology Edwin Boring (1950, pp. 323–324). With the centenary as its official theme, the convention in New York City was itself testimony to the momentousness of that fateful founding, for nearly twenty thousand psychologists came to participate in five days of programs organized by the forty-some divisions of an association that today has over 100 000 members.

A momentous founding, perhaps, but certainly modest, for as Boring (1965) points out, this "founding" consisted of nothing more than the decision to allow two students to conduct some research in a small room that had been assigned to Wundt three years earlier for the storage of his demonstration apparatus. This quite informal establishment of a psychological laboratory might in fact have gone unnoticed if Stanley Hall, one of the two students, had not later stirred up controversy by claiming for himself the honor of having founded the first genuinely significant psychological laboratory—in 1881 at Johns Hopkins University.

This historic squabbling over whose laboratory was the first was of no concern to those attending the 1979 APA convention. Nor, certainly, did many pause to wonder how Wundt would view the scientific psychology he is reputed to have spawned, or even to contemplate the curious notion that a scholarly field might be said to have been founded at a particular time and place. What captured their attention instead was the large number of convention offerings dedicated to observing the long-anticipated centenary. Particularly conspicuous was the well-orchestrated program of symposia and invited lectures co-sponsored by the Division of General Psychology (Division 1) and the

---

[1] A briefer version of this paper was given as the opening address to the 6th symposium of European Psychologists of Religion, Lund University, June 19, 1994.

Division of Philosophical Psychology (Division 24) and carefully assembled by Sigmund Koch—who happened to be the president of both divisions that year—and David Leary, an historian of psychology who agreed to be joint program chair for the two divisions. Entitled *A Century of Psychology as Science: Retrospections and Assessments*, their program engaged the efforts of 46 presenters and eventuated in 1985 in a 1000-page book containing revised and augmented versions of the convention presentations.

As Koch and Leary point out in their introduction to this book, the fractionation within contemporary psychology foreclosed the possibility of representing all of its many divisions. It is not even possible to hope for a consensus on what the overall structure of psychology might be—if indeed such a structure exists. "Current psychology," Koch and Leary write in their introduction, "is much like a jumbled 'hidden-figure' puzzle that contains no figure" (p. 2).

If no overall structure can be discerned, Koch is nevertheless willing to hazard identifying some basic trends that stood out for him as he reviewed the book's 42 chapters. Altogether, these chapters not only survey the traditional subdivisions of basic psychology but also address fundamental questions about psychology's disciplinary status, its connections to intersecting disciplines, and its relation to human and social affairs. In these diverse essays Koch discerns the following six trends:

1) a resurgence of sensitivity to and respect for history, after an extended period of ahistoricism;
2) growing doubt concerning psychology's formal status as a unitary discipline;
3) increasing awareness of the philosophical presuppositions and implications of psychology's concepts, theories, research strategies, and conclusions;
4) a growing sense of the experiment's limited applicability and its complexity of meaning in psychology;
5) a greater degree of modesty and tentativeness regarding the accomplishments, generality, and future prospects of the specialized areas of psychology as well as of the field as a whole; and
6) a growing concern over the negative effects of psychology on both individuals and society (pp. 935–950).

The restiveness in contemporary psychology, Koch observes,

> is now more extensive than at any preceding interval of the last hundred years, including even that unsettled period in the first quarter of this century marked by the constant polemical conflict of the "schools". But the pluralism *now* obtaining has a less embattled, thus less querulous and rhetorical quality. It is a pluralism of *search* rather than assertiveness, marked by humility, not hubris (p. 938).

One of the "happiest commonalities" of the essays, says Koch, is "a quality of undogmatic civility, [of] responsible tentativeness, that has rarely been conspicuous in the history of our field" (p. 940).

Although the psychology of religion was not among the fields represented by Koch and Leary's symposiasts, one would naturally assume that Koch's generalizations apply to this specialty no less than to the others. Certainly there is evidence of a growing tolerance if not also appreciation for the plurality of views that is no less evident in the psychology of religion, and even those in the field most committed in principle to experimental methods have recognized that these procedures are only minimally applicable in the realm of religion. Whether the other generalizations apply is less clear, however, and as one reads the individual chapters in Koch and Leary's book, the impression grows that the psychology of religion is in a position that is in various respects unique.

Let us begin a retrospective and assessment of this field by observing that the limited applicability of experimental methods in the study of religion would make it odd for the psychology of religion to trace its beginnings to Wundt's Leipzig laboratory. Wundt would have thought so, too, for he himself ruled out laboratory methods for the study of religion. For religion and other cultural expressions of higher mental processes he advocated the historical and ethnographic approach of folk psychology.

Those in the psychology of religion whose sense of history requires the reassurance of a founding date usually cite a public address given in Boston in 1881 by Stanley Hall, who claims to have been, on that occasion, the first to present empirical data linking conversion and adolescence (Kahoe, 1992). He briefly restated his conclusions in an article published the following year (Hall, 1882). Yet Hall's data would seem to have been rather unsystematic and impressionistic—collected, he said, both by correspondence and by studying the records of a midday prayer meeting in New York City (Hall, 1904, 2, p. 292n).

Although Hall, in his various roles, is as close to a founder as one can find in the psychology of religion, a closer parallel to Wundt's laboratory would be the questionnaires on conversion and religious development that Edwin Starbuck formulated and began circulating late in 1893 while a graduate student at Harvard. He gave an initial report of his findings in a lecture before the Harvard Religious Union in 1894. Thus, giving Starbuck priority would not only recognize his inaugural use of the chief research tool of the empirical psychology of religion but it would also have allowed us to celebrate the field's centenary during the 1993–94 academic year.

Setting aside these rather trivial differences in founding dates and circumstances, we may ask how the psychology of religion has otherwise gotten on in comparison with other subfields of psychology, notably those that Koch and Leary chose to represent. Without much effort one can find some common trends. One learns, for example, that the psychology of religion was not the only specialty to suffer a fallow period extending roughly from 1930 to 1960, during which behaviorism's hegemony in American psychology largely foreclosed research on a variety of subjective phenomena. But immediately we must note a significant difference: Unlike virtually all other subfields of psychology, the psychology of religion had a second home—the religious studies—where it could have thrived in spite of the strictures of behaviorism. Yet it suffered there as well, largely because of the post-war decline of the liberal evangelical outlook and the ascendancy of dialectical theology, in both Europe and America.

The oppressive influence of dialectical theology is just one example of a number of fundamental difficulties that distinguish the psychology of religion from other specialized areas within psychology. Although the word 'religion' gives the impression that one is speaking of a single, abstracted thing—akin, say, to perception or motivation—in reality it designates, on the individual level, an indeterminately complex realm of images, ideas, feelings, perceptual intimations, and aspirations. Giving expression to these often vague and ineffable experiences are the more observable elements that constitute the historic religious traditions, including doctrines, scriptures, temples, rituals, music, and dance. Daunting in themselves as objects for psychological study, these diverse manifestations of religion ultimately derive their meaning and significance from their association with a transcendent dimension, realm, or object, which lies utterly beyond the psychologist's professional competence and comprehension.

In a classic paper published at the beginning of this century, Swiss psychologist Theodore Flournoy (1903) argues that psychologists of religion should remain agnostic about the transcendent dimension or object, neither affirming nor denying its independent existence. In the ensuing decades, however, this "principle of the exclusion of the transcendent" has been violated far more frequently than it has been observed. It is difficult, certainly, to set aside one's own views of or attitudes toward the transcendent, which views otherwise silently inform all of one's experience.

More significant, however, is the fact that Flournoy's principle, when taken seriously, precludes many of the questions that bring inquirers to the psychology of religion in the first place. Without this constraint, deniers of the transcendent such as James Leuba, Sigmund Freud, and B. F. Skinner are free to ask the questions that most interest them. How is it that people experience as present someone who in reality is not there? Whence comes the illusory image of an omniscient and omnipotent god who is both loving and threatening? What is the origin of the odd gestures of religious ritual and why do they persist when in fact they have no objective effects? On the other hand, those who affirm the transcendent dimension, such as Gordon Allport, Antoine Vergote, and Adrian van Kaam, ask rather different types of questions. How may we distinguish individuals who are genuinely religious from those whose piety is a charade? What psychodynamic principles will explain the militant atheist's resistance to an all-powerful God? What forms does the search for spiritual direction take when people repress the spirit that lies at the core of human existence?

If we compare the questions preferred by the deniers of the transcendent with the questions posed by the affirmers, we will notice that the deniers frequently undertake to analyze and explain shared religious *content*—a tradition's image of God, for example, or some scriptural passage or a ritual observance—whereas the affirmers pass over content to focus on individual religious *persons*. For example, the widely cited Roman Catholic psychiatrist Ana-Maria Rizzuto (1992, p. 156) explicitly rejects the content-centered approach of both Freud and her fellow object-relations theorists in maintaining that psychologists are not competent to discuss religion in general but must limit themselves to individuals' idiosyncratic perceptions and feelings regarding the divine object. In expressing a similar view, Vergote (1993) declares that psychologists are not competent to speculate on the nature and origins of religion or to declaim on the appropriate or possible roles of religion in today's world. C. G. Jung, in contrast, takes the study of religious content and its dynamics in personal lives and the social order to constitute the psychology of religion proper, to which he dedicated much of his life's work. He was, of course, widely criticized—by secular psychologists for his interest in obscure religious imagery and by conservative religionists for reducing religion to a psychological function.

Viewed as a defender of religion—for he declares it to be an essential psychological function—yet charged, on the other hand, with the error of reducing religion to psychology, Jung exemplifies in attenuated forms the twin dangers that face the psychology of religion: apologetics and psychologism. One or the other of these errors seems in fact to be an occupational hazard for those contributing to the psychology of religion. A majority of those with a sustained interest in the field are likely to describe themselves as religious; moreover, many have formally studied theology, and some have obtained degrees from conservative Protestant seminaries. For many such persons, involvement in the psychology of religion seems to be more a religious than a scholarly commitment. The result, beyond an evident narrowness of focus, is an undercurrent of apologetics that sometimes surfaces without apology. I am thinking, for example, of the *Journal of Psychology and Theology*, which, edited at a school of theology that requires its faculty members to subscribe to the doctrine of the inerrancy of the Bible, accepts only those manuscripts that are consistent with the Evangelical Christian point of view. Usually, however, the attitude of apologetics is less sectarian and more subtle, as in the common search for evidence of religion's adaptive value.

On the other hand, the psychology of religion occasionally also attracts individuals who are adamant about not being religious. Typically convinced that religious persons are in every respect mistaken and that the religious traditions have inflicted enormous harm on humankind, these religiously hostile individuals wield psychology as a virtual weapon for attacking piety. Arguing that religious images, experiences, and practices can be wholly accounted for in such terms as infantile longings, brain anomalies, or environmental reinforcements, they conclude that reasonable persons will abandon religion altogether. It is no wonder that religious individuals sometimes view the psychology of religion as fundamentally antagonistic to religious faith whereas secular psychologists commonly see the field as hopelessly tainted by the religious sentiments of its practitioners.

We may be faced here with what seems to be an irresolvable dilemma. Being oneself religious, it has been argued by various scholars of religion, is essential if one is to gain direct access to the realm of religious experience and to avoid the clumsy misperceptions and misinterpretations to which the irreligious are prone. Yet persons with a religious outlook often begin with presuppositions and proceed with categories of analysis that invalidate their work when it is viewed from a different perspective, whether religious or scientific. Flournoy's exclusionary principle notwithstanding, perhaps what is required of psychologists of religion are two of the qualities that Karl Jaspers (1946, p. 808) attributed years ago to the ideal psychotherapist: a "profound existential faith," on the one hand, and "scientific attitudes of the sceptic" on the other. Possessing a deep sense of the transcendent dimension, such a psychologist would view the images and rites of the religious traditions as human constructs that give tangible form to the transcendent and provide various modes of human response.

This perspective, which liberal religionists have embraced for more than a century, seems increasingly reasonable in the light of today's pluralism and relativism. Yet its rejection of the notion of a final, revealed truth and thus its relativizing of all religious claims makes it unacceptable to many traditionally religious individuals, including some psychologists of religion. Moreover, it does not automatically solve the problem of how to discuss the experience and human representation of transcendence without at the same time implying something about the ontological nature of the transcendent and the metaphysical adequacy of its representations.

Such difficult issues, unparalleled in any other subfield of psychology, help us to understand why the psychology of religion has not thrived even in the best of times. Symptomatic of its struggle is the fateful history of its journals. In sharp contrast to the long-lived and successful journals mentioned by Koch and Leary's contributors, the journals of the psychology of religion have tended to flounder. The first such journal, *The American Journal of Religious Psychology and Education*, was founded in 1904 by Stanley Hall, who had earlier launched two other serials, *The American Journal of Psychology* in 1887 and *Pedagogical Seminary* in 1891. Hall was to collaborate in the founding of still another one, *The Journal of Applied Psychology*, in 1917. In sharp contrast to the latter three periodicals, which have been continuously published to this day (*Pedagogical Seminary* became the *Journal of Genetic Psychology* in 1954), the *Journal of Religious Psychology*, as it came to be called, appeared erratically from the outset and lasted only eleven years, in spite of the broadening of its content in 1911 to include anthropological and sociological material. An examination of Hall's record book for the journal shows that altogether it never had more than 100 subscribers, including libraries and other institutions. It likewise suffered from a lack of contributors. James Pratt and James Leuba, both of whom publish in the *Journal*, recorded elsewhere their deep disappointment in much of its contents (Pratt, 1908; Leuba, 1916).

A similar situation held in Europe, although there it was seriously complicated by adverse political circumstances. In 1907, just three years after the founding of Hall's journal, the first issue of the eclectic *Zeitschrift für Religionspsychologie* appeared. Its lead article was the famous and controversial paper, "Zwangshandlungen und Religionsübungen" (Obsessive Acts and Religious Practices) by Sigmund Freud, who for a short time served on the journal's board of advisers. In spite of a promising beginning, this journal lasted only six years, apparently for lack of a consistent point of view and the cooperation of authorities in the field.

Appearing almost immediately in the *Zeitschrift*'s place was the *Archiv für Religionspsychologie*, sponsored by *die Gesellschaft für Religionspsychologie* (the Society for Psychology of Religion), an association of scholars dominated by the Dorpat school of religious psychology, which was founded by theologian Karl Girgensohn. The *Archiv* made but a single appearance before it was interrupted by World War I, and only four more erratically appearing issues were published by 1936, when publication was once again suspended. Revived in 1962, it now appears about every two years, essentially as a record of the proceedings of the biennial conference of *Die Internationale Gesellschaft für Religionspsychologie und Religionswissenschaft* (the International Society for the Psychology and History of Religion) the current name of the *Archiv*'s founding sponsor.

The *Zeitschrift für Religionspsychologie* was itself revived in 1928 by Karl Beth, an Austrian historian of religion who positioned psychology at the very center of the scholarly study of religion. Declining overtures from the Dorpat school, whose exclusive dedication to the method of experimental introspection he considered too narrow, Beth formed instead a rival organization, pointedly named the *die Internationale Religionspsychologische Gesellschaft* (the International Society for Psychology of Religion), and founded under its sponsorship the Vienna Institute for Research on Psychology of Religion. The *Zeitschrift*'s second incarnation, however, was almost as short-lived as the first one. Along with the Institute, it succumbed in 1938 to the destructive forces of National Socialism.

More than half a century passed before there was again a regularly appearing journal—in this case, a quarterly—wholly dedicated to the psychology of religion. The *International Journal for the Psychology of Religion*, which began publication in 1991 under the editorship of L. B. Brown and Newton Malony, was conceived as a re-creation of Hall's old journal, the history and much of the contents of which are summarized in the Editors' Note in the first issue. Observing that Hall's three other journals survived whereas the one on religion did not, the editors speculate that the chief cause may lie in the psychology of religion's tendency to "window-shop through the current intellectual fashions" rather than addressing religious problems with scientific data (Brown & Malony, 1991, p. 4). For inclusion in the new journal, the editors declare, theories and reflections must at least in principle be subject to empirical testing.

Sensing the new journal's inhospitality to phenomenological, hermeneutical, and other qualitative methods of research, Finnish psychologist Kaisa Puhakka, of West Georgia College, and Indian historian of religion Arvind Sharma, of McGill University, founded an alternative, annual publication, *The Journal of the Psychology of Religion.* Oddly enough, the first issue, dated 1992 but published in 1993, contains neither an editors' introduction nor a statement of purpose. But its orientation is unmistakable in the call for papers that was circulated in advance, which invokes James's *The Varieties of Religious Experience* as the classic exemplar of the kind of research they wish to foster.

The founding in rapid succession of two new journals in the field—both nonsectarian and each dedicated in its own way to basic research and reflection—might seem cause for celebration. I confess, however, that these journals give me a disquieting feeling of *déjà vu.* I find it troubling, first of all, to see the old conflict between quantitative studies of ordinary piety and qualitative studies of exceptional experience so divisively reembodied today, and in the very names of those—Hall and James—who first squared off on this issue.

In some subfields of psychology, such as personality or clinical psychology, the abundance of both contributors and subscribers justifies the creation of specialized journals that divide the field up in terms of method, theoretical perspective, or subject matter. But that is not the situation in the psychology of religion. The modest size of these new journals, the rather uneven quality of the articles within them, and the struggle of both journals to attain a viable number of subscriptions is testimony, I think, to how few scholars are actively interested in this field. These journals, I fear, are at risk of repeating the sorry history of the earlier journals in the field.

The psychology of religion, perhaps more than any other subfield of psychology, has from its beginnings had to rely on the vision, energy, and even personal resources of a surprisingly small number of workers. Moreover, it is still today exceptionally dependent on a few classic contributors, especially James, Freud, and Jung. Even the extensive contemporary literature employing correlational and quasi-experimental methods finds itself largely grounded in the concepts and instruments developed by only a handful of researchers. The sustained institutional support, particularly in the form of professorships, that would at least ensure some degree of continuity is rarely to be found, especially in the United States.

The psychology of religion's dependence on a few dedicated scholars means that, more than most other subfields of psychology, it is highly vulnerable to the personal equation, the often subtle and unnoticed influences of an investigator's own dispositions, capacities, and experience. In addition to these influences, which are likely to become more conspicuous when the subject matter is religion, there are the effects of the unique life circumstances of the contributing individuals. For example, given the apparently crucial role that James's *Varieties* played in gaining academic respectability for the psychology of religion (Ames, 1959, p. 87), we may wonder what the fate of this field would have been had James not been invited to give the Gifford Lectures or had he finally abandoned them altogether, after twice postponing them because of ill health.

In spite of the paucity of scholars with long-term commitments to integrating and advancing the field, the literature that broadly constitutes the psychology of religion is paradoxically quite large. It is so in part because much of it has been produced by persons working on the periphery of the field—for example, in religious education or pastoral psychology—or by persons in allied fields, such as personality or social psychology, on the one hand, or the sociology and anthropology of religion, on the other. Moreover, a large number of contributions have also come from investigators who, like James, made but one or two incursions into the psychology of religion and then flew off to orbit somewhere else. Although no other contributors have left behind so momentous a work as James's, altogether their miscellaneous publications constitute a large part of the literature.

Although I make these generalizations primarily with the situation in the United States in mind, evidence suggests that they apply rather broadly. In a recent volume of the *Archiv*, for example, Jacob Belzen (1992, p. 267) reports that the considerable interest in psychology that is evident today in the theology faculties of the Netherlands is directed to pastoral psychology and applied clinical psychology, not the psychology of religion in the stricter sense. In the latter field, he reports, not much research is now being carried out.

Where, then, do all of these trends and difficulties leave us? A century of research and reflection has bequeathed to us today a striking plurality of theories and methods. In America, the most conspicuous approach is the objective empirical one initiated by Hall and Starbuck. Drawing on the evolving resources of scientific psychology, this approach has grown considerably more sophisticated in its development of questionnaires, its research designs, and its modes of statistical analysis. The extensive research on the intrinsic, extrinsic, and quest religious orientations comes most immediately to mind, but equally deserving of notice are programs of empirical research on such topics as mystical experience, religious coping, and the relation of God and parental images.

For those who are not drawn to the quasi-experimental and correlational research of these empiricists there is a variety of alternatives, the most notable of which originated in Europe. Standing out are the depth psychologies, specifically Jung's analytical psychology and the varieties of psychoanalytic thought, including object-relations theory and Kohut's self psychology. But there are also, on the subjective side, the phenomenological, humanistic, and transpersonal points of view and, on the objective side, the physiological, comparative, sociobiological, and behavioral perspectives.

When in 1926 Edwin Schaub remarked that the diversity evident even then in the psychology of religion was equally an indicator of immaturity and a sign of promising vitality, he apparently anticipated that the field would some day become united. Although the same hope for a unified science lives on in the broad field of psychology (e.g., Staats, 1987), there is, as Koch remarked, widespread doubt about such a possibility. In a book on the conflictual character of psychology today, Howard Kendler asserted in 1981 that

> The unity of psychology has all but collapsed. Psychology is a multidisciplinary field with different segments employing irreconcilable orientations. As a result, bitter disputes have occurred concerning the proper methodological position that psychology should adopt. . . . These differences are unavoidable considering the fundamental nature of psychology. A choice of competing methodological alternatives cannot be made by purely rational means. . . . The best that can be hoped for within psychology is a mutual understanding of the competing methodological positions and an appreciation of the decisions that led to their adoption (Kendler, 1981, p. 371).

A few years later, after participating in several symposia on the future of psychology, Kendler (1987, p. 56) decided that his hope for mutual understanding had been too optimistic. "Many psychologists," he says, "are so dominated by ideological commitments that they cannot understand competing conceptions of psychology, much less tolerate them. Consequently, the profession of psychology inevitably will be divided into warring camps that cannot achieve any real peace or even an armistice." Concluding that the search for unity is a romantic illusion and that a good divorce is better than a bad marriage, Kendler recommends that psychology be divided up into independent disciplines, each going its own way.

But what if we could bring representatives of these various camps together to discuss a common topic—say, religion? Such dialogue would not solve the problem of pluralism, but it might help to spread more widely the humility, undogmatic civility, and tentativeness that Koch perceives in the literature today. Focused on religion, this gathering of perspectives would help us come closer to fulfilling the mandate for the psychology of religion that Flournoy (1903) put forward nearly a century ago in his second principle, the "principle of biological interpretation." According to this principle, the psychology of religion is

> (1) *physiological* in its seeking out wherever possible the organic conditions of religious phenomena; (2) *genetic* or *evolutionary* in its attentiveness to both internal and external factors in their development; (3) *comparative* in its sensitivity to individual differences; and (4) *dynamic* in its recognition that the religious life is a living and enormously complex process involving the interplay of many factors (Wulff, 1991, p. 25).

Yet I, too, am undoubtedly too optimistic. There is first of all the long history of conflict that we have briefly reviewed—among competing psychologists of religion as well as among the field's handful of societies, journals, and research centers. Occasional scholars and organizations have striven to be hospitable to a variety of methods and perspectives, but most have not. Loyalty to a single theoretical or methodological framework is so common as to be the rule. An experimentally oriented reviewer of my book, for example, after writing with appreciation about the first five, empirically oriented chapters, described the remaining seven, interpretive chapters as a metastatic cancer. True to his own way of thinking, he determined the extent of the metastasis by counting the number of pages on which each of the unscientific psychologists—Freud, Erikson, and Jung, among others—was allowed to intrude.

Even if psychologists of religion developed a greater degree of tolerance and mutual understanding regarding psychological principles, there are still the problems introduced by the subject matter they share in common. Religion, more than almost any other other topic, tends to be highly divisive, even among researchers with the same psychological orientation. For example, although the debate between the advocates of the intrinsic religious orientation and the proponents of the quest orientation has been carried out largely in terms of psychometric criteria and empirical findings, the animus of the debate derives from an irresolvable underlying disagreement about what it means today to be genuinely or maturely religious. More generally, there is widespread disagreement about how religion should be defined and how the piety of individuals should then be measured or assessed.

Such diversity of views regarding subject matter, research methods, and goals is hardly to be found in any other academic field, remarks Hans-Günter Heimbrock (1978) in a literature review of the psychology of religion. If we posed the question in the title of this paper to a random sample of persons in the field, their answers would undoubtedly show a like diversity. A few might be tempted, I suspect, to give a reply similar to the pessimistic one provided by James Gibson in his summing up of research on sense perception for the Koch and Leary symposia. You may make, if you wish, the appropriate substitutions. He writes,

> The conclusions that can be reached from a century of research on perception are insignificant. The knowledge gained ... is incoherent. We have no adequate theory of perception, and what we have found in the search for sensations is a mixed batch of illusions, physiological curiosities, and bodily feelings. The implications are discouraging. A fresh start has to be made ... (Gibson, 1985, pp. 229–230)

Somewhat less pessimistically, others might provide answers akin to Henry Gleitman's regarding the study of cognition. Here we could substitute James for Wundt.

> I do not know whether we have progressed much beyond [Wundt]. Our techniques are more sophisticated, and there are many more of us, so we can inundate each other in a mass of facts. But much of what we now do and think was already implicit in Wundt, and in other nineteenth century figures. We could do worse than to go back for an occasional glance at our intellectual origins ... (Gleitman, 1985, p. 434).

I suppose it is unlikely that any of our respondents would give an answer like Kenneth Gergen's, in an essay on social psychology in the same volume. It is one worth hearing, however, for beyond recognizing the situation we are in, it anticipates the possibility of renewal and a new direction.

> ... During the past century social psychology has participated in one of humankind's greatest intellectual adventures. It has, in J. L. Austin's (1962) terms, joined in the "pursuit of the incorrigible," or certain knowledge, a pursuit that has challenged thinkers from Heraclitus to the present. Early in this century it appeared that the means had been discovered for gaining certainty in the behavioral sciences. Yet, subsequent examination has found such means sadly wanting. The search for certainty is a child's romance, and as in most romances, one holds fast to even the most fragile shard attesting to continued life. The question that must now be confronted is how to pass successfully into the maturity of a second century. A new romance may be required to extinguish the old, and possibly the signals of its inception are at hand (Gergen, 1985, p. 551).

The signals Gergen has in mind are issuing out of the postmodernist movement, which, particularly in the form of social constructivism, possesses the potential for revolutionizing the human sciences. Social constructivism, it is perhaps unnecessary to say, maintains that knowledge is not an impartial or 'objective' representation of 'the way things are,' as the empiricists have assumed, but is a product reflecting the investigative context as well as the interests and commitments of those carrying out the research. Rather than being universal and ahistorical, knowledge is understood as constituted through a process of social negotiation and hence it is always relative to the factors influencing that process (Danziger, 1990; Gergen, 1985).

From a social constructivist perspective, a plurality of views such as we find in the psychology of religion is not only an inevitable feature of free inquiry but also a desirable one. Distinctly undesirable is the marked tendency toward methodological and theoretical imperialism that is evident throughout psychology. One might suppose that at least psychologists of religion would be less prone to such imperialism, given that, in general, scholars of religion are ahead of psychologists in assimilating the implications of the hermeneutics of postmodernism, especially the relativity of their own points of view. According to John Cobb (1990), many of his colleagues in religious studies are motivated by

> the desire to overcome the parochial and doctrinaire attitudes that pervasively affect the climate of most religious communities. Our passion has been to open the minds of religious people to the values of other traditions, and thus to relativize their own beliefs and practices. We emphasize the relativity of those beliefs and practices to historical and cultural experience, hoping to break the shackles of absolutist thinking and feeling (p. 603)

But such motives, I have already suggested, are not characteristic of psychologists of religion, at least those who come to the field out of psychology rather than religious studies. Convinced that the empiricist model of psychology—and only this model—will in time establish an enduring set of truths, they are similarly content to conceive of religion in the terms of but a single tradition, most often their own. Such knowledge as they might be thought to have attained is at best local knowledge, generalizable only to certain groups of Protestant Christians living in the West near the end of the twentieth century. And even to them we should hesitate to generalize, given the doubts that have been raised not only about particular scales but also about the whole scaling enterprise.

If I may be pardoned for saying so, I think Gibson's conclusion regarding research on perception applies equally well to the empirical tradition in the psychology of religion, if not to the field as a whole: A fresh start has to be made. So also Gleitman's conclusion, though rather than giving only an occasional glance at our intellectual origins I would have us engage in a sustained reexamination of them, especially the works of William James and James Pratt.

Even though James and Pratt wrote before the psychological and religious pluralisms of the twentieth century had fully emerged, both possessed personal and metatheoretical perspectives for making sense of pluralism and both actively rejected dogmatic loyalty to a single point of view. The somewhat greater inclusiveness of religious traditions that set James's *Varieties* apart from other works appearing at the turn of the century became thematic in Pratt's research and writings. As Pratt remarks in the Preface to his classic book *The Religious Consciousness* (1920), he sought above all else to avoid geographical and intellectual provincialism. "In order not to be confined to the American Protestant point of view," he writes, "I have seen what I could of Roman Catholicism in Europe, and of Hinduism and Buddhism in India, Burma, and Ceylon" (p. viii). As historians of religion have acknowledged, Pratt viewed these diverse religious expressions not only with brilliance but also with extraordinary sympathy (Smith, 1959, p. 36).

When Pratt undertook his travels to India and nearby lands early in the twentieth century, there was virtually no other way for him to become directly acquainted with the Asian religious traditions. Today, a few hours' drive would suffice, for in almost every American city, one can find Hindu and Buddhist temples as well as Muslim mosques, some of them as large and imposing as their counterparts in Asia and the Middle East. Throughout the United States can also be found some 60 Jain temples and centers as well as communities of Zoroastrians and Sikhs. This new religious plurality is similarly evident in England, where there are now more than one million Muslims, 400 000 Hindus, and 400 000 Sikhs. In France, Germany, and Sweden the story is much the same (Eck, 1993, pp. 37–41).

Religious diversity per se is hardly a new fact, for as long as human beings have sought to trade with, conquer, or convert the peoples of other lands they have been confronted by such differences and the challenge of making sense of their neighbors' traditions. What is new today, notes Harvard Indologist Diana Eck (1993, pp. 42–43), "is our sharply heightened awareness of religious diversity in every part of our world and the fact that today everyone—not just the explorers, the missionaries, the diplomats, and the theologians—encounters and needs to understand people and faiths other than their own."

This new awareness of diversity must be, I think, the starting point for renewed effort in the psychology of religion. Our definitions and our assessment instruments must be inclusive enough to do justice to the religious faiths fostered by other traditions. The new sensitivity to plurality must also be allowed to recast the questions we ask and the theoretical constructs we use to shape provisional answers. Especially urgent are questions that address the 'crisis of belief' precipitated by today's plurality of traditions and the defensive retreat into exclusivist positions signaled by the world-wide resurgence of fundamentalism. Although psychology is distinctly not competent to assess the validity of any particular religious position, it surely ought to be able to discuss the full range of such positions and to explore the cognitive and other psychological processes that underlie them. And in clarifying what the alternatives are and what their sources and functions might be, the psychology of religion may even hope to foster those religious forms that thoughtful and well-informed people today take to be most desirable for the social and spiritual well-being of all of humankind.

A new, more religiously inclusive psychology of religion will also need to be more psychologically inclusive. Of course, the field is already inclusive in the sense that many points of view can be found within its boundaries. But what I have in mind is the more humble and open-minded pluralism that Koch perceives within psychology as a whole. This emerging 'pluralism of *search*,' which is now being systematized in the constructivist movement, recognizes not only the relativity and hence limitations of any one psychological point of view but also the commonalities and strengths of alternative perspectives. In seeking insight into the exclusivist impulse in religion, psychologists of religion may simultaneously gain understanding into their own history of conflicting perspectives.

Whether humankind may someday transcend today's pluralisms of religion and of psychology we cannot now anticipate. But for the present, they may be the "new romance" that Gergen says may be necessary "to extinguish the old". However one conceives of them, these pluralisms are a challenge that psychologists of religion must take into account if they are "to pass successfully into the maturity of a second century".

Bibliography

Ames, E. S. (1959). *Beyond theology; The autobiography of Edward Scribner Ames* (V. M. Ames, Ed.). Chicago: University of Chicago Press.
Austin, J. L. (1962). *Sense and sensibilia*. London: Oxford University Press.
Belzen, J. A. van. (1992). Der Chiasmus der niederländischen Religionspsychologie. *Archiv für Religionspsychologie, 20,* 256–269.

Boring, E. G. (1950). *A history of experimental psychology* (2nd ed.). New York: Appleton-Century-Crofts.
Boring, E. G. (1965). On the subjectivity of important historical dates: Leipzig 1879. *Journal of the History of the Behavioral Sciences, 1,* 5–10.
Brown, L. B., & Malony, H. N. (1991). Editors' note. *International Journal for the Psychology of Religion, 1,* 1–4.
Cobb, J. B., Jr. (1990). Responses to relativism: Common ground, deconstruction and reconstruction. *Soundings, 73,* 595–616.
Danziger, K. (1990). *Constructing the subject; Historical origins of psychological research.* Cambridge: Cambridge University Press.
Eck, D. (1993). *Encountering God; A spiritual journey from Bozeman to Banaras.* Boston: Beacon Press.
Flournoy, T. (1903). Les principes de la psychologie religieuse. *Archives de Psychologie, 2,* 33–57.
Gergen, K. J. (1985). Social psychology and the phoenix of unreality. In Koch, S. & D. E. Leary (Eds.), *A century of psychology as science* (pp. 528–557). New York: McGraw Hill.
Gibson, J. J. (1985). Conclusions from a century of research on sense perception. In S. Koch & D. E. Leary (Eds.), *A century of psychology as science* (pp. 224–230). New York: McGraw Hill.
Gleitman, H. (1985). Some trends in the study of cognition. In Koch, S. & D. E. Leary (Eds.) *A century of psychology as science* (pp. 420–436). New York: McGraw Hill.
Hall, G. S. (1882). The moral and religious training of children. *The Princeton Review, 9,* 26–48. (Reprinted in *Pedagogical Seminary,* 1891, *1,* 196–210).
Hall, G. S. (1904). *Adolescence; Its psychology and its relations to physiology, anthropology, sociology, sex, crime, religion, and education* (2 vols.). New York: D. Appleton.
Heimbrock, H.-G. (1978). Wahrheit in der Wirklichkeit? Ein Literaturbericht zur Religionspsychologie. *Theologia Practica, 13,* 148–158.
Jaspers, K. (1946). *General psychopathology.* Translated by J. Hoenig and M. W. Hamilton. Chicago: University of Chicago Press, 1963. (Revised fourth German edition 1946).
Kahoe, R. D. (1992). A birthday for psychology of religion? *Newsletter of Division 36, American Psychological Association,* 17(3), 9.
Kendler, H. H. (1981). *Psychology: A science in conflict.* New York: Oxford University Press.
Kendler, H. H. (1987). A good divorce is better than a bad marriage. *Annals of Theoretical Psychology, 5,* 55–89.
Koch, S., & Leary, D. E. (Eds.) (1958). *A century of psychology as science.* New York: McGraw Hill.
Leuba, J. H. (1916). Religious psychology. *Psychological Bulletin, 13,* 466–471.
Pratt, J. B. (1908). The psychology of religion. *Harvard Theological Review, 1,* 435–454.
Pratt, J. B. (1920). *The religious consciousness; A psychological study.* New York: Macmillan.
Rizzuto, A.-M. (1992). Afterword. In M. Finn & J. Gartner (Eds.), *Object relations theory and religion* (pp. 155–175). Westport, Conn.: Praeger.
Schaub, E. L. (1926). The psychology of religion in America during the past quarter-century. *Journal of Religion, 6,* 113–134.
Smith, W. C. (1959). Comparative religion: Whither—and why? In Eliade, M. & J. M. Kitagawa (Eds.), *The History of Religions; Essays in Methodology* (pp. 31–58). Chicago: University of Chicago Press.
Staats, A. W. (1987). Unified positivism: Philosophy for the revolution in unity. *Annals of Theoretical Psychology, 5,* 11–54.
Vergote, A. (1993). What the psychology of religion is and what it is not. *International Journal for the Psychology of Religion, 3,* 73–86.
Wulff, D. M. (1991). *Psychology of religion: Classic and contemporary views.* New York: John Wiley & Sons.

Author Index

Allport, G. W., 23, 33, 63, 64, 65, 90, 129, 174
Aristotle, 31, 161
Argyle, M., 19, 31, 33
Augustine, 31, 46, 161

Bainton, R., 43, 44
Bakan, D., 38, 53
Barth, K., 74, 76, 100, 161
Beit-Hallahmi, B., 22, 134
Berger, P., 130
Berger, P. & Luckmann, T., 92, 94, 128, 172, 176
Berggrav, E., 127
Boring, E. G., 38
Browning, D., 19
Buber, M., 32, 172

Camus, A., 179
Capps, D., 137
Cassirer, E., 164

Danziger, K., 28
Derrida, J., 32, 50
Dilthey, W., 78
Dittes, J., 38, 44
Dostoevsky, F., 178, 179
Duchamps, M., 19

Eck, D., 195
Edwards, J., 138
Ekström, Hj., 83
Eliade, M., 48, 159, 172
Erikson, E., 43, 44, 46, 47, 50, 51, 71, 74, 75, 127, 148, 155, 159, 193

Festinger, L., 94, 165
Feuerbach, L., 97
Flournoy, T., 96, 186, 188, 192
Fortmann, H., 23

Fowler, J., 129, 130, 131, 174
Frankl, V., 21
Freud, S., 19, 22, 56, 58, 75, 98, 127, 146, 163, 174, 186

Gadamer, H., 139, 146
Geertz, C., 172
Gergen, K., 30, 194
Girgensohn, K., 189
Glasser, B. G. & Strauss, A. L., 87, 88
Goldmann, R., 155
Grønbaek, V., 139, 141, 142

Habermas, J., 137
Hall, S., 22, 62, 63, 174, 185, 187, 190
Hedenius, I., 104
Hegel, G. W. F., 161
Heiler, F., 172
Heidegger, 71, 74, 76, 78, 160
Heisenberg, W., 56
Husserl, E., 71, 146, 169
Høffding, H., 137, 141, 142

James, W., 22, 39, 40, 41, 46, 47, 48, 51, 58, 59, 60, 62, 63, 64, 78, 95, 99, 120, 127, 148, 151, 160, 190, 187
Jaspers, K., 71, 168
John of the Cross, 168, 174
Jones, J., 104
Jung, C. G., 62, 63, 75, 129, 159, 165, 174, 187, 193

Kant, I., 72, 129, 161
Katz, S. T., 114
Kierkegaard, S., 162
Koch, S., 184, 195
Kohut, H., 191

Laans, van der, J., 117, 130, 131
Lacan., J., 163

Levi-Strauss, C., 163
Levinas, E., 32, 72, 78, 150
Luther, M., 43, 47, 50
Leuba, J. H., 90, 100, 186

Marx, K., 163
Mead, G. H., 172
Merlau-Ponty, M., 163

Newman, J. H., 44, 45, 47, 49, 53
Nietzche, F., 73
Nuttin, 159, 168
Nygren, A., 100

Miller, A., 92
Mitzerlich, A., 68, 73

Otto, O., 78, 97, 148, 159, 172

Pascal, B., 162
Pfister, O., 12
Piaget, J., 163, 166
Plato, 161
Popper, K., 29, 113
Powy, J. P., 176, 177
Pratt, J. B., 99, 174, 195
Proust, M., 176, 177
Pruyser, P., 23, 49, 53, 70, 177

Ricour, P., 146, 152, 153, 162, 165
Ritschl, A., 100
Rizutto, A. M., 173, 184

Russel, B., 177

Tengberg, V., 84
Thomas Aquino, 161
Thouless, R. H., 99
Tillich, P., 19
Trevor-Roper, P., 47
Turner, V., 37, 177

Sartre, J.-P., 71, 72, 172, 174
Schleiermacher, F., 87, 100
Shibutani, I., 92
Skinner, B. F., 165, 186
Stace, W. T., 114
Starbuck, E. D., 62
Stern, W., 19
Sundén, Hj., 42, 43, 137, 160
Söderblom, N., 97, 137

Vergote, A., 146, 155, 186, 187

Weber, M., 19, 130
Winnicott, D., 177
Wikström, O., 43, 44
Wittgenstein, L., 20, 26, 104
Wulff, D., 70, 77, 165
Wundt, W., 184

Yinger, J. M., 133

Zaleskij, C., 44